当代国外语言学与应用语言学文库（升级版）

普通语言学教程

Course in General Linguistics

F. de Saussure 著
Roy Harris 编译
张绍杰 导读

外语教学与研究出版社
FOREIGN LANGUAGE TEACHING AND RESEARCH PRESS
北京 BEIJING

京权图字：01-2001-2865

图书在版编目（CIP）数据

普通语言学教程 = Course in General Linguistics ：英文 /（瑞士）F. 德 · 索绪尔（F. de Saussure）著 ；（英）罗伊 · 哈里斯（Roy Harris）编译 ；张绍杰导读. —— 北京 ：外语教学与研究出版社，2021.9
（当代国外语言学与应用语言学文库 ：升级版）
ISBN 978-7-5213-2959-9

Ⅰ. ①普… Ⅱ. ①F… ②罗… ③张… Ⅲ. ①普通语言学－教材－英文 Ⅳ. ①H0

中国版本图书馆 CIP 数据核字（2021）第 173195 号

出 版 人　徐建忠
项目负责　姚　虹　李亚琦
责任编辑　徐　宁
责任校对　都楠楠
装帧设计　李　高
出版发行　外语教学与研究出版社
社　　址　北京市西三环北路 19 号（100089）
网　　址　http://www.fltrp.com
印　　刷　唐山市润丰印务有限公司
开　　本　650×980　1/16
印　　张　18
版　　次　2021 年 9 月第 1 版　2021 年 9 月第 1 次印刷
书　　号　ISBN 978-7-5213-2959-9
定　　价　45.00 元

购书咨询：（010）88819926　电子邮箱：club@fltrp.com
外研书店：https://waiyants.tmall.com
凡印刷、装订质量问题，请联系我社印制部
联系电话：（010）61207896　电子邮箱：zhijian@fltrp.com
凡侵权、盗版书籍线索，请联系我社法律事务部
举报电话：（010）88817519　电子邮箱：banquan@fltrp.com
物料号：329590001

当代国外语言学与应用语言学文库

（升级版）

出版前言

“当代国外语言学与应用语言学文库”（以下简称“文库”）从2000年至今已出版近200个品种，深受语言学与应用语言学专业师生和研究者的欢迎，大家既把“文库”视为进入语言学与应用语言学百花园的引路人，又把“文库”视为知识更新的源泉，还把“文库”当成点亮科研之路的明灯。

为了追踪相关领域的研究进程，并满足广大读者的需求，外语教学与研究出版社从2020年开始启动了“文库”的更新升级工作，与牛津大学出版社、剑桥大学出版社、劳特利奇出版社等世界知名出版机构合作，推出“文库”（升级版）。

“文库”升级的原则如下：

1. 对原有经典图书，若无新版，则予以保留，并予以必要修订；若有新版，则以新版代替旧版，并请相关领域学者撰写新版中文导读。

2. 引进语言学与应用语言学领域的新锐力作，进一步拓展学科领域。

3. 用二维码代替CD-ROM，帮助读者更加快捷地获取内容。

“文库”（升级版）定位为一套大型的、开放性的系列丛书，希望它能对我国语言学教学与研究和外语教学与研究起到积极的推动作用。外语教学与研究出版社亦将继续努力，力争把国外最新、最具影响力的语言学与应用语言学著作奉献给广大读者。

外语教学与研究出版社

2021年8月

当代国外语言学与应用语言学文库（升级版）

2021年出版书目

——Cognitive Linguistics 认知语言学

Cognitive Linguistics and Language Teaching
《认知语言学和语言教学》
Randal Holme

An Introduction to Cognitive Linguistics (Second Edition)
《认知语言学入门（第二版）》
F. Ungerer & H.-J. Schmid

——First Language Acquisition 第一语言习得

An Introduction to Child Language Development
《儿童语言发展引论》
Susan H. Foster-Cohen

——Functional Linguistics 功能语言学

Genre Relations: Mapping Culture
《语类关系与文化映射》
J. R. Martin & David Rose

An Introduction to Functional Grammar (Third Edition)
《功能语法导论（第三版）》
M. A. K. Halliday, revised by Christian Matthiessen

——General Linguistics 普通语言学

Course in General Linguistics
《普通语言学教程》
F. de Saussure

General Linguistics (Fourth Edition)
《普通语言学概论（第四版）》
R. H. Robins

An Introduction to Linguistics
《语言学入门》
Stuart C. Poole

—— **History of Linguistics 语言学史**

A Short History of Linguistics (Fourth Edition)
《语言学简史（第四版）》
R. H. Robins

—— **Intercultural Communication 跨文化交际**

Intercultural Interaction: A Multidisciplinary Approach to Intercultural Communication
《跨文化互动：跨文化交际的多学科研究》
Helen Spencer-Oatey & Peter Franklin

—— **Lexicography 词典学**

Dictionary of Lexicography
《词典学词典》
R. R. K. Hartmann & Gregory James

—— **Philosophy of Language 语言哲学**

How to Do Things with Words
《如何以言行事》
J. L. Austin

—— **Pragmatics 语用学**

Meaning in Interaction: An Introduction to Pragmatics
《言谈互动中的意义：语用学引论》
Jenny Thomas

—— **Psycholinguistics 心理语言学**

The Articulate Mammal: An Introduction to Psycholinguistics (Fourth Edition)
《会说话的哺乳动物：心理语言学入门（第四版）》
Jean Aitchison

—— **Research Method 研究方法**

Research Perspectives on English for Academic Purposes
《学术英语的多维研究视角》
John Flowerdew & Matthew Peacock

—— **Second Language Acquisition 第二语言习得**

Fossilization in Adult Second Language Acquisition
《成人二语习得中的僵化现象》
韩照红（Zhaohong Han）

Linguistics and Second Language Acquisition
《语言学和第二语言习得》
Vivian Cook

Strategies in Learning and Using a Second Language
《学习和运用第二语言的策略》
Andrew D. Cohen

Tasks in Second Language Learning
《第二语言学习中的任务》
Virginia Samuda & Martin Bygate

——Semantics 语义学

Meaning in Language: An Introduction to Semantics and Pragmatics (Third Edition)
《语言的意义：语义学与语用学导论（第三版）》
Alan Cruse

Semantics (Fourth Edition)
《语义学（第四版）》
John I. Saeed

——Sociolinguistics 社会语言学

The Handbook of Sociolinguistics
《社会语言学通览》
Florian Coulmas

An Introduction to Sociolinguistics (Seventh Edition)
《社会语言学引论（第七版）》
Ronald Wardhaugh & Janet M. Fuller

——Stylistics 文体学

A Linguistic Guide to English Poetry
《英诗学习指南：语言学的分析方法》
Geoffrey N. Leech

Patterns in Language: Stylistics for Students of Language and Literature
《语言模式：文体学入门》
Joanna Thornborrow & Shân Wareing

Style in Fiction: A Linguistic Introduction to English Fictional Prose
《小说文体论：英语小说的语言学入门》
Geoffrey N. Leech & Michael H. Short

Stylistics: A Practical Coursebook
《实用文体学教程》
Laura Wright & Jonathan Hope

—Syntax 句法学

Chomsky's Universal Grammar: An Introduction (Third Edition)
《乔姆斯基的普遍语法教程（第三版）》
V. J. Cook & Mark Newson

—Testing 语言测试

Language Testing and Validation: An Evidence-Based Approach
《语言测试与效度验证：基于证据的研究方法》
Cyril J. Weir

—Text Linguistics 语篇语言学

The Language of Evaluation: Appraisal in English
《评估语言：英语评价系统》
J. R. Martin & P. R. R. White

Metadiscourse
《元话语》
Ken Hyland

导　读

张绍杰

《普通语言学教程》(以下简称《教程》)是费尔迪南·德·索绪尔(Ferdinand de Saussure)留给20世纪语言学最宝贵的遗产，在现代西方语言学思想史中占有不可动摇的地位。这部《教程》使Saussure成为“现代语言学之父”，他所发起的这场语言学革命也被誉为“哥白尼式革命”。对于这样一部重要的理论著作，我国的读者是早已熟知的，因此，这里我们不打算向读者具体介绍《教程》的内容，而重在评析Saussure语言学思想及其研究。为了使读者更多地了解Saussure从而理解他的语言符号学思想，有必要先简要介绍Saussure的生平。

一、Saussure生平简介

Saussure于1857年11月26日生于瑞士日内瓦一个学者家庭。他的家族以科学世家而著称，近一个半世纪人才辈出，其中有生物学家、植物学家、博物学家、物理学家和地质学家。Saussure 的父亲既是一位动物学家，也是一位昆虫学家；母亲是一位聪慧的女性，也是一位出色的音乐家。出生在这样一个美好的家庭，Saussure 从小就受到良好的文化和科学思想的熏陶。他幼年就学会了法语、德语、英语、拉丁语和希腊语。少年时期，他深受语文学家 A. Pictet 的影响，对语言产生了某种特殊的偏爱和浓厚的兴趣，1872 年在不满 15 岁时便写出了第一篇《论诸语言》的论文。[1] 1873 年，Saussure 进入高中学习，1874 年，在 Pictet 的劝导下开始自学梵语。1875 年，他进入日内瓦大学学习，继承家族的传统主修化学和物理，但他本人对自然科学毫无兴趣，确信自己的潜能在于语言研究方面。所以，作为理科学生他越发对语言学课程感兴趣，并且于 1876 年春天申请加入了巴黎语言学会。Saussure 致力于语言学研究的信念得到了其父母的理解和支持，于是他在 1876 年秋离开日内瓦大学转入德国的莱比锡大学文学系攻读历史语言学。

事实证明，Saussure 的选择是正确的，德国的留学时代对 Saussure 的学术生涯具有极其重要的意义。当时德国莱比锡大学是“新语法学派”的中心，他不但能聆听那个时代最杰出的历史语言学家，如新语法学派的年轻教授 Leskien、Osthoff 等的讲课，而且还能够同新语法学派的旗手 Brugmann、Paul 等密切交往，并与同学术界知名学者如 Curtius、Noreen 等拜师结友。正是在莱比锡大学学习期间，年仅 21 岁的青年 Saussure 于 1878 年发表了《论印欧系语言元音的原始系统》这篇著名论文，成功地把一个在印欧系语言元音的原始系统中起着重大作用的音拟构出来，

---

1 在这篇论文中索绪尔提出这样一种假设：所有语言都根源于由两三个辅音构成的系统。这种假设当然有些奇思异想，但它反映出索绪尔少年时就表现出对语言有天赋的抽象能力。参见 Culler，J. 1976. *Ferdinand de Saussure*. Harmondsworth：Penguin Books，p. 2.

为理解印欧语元音交替的复杂关系做出了突出贡献，这引起了欧洲语言学界的广泛关注。1878 年 7 月 Saussure 离开莱比锡赴柏林大学，次年末他返回莱比锡大学，提交了他的博士论文《梵语绝对属格的用法》。1880 年 2 月，他通过论文答辩，获博士学位。

1880 年秋，Saussure 离开德国前往法国巴黎定居。是年 10 月巴黎高等研究院决定委任 Saussure 为哥特语和古高德语讲师。在巴黎高等研究院工作的十年中，他先后讲授过哥特语、古高德语、希腊语、拉丁语比较语法、立陶宛语、梵语等。他的讲授因其知识广博、逻辑严密、思想深刻、格调清新、语言精练而对学生产生了极大的魅力。他同时还积极参加巴黎语言学会的学术活动。Saussure 的思想对法国年轻一代语言学者产生了重要影响，他的学生有一批后来成为法国著名语言学家，如 Meillet、Grammont、Passy。大概就是在巴黎高等研究院这一时期，Saussure 的语言学思想框架已开始形成。[1] Saussure 在法国学术界的地位日益增高，被认为是当时印欧比较语言学的最高权威。巴黎高等研究院准备授予他教授职位，这是法国的最高待遇和荣誉。但是，Saussure 出于爱国之心，毅然放弃了这一殊荣，于 1891 年由巴黎回到日内瓦。

同年 10 月，Saussure 就任日内瓦大学文学社会科学系教授，主要讲授梵语和印欧语的课程，后期讲过日耳曼历史语言学。1906 年讲语言学课的一位教授退休，Saussure 继任他的位置，被任命为主任教授。于是，他从次年 1 月开始并在此后连续三次（1907 年、1908—1909 年、1910—1911 年）讲授普通语言学课程。但在日内瓦听讲普通语言学课程的学生较少，也不都是来自

1 19 世纪 90 年代初的文献记录表明，那个时期索绪尔投入很大精力去思考后来在《教程》中体现出来的普通语言学问题。见 Aarsleff, H. 1982. *From Locke to Saussure*. Minneapolis: University of Minnesota Press, p. 359-360.

语言学专业。因此为了使学生听懂自己的语言理论，Saussure 费尽心血，耐心教学，严格指导。后来，这些学生当中也出现了许多杰出语言学家，如 Bally、Sechehaye、Karcevskij 等。1909 年，Saussure 被评选为丹麦科学院会员，1910 年被授予法国研究学院通讯院士。在日内瓦这段时期，尤其从 1894 年之后，Saussure 几乎保持沉默，发表的论述较少，同外界的接触以及同亲属朋友的书信来往也日益减少。[1]关于 Saussure 沉默的原因，有关资料显示，除了专注于普通语言学的理论问题之外，他对自己学术上的要求几乎达到尽善尽美、十分苛刻的程度。他认为自己的语言理论不成熟，尚未达到出版的水平，所以即使抄得干干净净的手稿也未送出去出版。更令人遗憾的是，Saussure 第三次普通语言学课程的计划还未全部完成，病魔就使他卧床不起了。

1913 年 2 月 22 日，Saussure 在日内瓦病逝，享年 55 岁。Saussure 毕生致力于语言教学和语言研究，但他生前发表的重要著作不多，他的学术思想主要体现在他三次普通语言学讲授之中。1916 年，Saussure 逝世后的第三个年头，他的学生 Bally 和 Sechehaye 根据他三次讲授普通语言学时学生们所做的课堂笔记，以及其他有关资料整理编辑出版了《普通语言学教程》。在《教程》中，Saussure 创造性地提出了一套语言研究理论和研究方法，改变了 20 世纪语言学研究的发展方向，从而奠定了 Saussure“现代语言学之父”的地位。

二、关于《教程》的译本

Saussure 的《教程》是一部不朽的著作，自 20 世纪初问世至今多次再版重印，并被译成多种语言出版，包括日译本（1928）、

---

1 见 Culler, J. 1976. *Ferdinand de Saussure*. Harmondsworth: Penguin Books, p. 4.

德译本（1931）、俄译本（1933）、西班牙语译本（1945）、英译本（1959）、波兰语译本（1961）、意大利语译本（1967）、匈牙利语译本（1967）、塞尔维亚－克罗地亚语译本（1969）、瑞典语译本（1970）、葡萄牙语译本（1971）、越南语译本（1973）、朝鲜语译本（1973）、阿尔巴尼亚语译本（1977）、土耳其语译本（1976—1978）、中译本（1980）等（参见戚雨村，1997）。1959年的英文版《教程》是由 Baskin 所译，在纽约出版，1966 年再版重印。

本英文版《教程》是由英国牛津大学著名语言学家 Harris 根据原文第二版翻译的，1983 年在伦敦出版，到 1998 年五次再版重印。这部由 Harris 翻译的英文版《教程》，自 80 年代以来在学术界产生的影响较大，基本上取代了 Baskin 所译的英文版《教程》。如果读者把这两个英译本加以对照，便会发现 Harris 的译文自然流畅、清晰准确，并对原版中的印刷错误作了纠正。同时，译者对某些重要的术语或概念采用了新的译法，比如通常我们所说的所指（signified）和能指（signifier）被重译成指号（signal）和指称（signification），听觉形象（accoustic image）或声音形象（sound image）被重译成声音结构（sound pattern）或声音序列（sound sequence），“语言”这一术语的译法尤其完全与众不同，有时被译成英语的类指用法（the language），有时被译成具体指用法（a language），在一些场合还被译成“语言结构”（linguistic structure）。这方面读者可细致观察。更值得指出的是，在 Baskin 的英译本里，我们很难读到“结构”（structure）一词，而在 Harris 的译本里，我们会发现“结构”“语言结构”这样的概念多次出现，这不同程度地反映出译者对 Saussure 所使用的概念的独到理解。诚然，Harris 是一位 Saussure 研究专家，他早在 1987 年就出版了《读索绪尔》一书，后来又出版或发表了许多关于 Saussure 思想研究的论著或论文。1993 年，根据 Constantin

的课堂笔记，他合作编辑并翻译出版了 Saussure 于 1910—1911 年第三度讲授的《普通语言学教程》（法英对照本）。[1] 所以，本英文版《教程》的引进，对于我国读者能更准确地理解 Saussure 以及我国的 Saussure 研究会起到积极的引导作用。

现已在我国出版的中文版《教程》，是由已故著名语言学家高名凯先生翻译，并由岑麒祥、叶蜚声校注的，1980 年由商务印书馆印刷。实际上，早在 20 世纪 60 年代初高名凯就已完成了《教程》的译稿，但由于后来政治形势的变化，迟至 80 年代初才正式出版。中译本的出版为国内更多读者了解和研究 Saussure 创造了条件。我们今天所使用的术语基本上仍沿用高名凯的译法。但如果有些读者想借用汉译本去理解 Harris 的英译本，那将会遇到不少的困难，因为在许多地方你会找不到对应的关系。不过假如以英译本为读本去理解其中的细微差别，可能对我们会更有帮助。

三、关于《教程》的思想研究

Saussure《教程》的问世虽然已跨越了一个世纪，但在世界范围内 Saussure 思想研究仍经久不衰，经历了解释与再解释、认识与再认识的过程，这一过程可概括为以下四个时期。

1. 传播时期。从《教程》1916 年出版至 50 年代初，近 30 年的时间里，Saussure 的语言学理论并未引起学术界的极大震动和广泛认同。虽然在《教程》出版后的五年时间里有不少评论文章发表，但是理解 Saussure 思想的人却为数不多，许多学者，包括 Meillet、Jesperson 等这些名家都持谨慎或否定的态度。尤其在英美国家，Saussure 的学术思想未引起足够的重视。在英国，其

1 索绪尔 1910—1911 第三度讲授的《普通语言学教程》由张绍杰译成中文，于 2001 年由湖南教育出版社出版。

原因之一是语义学家 Ogden 和 Richards 对 Saussure 语言理论的评价持否定态度；而在美国，其主要原因在于 Bloomfield 的语言理论当时统治着整个美国语言学界，尽管他对 Saussure 的语言理论有过正面的评价。[1] 为了使 Saussure 的思想传播于世，日内瓦学派第一代的代表 Bally、Sechehaye、Karcevskij，第二代的代表 Frei、Godel、Burger 等人，不遗余力地撰文阐发《教程》所包含的思想观点。[2] 1941 年，日内瓦学派创办《索绪尔研究集刊》(*Cahiers F. de Saussure*)，刊登研究 Saussure 的论文、札记以及 Saussure 的遗稿、传记等。这进一步推动了 Saussure 研究的开展。随着对 Saussure 理论观点之争的展开，一些学者发现《教程》中存在"自相矛盾之处"，还有些学者对《教程》本身的"忠实性"和内部的"一致性"提出疑义。看来，要把 Saussure 研究引向深入，对《教程》作全面考证势在必行。正是在这样的背景下，Saussure《教程》的性质和地位问题被提了出来。这个时期学术界未对 Saussure 作出公正的评价。

2. **重新发现时期**。Saussure 思想的追随者非常认真地对待《教程》的"真实性"问题，于是从 50 年代初开始了《教程》的考证工作。考证的方法是把现行的《教程》的文本同现存的手稿笔记加以比较。到 60 年代后期，这项艰巨工作取得重大成果，在欧洲先后出现了三部研究《教程》的专著或 Saussure 版本学专著——瑞士学者 Godel 著：Saussure《普通语言学教程》稿本溯源（日内瓦 / 巴黎版，1957 年）；意大利语言学家 Mauro 著：评

---

1 有关详细情况，见 Harris, R. 1987. *Reading Saussure*. London: Duckworth, Preface；还可参见许国璋，1983，"关于索绪尔的两本书"，载《国外语言学》1983 年第 1 期；戚雨村，"索绪尔的重新被发现"，载于《语文研究群言集》，中山大学出版社，1997 年，第 28—41 页。

2 徐志民对 30 年代学术界的争论情况作了较为详细的概述，见徐志民，1983，"索绪尔研究的新阶段"，载于《语文现代化》，1983 年第 2 期，85—105 页。

注 Saussure《普通语言学教程》(意大利文版，1967 年；法文版，1972 年)；瑞士学者 Engler 著：Saussure《普通语言学教程》评注(德国 Harrassowitz 版，1967—1974 年)。这三部 Saussure 版本学专著证明，尽管《教程》现行本有编辑者“再创造”的成分，也存在某些“前后不一”之处，但是编辑者最大程度地保证了对 Saussure 思想的忠实，基本上反映出 Saussure 思想的原貌。因此，50 年代后研究《教程》的三部专著的问世，标志着 Saussure 研究进入一个新阶段，50—60 年代这一时期的考证研究过程通常被称为“索绪尔语言学思想的重新发现”。[1] 这个时期的 Saussure 研究实际上是《教程》的文本研究，也可说是对《教程》作了“语文学”式的解读。虽然这种研究未对 Saussure 思想体系作深入探究，但它证实了《教程》的真实性，从而成为 Saussure 研究的转折点。50 年代初英国语言学家 Firth 把语言研究者分为四种类型：索绪尔主义者、反索绪尔主义者、后索绪尔主义者、非索绪尔主义者。而到 50 年代后期另一位英国语言学家 Spence 则宣称“我们现在都是索绪尔主义者了”。

3. **再认识时期**。进入 70 年代，Saussure 评传性研究著作和专题性研究著作相继问世，这不仅说明《教程》的学术思想已产生广泛影响，而且说明 Saussure 的学术地位在语言学研究中已完全得到确认。这一时期的主要研究著作有：Koerner 的《索绪尔：他的语言学思想、西方语言研究的起源与发展》(1973)、Calvet 的《索绪尔：支持与反对》(1975)、Culler 的《索绪尔》(1976)等。其中尤以 Culler 的研究影响最大，他不但阐述了 Saussure 语言理论的基本思想，而且对 Saussure 在符号学领域所做出的贡献及其对人文科学的影响给予了较高评价。80 年代，英国语言学家 Harris 的《读索绪尔》(1987)和《语言、索绪尔和维特根斯坦》

1 参见戚雨村，1997，“索绪尔的重新被发现”，载于《语文研究群言集》，中山大学出版社。

（1988）是这个时期两部重要代表著作。这两部著作以《教程》为依据，以挖掘其思想内涵为目的，分别对 Saussure 的语言学思想和哲学思想进行独到的思考和探究，拓宽了人们对 Saussure 思想的认识。这个时期的研究提出了三种不同的看法：一种对《教程》作出"结构主义"的解读，认为《教程》的基本精神是结构主义的，为结构主义的发展提供了理论前提和思想来源；第二种对《教程》作出"语言系统理论"的解读，认为《教程》是关于语言系统的理论，阐述的是语言自身的普遍规律；第三种对《教程》作出"符号学"的解读，认为《教程》是关于符号学的理论，阐述了符号的基本性质和功能及符号学的学科地位。[1] 经过这个时期的再认识过程，Saussure 丰富的思想内涵被揭示出来。

4. 重新认识时期。所谓重新认识，既包含对 Saussure 思想理论体系的重新思考，也包括对前人关于 Saussure 研究结论的重新审视。90 年代的研究表明，一方面对 Saussure 原始思想的考证工作仍在进行并有新的发现，如 Saussure 于 1910—1911 年第三度讲授《普通语言学教程》（法英对照本）（1993）已公开出版发行，1996 年他的橘园手稿被发现，并于 2002 年由 Gallimard（伽里玛）出版社以《普通语言学手稿》为名出版，汉译版于 2011 年由南京大学出版社出版。同时，日内瓦大学语言学教授 René Amacker 编辑的校注本索绪尔手稿《语言科学——论语言的二元本质》2011 年由日内瓦 Droz 书店出版。另一方面，研究成果在理论上有突破性进展，其深度和广度都是前所未有的。这标志着 Saussure 研究步入了一个新的历史发展时期。这个时期有两部著作代表了 90 年代 Saussure 研究的特点及发展趋向。一部是

---

1 蒂保尔特（Thibault）提出对索绪尔《教程》的解读只有前两种模式，但笔者认为第三种模式也是客观存在的。参见 Thibault, P. J. 1997. *Re-reading Saussure: The Dynamics of Signs in Social Life*. London: Routledge, pp. 4-5.

Holdcroft 所著的《索绪尔：符号、系统和任意性》(1991)。这部专著对 Saussure 思想的基本观点作了全面阐发并给予了批评性评价，并对 Saussure 的某些观点及前人的看法提出了质疑。另一部著作是 Thibault 所著的《重读索绪尔：社会生活中符号的动态性》(1997)。这部著作是这个时期 Saussure 研究发展趋向的代表作。Thibault 在这部著作中对前人的研究提出了挑战，以全新的视角对 Saussure 理论作出“结构主义”或“形式主义”解读的结论进行了批判，提出并阐述了 Saussure 社会–符号元理论的思想，即认为 Saussure 语言理论是关于如何使用语言系统创造意义的理论。Saussure 研究的最新进展表明，人们已冲破了传统的认识模式，对《教程》作出了“结构–功能”式的解读。这是一种综合性的理解，综合蕴涵着“创造”，它标志着 Saussure 研究发展到更高的水平。

四、关于我国的 Saussure 思想研究

虽然《教程》的中译本迟至 20 世纪 80 年代初才在我国正式出版，我国的 Saussure 研究可追溯到 30 年代，从那时起，除了“文革”时留下空白之外，Saussure 研究一直没有间断，至今对许多研究者仍具吸引力。按照时间顺序，Saussure 思想研究在我国大致经历了三个阶段。

1. 引进与传播（30—60 年代初）。Saussure 语言学思想研究在我国可追溯到 30 年代，陈望道和方光焘是早期接触和引进 Saussure 思想的两位学者。1938 年，陈望道就发表文章，区分言语行为（langage）、语言（langue）和言语（parole）三个概念，并分别译为“言语活动”“话语”和“言谈”。方光焘在早年讲授普通语言学理论课程时就把《教程》作为重要参考书目（戚雨村，1997），并在 50—60 年代对《教程》有过深入讲解和研

究。1938—1943年以上海为阵地展开的“文法革新讨论”，对于Saussure思想的传播起到了巨大推动作用。新中国成立以后，通过译介苏联有关Saussure研究的资料，我国更多学者开始了解Saussure。50年代初和60年代末开展的关于语言和言语问题的大讨论进一步推动了索绪尔语言学思想的广泛传播。在这个时期，岑麒祥和高名凯是主要代表，尽管在他们的著述中明显有“左”的思想倾向。引进和传播这个时期体现出这样的特点:（1）Saussure思想的传播在中国早期是悄然而入的，在较长一段时间里，引进是零散的，缺乏系统性;（2）许多理论观点是通过苏联间接引进的，因此在引进和传播过程中不同程度地受到苏联学术观点的影响;（3）在“左”的思想的干扰下，对Saussure思想的理解有简单化倾向，同时存在片面性，所持的态度是否定大于肯定。

2. 解释与评价（70—80年代末）。1978年改革开放以后，随着思想的解放，学术研究呈现出异常活跃的局面。1980年《教程》的中译本出版，为我国更多读者了解和研究Saussure创造了必要条件，我国的Saussure研究步入了一个全面解释与评价的阶段。这个时期的研究主要是围绕三个方面展开的。（1）基本语言理论的系统介绍与评述：由于受历史的局限和时代背景的影响，Saussure思想早期在我国的引进与传播明显不足，因此改革开放后岑麒祥（1980）等许多学者撰文，全面、系统地介绍和评述了Saussure的语言理论，涉及了《教程》所包含的重要理论观点。这些评介不但充分肯定了Saussure语言理论在20世纪语言学中的地位，而且指出了它的某些缺憾。（2）国外Saussure研究的译介与评述：在国外，60年代后Saussure的理论被重新发现，而这个时期在我国正是十年浩劫，Saussure研究与国外隔绝。所以，改革开放后，引进国外Saussure研究成果，介绍国外的研究状况以促进学术争鸣是完全必要的。徐志民（1983）对Saussure自

1878 年发表他的成名作《论印欧系语言元音的原始系统》至 20 世纪 70 年代近一个世纪的研究和背景情况作了翔实的评介。许国璋（1983）率先介绍了 Godel 和 Mauro 所著的两部《教程》评注本，并以丰富翔实的资料和独特的理解受到学术界的重视。（3）重要理论问题的讨论与评价:《教程》包含诸多重要的理论问题，如语言和言语的区分、语言符号的任意性、语言的共时性和历时性、组合关系和联想关系、语言符号的价值等。这些问题在学者（许国璋，1988；王钢，1988；徐思益，1980；索振羽，1983；孙力平，1987）中都有深入的探讨和评价。这个时期 Saussure 研究体现出全面解释、客观评价、批判吸收、大胆探索的特点。

3. **重新认识与再认识**（90 年代至今）。所谓重新认识和再认识，即吸收国外研究成果，冲破传统认识上的局限，挖掘 Saussure《教程》丰富的思想内涵，重新认识 Saussure 的思想理论体系和审视前人对 Saussure 的评价。这个阶段的研究涉及对 Saussure 的符号学思想（刘润清，1995）以及语言学和符号学的关系的认识（乐眉云，1994，1997）；涉及对 Saussure 语言学哲学（linguistic philosophy）思想的进一步阐释，包括他的方法论和认识论（皮鸿鸣，1994），以及对任意性思想的重新评价（刘润清、张绍杰，1997）和理论之争（李葆嘉，1994；索振羽，1995）；同时还涉及对 Saussure 语言理论根源的探究（姚小平，1993）。更重要的是澄清了 Saussure 研究中一些有争议的理论问题（信德麟，1993；戚雨村，1997；张绍杰、王克非，1997），如 Saussure 是不是把语言和言语割裂开来，是不是强调研究语言的关系（结构）而忽视语言的价值（意义），他的认识论是不是唯心的等问题。90 年代以来的研究表明，我国的 Saussure 研究能积极借鉴国外研究的新成果，在广度和深度上都有新的进展，

Saussure 研究对我国语言理论工作者仍具吸引力。[1] 2013 年，索绪尔 100 周年诞辰。为纪念这位伟大的语言学家，《外语学刊》开辟专栏发表 Saussure 研究的论文，反映出 Saussure 思想研究的最新成果。新世纪之后的文献显示，我国学者对 Saussure 的研究兴趣有增无减，其研究成果也体现了研究的深度和广度。

五、Saussure 留给 20 世纪语言学的遗产

综观整个 20 世纪语言学的发展，几乎所有不同语言理论和不同语言学派，都曾不同程度地受到 Saussure 思想的影响，如 Bloomfield 的语言理论、Chomsky 的语言理论、Halliday 的语言理论，以及布拉格学派、哥本哈根学派、伦敦学派等等。不仅如此，他的符号学思想对 20 世纪人类学、文学批评等人文学科都产生了重要影响。所以，《教程》是 Saussure 留给 20 世纪语言学的宝贵遗产。

近一个世纪以来，Saussure 作为现代语言学创始人的地位从未受到挑战，正如本《教程》英译者 Harris 在译者前言中指出的那样，居于两方面原因：其一，在同时代的语言学家当中，Saussure 是第一位认识到语言学要在科学中占有一席之地，就必须要回答一系列理论问题的语言学家；其二，他本人对这些问题提供了答案，而这些答案为后来语言研究领域各种语言理论或所谓“语言学”的建立提供了基础或出发点。《教程》所涉及的这些理论问题很多，内容十分丰富，下面我们概括地加以评介。

1. 语言研究的对象不是给定的而是建构的

Saussure 认为，语言学是一门科学，语言学研究是对语言的科学研究，作为一门科学的语言学必须有它确定的研究对象。但

---

1 关于我国的索绪尔研究情况，详见张绍杰，1999，“索绪尔研究在中国”，《外语与外语教学》，1999 年第 3 期。

语言学这门学科不同于其他学科，这种差别在于其他学科的研究对象是预先给定的，然后我们采用不同的观点加以研究，而语言学的对象不是事先给定的，是先有观点然后才有研究对象，即“所采用的观点创造了研究对象”（8）[1]。因此，Saussure 首先从符号学的观点来阐释语言的性质。Saussure 指出，语言是一种社会惯例，但它不同于其他社会惯例，它是表达概念的符号系统（15）。也就是说，语言具有社会符号的性质，表现在它具有符号性、社会性和规约性。语言的这种性质揭示了语言在人类社会生活中的作用。正如 Harris（1989：177）指出的那样，在 Saussure 看来，“语言是人类用来对他们所生活的世界进行理性认知的工具，语言不仅仅被看作我们理解现实的依附品，反之，我们对现实的理解被看作基本上是依赖于构成语言系统的言语符号在社会中的使用”。

另一方面，我们必须看到，语言是一种特殊的符号系统。人类的言语行为既包含个人的方面，也包含社会的方面，对于现在时来说，它是一种惯例，而同时又是过去的产品。这种二重性为语言研究带来了困难，因此，Saussure 认为，为了使语言学成为一门科学，“语言学家必须把语言结构作为主要的研究对象，并把言语行为的全部表现形式与其联系起来”（9）。换言之，要对语言进行科学的研究，我们必须区分语言和言语。Saussure 所说的“语言”指的是语言的结构，或是语言的结构系统，它是超个人的。“言语”指个人的说话行为。人类所从事的各种各样的语言活动即“言语行为”中正包含语言和言语两个部分，语言是本质的（essential），言语是次要的（secondary）。语言和言语之间的本质区别，为我们建立不同的语言学科提供了前提（参见 8—17 页）。因此，Saussure 提出，“语言研究包括两个部分，本质的部分把

1 括号里的数字表示本《教程》的参照页码。

本质上是社会的和独立于个人的语言系统本身视为研究对象，这是纯粹的心理研究；次要的部分把言语行为中个人的方面即言语也包括发音视为研究对象，这是心理 – 物理研究”（19）。这两种研究分别称作语言的语言学和言语的语言学，进而他又区分了内部语言学和外部语言学，内部语言学研究语言的结构系统，外部语言学研究与其相关的文学、文化、历史等（18—23）。Saussure 主张科学的语言研究应把语言作为对象，而不是把言语作为研究对象。所以，Saussure 坚持区分语言和言语完全是由他对语言性质的认识所决定的，也可以说完全是为了理论上的建构，并非要把两者割裂开来。

如果说语言具有社会符号的性质，以揭示语言社会符号本质为目的的 Saussure 语言理论，就可以称为“社会符号元理论”（Thibault，1997），这种理论不同于以心理学为基础、以人类生物基础为解释目标的 Chomsky 的语言理论。过去学术界认为 Saussure 和 Chomsky 两人有承袭关系，这是一种误解。但是 Saussure 提出的社会符号元理论到底有没有引发一场语言学革命，对这个问题有不同看法。Tobin（1990）认为，“索绪尔的符号革命”实际上并没有发生，语言学和符号学至今仍被视为两个独立的学科。事实上，“Saussure 的符号革命”昭示着符号学和语言学两者之间的统合。这不能不唤起人们对 Saussure 符号学语言观的重新思索。

2. 语言符号的根本特征：任意性和线性

语言学的研究对象既然是语言符号系统或语言的结构，那么如何认识语言符号的性质便成为必须给以回答的问题。Saussure 是在批判了命名主义（nominalism）的基础上阐述语言符号的任意性和线性特征的。西方哲学史上长期存在着两种根本不同的观点：经验论和唯理论。虽然两者的观点是相互对立的，却有一个共同的前提，即都假定有一个完整的、明晰的、自在的宇宙存在。

因此，两派都承认语词与外部世界之间存在着联系，但看法截然不同。一派认为名称和它所代表的事物之间没有内在的必然联系；一派认为名称和它所代表的事物之间存在着必然联系。前者称约定论，以亚里士多德为代表；后者成自然论，以柏拉图为代表。命名主义就是在这两种哲学观的基础上发展而来的。

Saussure 指出，有些人认为语言是一套命名集，它的要素与事物存在着对应的关系。Saussure 批评说，这种观点没有搞清名称是一个声音实体还是心理实体（65）。按照命名主义的观点，一个名称（词）只是简单的一串声音，它的意义存在于它的外部。Saussure 认为，这样的认识方法是幼稚可笑的。语言符号和外部世界之间不存在对应的关系，符号的意义产生于语言系统的内部，是“系统的结构自身创造了语言单位并在它们之间建立起关系”（Harris，1989：179）。所以，Saussure 明确指出，语言符号联系的不是事物和名称，而是概念和声音结构，它是一个二元的心理实体。构成语言符号的两个成分概念和声音结构又称为指称（signification）和指号（signal），通常称为所指和能指，它们之间的联系或两者的结合是任意的（66—67）。Saussure 把语言符号的任意性特征称作“第一原则”。语言符号的任意性是区别于所有其他社会符号系统的根本特性，也是我们认识和理解 Saussure 语言学思想的出发点。正如 Saussure 所言，“整个语言系统都建立在符号任意性的非理性的原则基础之上”（131）。不过应当指出，长期以来国内学术界对任意性的看法存在着分歧。诚然，有理有据的学术之争是正常的，但由于误解导致分歧就是不正常的了。读者在这方面应有自己的观察和分析。

语言符号的第二原则，即指号的线性特征。这一特征是我们认识语言系统内部结构关系的基础（69—70）。由于篇幅的限制，这里不加以赘述。

3. 语言研究的两种观点：共时研究和历时研究

Saussure 认为，语言研究可采用两种观点，一种是共时的观点，一种是历时的观点，这两种观点分别称作共时研究和历时研究。前者涉及共时事实，即共存于同一个系统中的事实，后者涉及历时事实，即随时间变化但不影响整个系统的事实，或者说是跨越时间所产生的事实。为什么语言中会存在这两种事实？这个问题与语言符号的另一个特性即不可变性和可变性有关，这一特性也是区分共时语言学和历时语言学的前提。

语言符号一方面是可变的，另一方面是不变的。这似乎是一对无法调和的矛盾，对这个问题的解释涉及语言符号任意性、规约性和社会性的关系。Saussure 认为，这一特性可联系非理性的任意性原则和时间的连续性原则给以解释。从语言的内部看，符号的指号和指称之间的联系是任意的，因而指号对指称的选择似乎是自由的（71）。这一点看起来符号是容易改变的，可正是因为语言符号以任意性为基础，说话大众才没有讨论改变符号的基础。从语言的外部看，也就是从符号和使用它的语言社团成员的关系看，符号不是自由的而是受制约的，一种符号不能随随便便被另一种符号所代替，这体现出语言符号的规约性。随着时间的流逝，语言符号注定是要变化的。这种不变性和可变性是时间的连续性原则在起作用的结果。也就是说，时间因素既使语言符号具有不变性的一面（体现在语言的历史继承性），也使语言符号具有可变性的一面（体现在语言的历时变化性）。同时必须看到，语言是社会事实，随着时间的推移，说话大众将产生改变它的社会力量（72—78）。所以，符号的不变性和可变性包含着自由和非自由之间的矛盾，如果不考虑时间因素，语言符号具有任意性，因此是自由的；而考虑时间因素，语言符号既是非自由的，具有不变性，也是变化的，具有某种程度的可变性（Saussure，1993：98）。

正是语言符号的不变性和可变性的特征导致了两种语言事实的产生。在Saussure看来，由于这两种事实完全属于不同的秩序，这就决定了我们必须区分静态语言学和演化语言学或共时语言学和历时语言学。Saussure指出，“共时语言学研究同一个集体意识所感知的构成一个系统的共存要素间逻辑的和心理的关系，而历时语言学研究非同一个集体意识所感知的连续要素间的关系，这些要素彼此可以取代但不构成系统”（98）。Saussure指出，在共时语言学和历时语言学的十字路口，我们应选择前者，也就是研究语言的共时符号系统的关系和价值。但同时Saussure通过语言和下棋的比喻，说明了共时研究和历时研究既相对独立又相互依赖的关系（87—89）。

4. 语言符号系统是一个关系网络系统

既然共时研究涉及的是关系和价值，那么什么是价值？语言符号的价值是如何实现的？这是Saussure必须给以回答的问题。根据Saussure的解释，语言符号系统是一个价值系统，价值是通过系统中内部的关系所体现的或生成的。

Saussure首先指出，一个词的价值主要指它所代表的一定的概念，单从概念的方面来看，价值无疑是意义的一部分，但我们决不能轻易地得出结论，价值和意义两者之间只存在这样的差别。从构成一个符号的两个成分之间的关系来看，意义就是声音结构的对等物，但另一方面，语言符号作为两个构成成分的结合体，同样具有它的对等物，这就是语言中的其他符号。所以，任何成分的价值取决于与其他成分在系统中的同时共存（112—113）。Saussure通过与货币价值的比较来解释语言符号的价值。他指出价值是由（1）非类似物所决定（比如五法郎的硬币可与一定量的面包相交换）；也由（2）可比较的类似物所决定（比如五法郎的硬币可兑换五法郎的纸币）。同样，一个词可替换非类似的东西即概念，同时它可与相似的东西另一个词相比较。所以，一个词的价值不仅仅是由它的概念或意义所决定，还必须通过参照与其他词的可比价值加以确定（113—114）。这里 Saussure 要阐明的是，语言符号价值的概念有两个含义：一是价值体现于差别，二是价值体现于关系。

因此，无论从构成符号的概念方面看，还是从物质方面的声音看，或者从作为整体的符号看，语言中只存在差别（118）。差别意味着价值，价值来源于语言系统中不同成分之间的关系。

语言系统中存在着由要素－符号－系统构成的不同层次的网络关系。在符号内部，存在着构成符号的两个成分指号与指称之间的关系；在符号外部，存在着作为构成符号的两个成分的整体与其他符号的关系，还存在着作为部分的符号和作为整体的系统之间的关系。这些关系集中表现为时间上的组合关系和空间上的联想关系，构成一个关系网络系统，语言符号的价值或意义正是通过这个关系网络系统实现的。也就是说，组合关系和联想关系不但构成了语言的结构，而且决定着语言的功能（126）。在 Saussure 看来，语言系统的机制表现在，它允许同时进行组合关系和联想关系的选择，从而实现语言系统的功能。这一选择的过程体现出语言符号的任意性和相对任意性相互作用的结果：一方面，任意性意味着系统对概念和声音结构的选择是自由的，这两个成分的结合产生了新的符号，同时也产生了价值，另一方面，组合关系和联想关系是相对任意的，相对任意性意味着系统对组合关系和联想关系的选择正是对任意性的限制（131），也就是对意义选择的限制（详见张绍杰，2013）。语言系统的功能正是在这样的过程中实现的。

从 Saussure 的论述中我们认识到，语言符号系统是一个关系网络系统，它为人们进行言语交际提供了可能的选择。语言系统实现其功能的过程，就是人们在使用语言的过程中对意义进行选择的过程。不过，由于时代的局限，Saussurc 尚不能解释，使用语言的选择过程不但受语言系统的限制，而且受语境等因素的限制，他只是阐述了以任意性为基础的符号系统如何使交际成为可能的问题。因此，纵观 Saussure 的语言理论，它实质上是关于人类如何使用符号系统作为资源创造意义的社会符号元理论。

六、结束语

Saussure《普通语言学教程》的思想的内涵极其丰富，我们很难在一篇导读中给以全面的介绍和评价。最后我们只想提出几点看法供读者思考。

首先，如何重新评价 Saussure 的语言理论？当今 Saussure 研究表明，Saussure 的语言理论是社会符号元理论。我们不应当受传统学术观点的影响，对《教程》作出结构主义的解读，而应从结构和功能的观点解释它的思想体系。

其二，如何以 Saussure 的语言理论为依据解释语言、社会和文化的关系？语言系统是一套社会惯例或规约，对于说同一语言的全体成员来说，对它的使用似乎是自由的，但对于每个人来说，他的使用却是不自由的，个人的理性思维必须按照该语言的价值系统去表达。作为社会惯例的语言也是文化的重要组成部分。这是否说明人类对世界的认知依赖于我们所说的语言？

其三，为什么任意性原则是语言符号的根本特征？任意性与语言的符号性、系统性、规约性、社会性有着内在的联系。从说话人的视角来看，任意性是语言系统建构意义的基础，因此使人类交际成为可能。任意性从某种意义上说体现了作为符号的人的特性。人首先是社会人，其次才是自由人。作为社会人，他的自由理性无法摆脱社会的约束，这就好比任意性必然受到语言关系网络系统的限制一样。

最后，如何看待国外学者近期对 Saussure 的否定性评价？

Pieter Seuren 于 2018 年出版了一本书，题为《索绪尔与施多霭：神话与天才》(*Saussure and Sechehaye: Myth and Genius*)。在此书中，Seuren 全面否定了 Saussure 现代语言学之父的地位，试图将这位举世公认的语言学集大成者拉下神坛。Seuren 认为，Saussure 的学生 Sechehaye 才是真正的语言学天才。其原因是前者的语言学思想多半都与后者存在渊源关系，然而前者在讲课手稿中并未提供他的思想来源，后者出于对老师的尊重而保持沉默。全书通过对两者的对比，对 Saussure 进行了全盘否定。这种貌似公允的否定令人难以接受，读者不妨阅读此书给出自己的评判。

参考书目：

Aarsleff, H. 1982. *From Locke to Saussure*. Minneapolis: University of Minnesota Press.

Culler, J. 1976. *Ferdinand de Saussure*. Harmondsworth: Penguin Books.

Harris, R. 1987. *Reading Saussure*. London: Duckworth.

Harris, R. and Taylor, T. J. 1989. *Landmarks in Linguistic Thought*. London: Routledge.

Joseph, J. E. 2011. Harris's Saussure–Harris as Saussure: The Translations of the Cours and the Third Course. *Language Sciences* 33 : 524-530.

Saussure, F. de. 1993. *Saussure's Third Course of Lectures on General Linguistics* (1910-1911). Edited and translated by Eisuke Komatsu & Roy Harris. Oxford: Pergamon Press.

Saussure, F. de. 2002. *Ecrits de linguistique générale*. Paris: Gallimard.

Thibault, P. J. 1997. *Re-reading Saussure: The Dynamics of Signs in Social Life*. London: Routledge. pp. 4-5.

Tobin, Y. 1990. *Semantics and Linguistics*. London: Longman.

Zhang, Shaojie and Zhang, Yanfei. 2015. Scalar Implicature: A Saussurean System-based Approach. *Language Sciences* 51: 43-53.

Zhang, Yanfei and Zhang, Shaojie. 2014. How and Why Saussure is Misread in China: A Historical Study. *Language and History* 57: 155-173.

Zhang, Yanfei and Zhang, Shaojie. 2021. How Saussure is Misinterpreted in Cognitive Grammar. *Semiotica Issue* 239: 243.

岑麒祥，1980，瑞士著名语言学家索绪尔和他的名著《普通语言学教程》，《国外语言学》第1期。

陈望道，1980，《陈望道语文论集》。上海教育出版社。

方光焘，1997，《方光焘语言学论文集》。商务印书馆。

高名凯，1995，《语言论》。商务印书馆。

李葆嘉，1994，论索绪尔符号任意性原则的失误与复归，《语言文字应用》第3期。

刘润清，1995，《西方语言学流派》。外语教学与研究出版社。

刘润清、张绍杰，1997，也谈语言符号的任意性问题，载于《语文研究群言集》。中山大学出版社。

皮鸿鸣，1994，索绪尔语言学的根本原则，《武汉大学学报》(哲学社会科学版)第4期。

戚雨村，1997，索绪尔的重新被发现，载于《语文研究群言集》。中山大学出版社。

孙力平，1987，应如何理解语言符号的任意性，《江西大学学报》第1期。

索绪尔，2011，《普通语言学手稿》，于秀英译。南京：南京大学出版社。

索振羽，1983，德·索绪尔的语言价值理论，《新疆大学学报》第2期。

索振羽，1995，索绪尔的语言符号任意性原则是正确的，《语言文字应用》第2期。

王　钢，1988，符号性·语言单位·意义，《现代外语》第1期。

信德麟，1993，索绪尔《普通语言学札记》(俄文版)评介，《国外语言学》第4期。

许国璋，1983，关于索绪尔的两本书，《国外语言学》第1期。

许国璋，1988，语言符号的任意性问题，《外语教学与研究》第3期。

徐思益，1980，论语言的共时性和历时性,《新疆大学学报》第 1 期。

徐志民，1983，索绪尔研究的新阶段,《语文现代化》第 2 期。

姚小平，1993，索绪尔语言理论的德国根源,《外语教学与研究》第 3 期。

乐眉云，1994，索绪尔的符号学语言观,《外国语》第 6 期。

乐眉云，1997，再论索绪尔的符号学语言观,《外国语》第 4 期。

张绍杰、王克非，1997，索绪尔两个教程的比较与诠释,《外语教学与研究》第 3 期。

张绍杰，1999，索绪尔研究在中国,《外语与外语教学》第 3 期。

张绍杰，2013，语言机制对任意性的限制：语言系统运行机理探究,《外语学刊》第 4 期。

Contents

PART ONE
GENERAL PRINCIPLES

PART TWO
SYNCHRONIC LINGUISTICS

PART THREE
DIACHRONIC LINGUISTICS

Translator's Introduction

Saussure's *Cours de linguistique générale* occupies a place of unique importance in the history of Western thinking about man in society. It is a key text not only within the development of linguistics but also in the formation of that broader intellectual movement of the twentieth century known as 'structuralism'. With the sole exception of Wittgenstein, no thinker has had as profound an influence on the modern view of *homo loquens* as Saussure.

The revolution Saussure ushered in has rightly been described as 'Copernican'. For instead of men's words being seen as peripheral to men's understanding of reality, men's understanding of reality came to be seen as revolving about their social use of verbal signs. In the *Cours de linguistique générale* we see this new approach clearly articulated for the first time. Words are not vocal labels which have come to be attached to things and qualities already given in advance by Nature, or to ideas already grasped independently by the human mind. On the contrary languages themselves, collective products of social interaction, supply the essential conceptual frameworks for men's analysis of reality and, simultaneously, the verbal equipment for their description of it. The concepts we use are creations of the language we speak.

Saussure's standing as the founder of modern linguistics remains unchallenged more than half a century after his death. It is based on two facts. One fact is that Saussure, although only one among many distinguished linguists of his day, was the first to recognise the particular range of theoretical questions which had to be answered if linguistics was ever to take its place among the sciences. The other fact is that Saussure himself proposed answers to those questions which have remained either the basis or the point of departure for all subsequent linguistic theory within the academic discipline which thereafter claimed the designation 'linguistics'.

This dual achievement suffices to explain Saussure's pivotal place in the evolution of language studies. But he plays a no less crucial role when his work is seen in a wider cultural context. For the founder of modern linguistics at the same time founded semiology, the general science of signs, within which linguistics was to be one special branch. In so doing, Saussure opened up a new approach to the study of many other human patterns of behaviour. It was an approach later to be exploited by theorists in such diverse fields as art, architecture, philosophy, literary criticism and social anthropology. The implications of Saussure's technique for dealing with linguistic analysis extend far beyond the boundaries of language, in ways which make the *Cours de linguistique générale* without doubt one of the most far-reaching works concerning the study of human cultural activities to have been published at any time since the Renaissance.

* * *

Saussure's proposals for the establishment of linguistics as an independent science may – at the risk of making them sound rather unexciting – be summarised as follows. He rejected the possibility of an all-embracing science of language, which would deal simultaneously with physiological, sociological, philosophical and psychological aspects of the subject. Instead, he proposed to cut through the perplexing maze of existing approaches to the study of linguistic phenomena by setting up a unified discipline, based upon a single, clearly defined concept: that of the *linguistic sign*. The essential feature of Saussure's linguistic sign is that, being intrinsically arbitrary, it can be identified only by contrast with coexisting signs of the same nature, which together constitute a structured system. By taking this position, Saussure placed modern linguistics in the vanguard of twentieth-century structuralism.

It was a position which committed Saussure to drawing a radical distinction between *diachronic* (or evolutionary) linguistics and *synchronic* (or static) linguistics, and giving priority to the latter. For words, sounds and constructions connected solely by processes of historical development over the centuries cannot possibly, according to Saussure's analysis, enter into structural relations with one another, any more than Napoleon's France and Caesar's Rome can be structurally united under one and the same political system.

Truism though this may now seem, there is no doubt that in arguing along these lines Saussure was swimming against the prevailing tide in language studies throughout his lifetime. For the great philological achievements of the nineteenth century had all been founded upon a historical and comparativist approach to language. Late-nineteenth-century philology was as uncompromisingly 'evolutionary' in outlook as Darwinian biology. Saussure was the first to question whether the historical study of languages could possibly provide a satisfactory foundation for a science of linguistics. The question was as profound as it was startling: for the assumption most of Saussure's contemporaries made was that historical philology already *had* provided the only possible scientific foundation. They believed, as Max Müller optimistically put it in the 1860s, that linguists were already dealing with the facts of language just as scientifically as 'the astronomer treats the stars of heaven, or the botanist the flowers of the field'. In Saussure's view, nothing could have been more profoundly mistaken.

Where historical philology had failed, in Saussure's opinion, was in simply not recognising the structural nature of the linguistic sign. As a result, it had concentrated upon features which were merely superficially and adventitiously describable in mankind's recorded linguistic history. The explanations philological historians provided were in the final analysis simply appeals to the past. They did not – and could not – offer any analysis of what a language is from the viewpoint of its current speakers. Whereas for Saussure it was *only* by adopting the users' point of view that a language could be seen to be a coherently organised structure, amenable to scientific study. For linguistic signs, Saussure insisted, do not exist independently of the complex system of contrasts implicitly recognised in the day-to-day vocal interactions of a given community of speakers.

Similarly, in all other fields of human activity where signs are arbitrary, it is the system of structural contrasts implemented in human interaction which must become the focus of attention for any scientific semiological investigation. For signs are not physical objects. We cannot study them as we can plants, or animals, or chemical substances. Signs are not to be equated with sounds uttered, or marks on paper, or gestures, or visual configurations of various kinds. These are merely the vehicles by which signs are expressed. To confuse the two would make it impossible to establish a science of signs at all, in Saussure's estimation, whether in the domain of language or any other.

Nor, although the terminology of the *Cours* itself falls short of ideal consistency on this point, are signs to be equated simply with the signals (*signifiants*) by which they are identified. Each sign is a dual entity, uniting signal with signification (*signifié*). Neither facet of this duality exists independently of the other, just as no sign exists independently of the other signs united in the same system of structural contrasts. A language (*langue*) is for Saussure this whole system which alone makes it possible to identify and describe constituent parts: it is not a whole fortuitously built up out of parts already existing in their own right. Linguistic signs are therefore not like individual bricks, put together in a certain way to form an architectural structure. Unlike bricks, they are not separate self-contained units. Except as parts of the total structure, they do not even exist, any more than the circumference or the radii of a circle exist without the circle.

Thus to treat words as linguistic units somehow capable of surviving through time from Latin down to modern Italian is, for Saussure, no more than a historian's metaphor. It is a metaphor which does no harm provided we recognise it as a projection based on our own acquaintance, as language-users, with the reality of the linguistic sign. But it is not a metaphor which can provide us with any genuine understanding of the reality, nor any foundation for a scientific account of it either.

This is not the place to discuss how far Saussure succeeded in answering his own searching questions about language and human signs in general, or in providing modern linguistics with the satisfactory theoretical basis he thought it lacked. These are issues which have been and still are controversial. There is no doubt, however, that it was Saussure who was responsible not merely for sparking the controversy, but also for giving that controversy the particular intellectual shape which it has taken ever since. Whether or not it is the right shape is another matter. But anyone who wishes to understand modern linguistics needs to be able to recognise that shape. In just the same way, although we may not agree with the terms in which the controversy between anomalists and analogists was formulated in Classical antiquity, we need to be able to recognise the shape that controversy took in order to appreciate both the achievements and the limitations of the linguistic theorising of that age.

* * *

When Saussure died in 1913, he left no manuscript setting out his theories in detail. What was published three years later as the *Cours de linguistique générale* was put together by his colleagues, mainly from lecture notes taken by his pupils. The notes in question have now – belatedly – been published in full by R. Engler in his critical edition of the text (1967–74). On the evidence of this material, it has sometimes been suggested that by no means all the ideas in the *Cours de linguistique générale* are a faithful reflexion of Saussure's.

Understandably, a great deal of the blame has been laid at the door of Saussure's editors. What is beyond dispute is that they subsequently admitted to having failed to represent Saussure's view of the phoneme correctly. What is also beyond dispute is that since the publication of the original material on which their text was based, and the detailed analysis of this material by Saussurean scholars, there is ample scope for doubt or scepticism on a variety of points. Indeed, it seems clear that in certain instances the editorial treatment of the original notes, far from clarifying what Saussure said, introduces an element of uncertainty as to the correct interpretation. Even the much-quoted final sentence of the *Cours* turns out to be an editorial pronouncement for which there is no specific textual authority in the manuscripts.

It is, however, a somewhat crude critical procedure constantly to compare the published text of the *Cours* with the available notes, and complain that the editors have misrepresented Saussure every time a discrepancy is found. There may be discrepancies both of detail and of arrangement. But what they prove is another matter. If we take the published text as a whole, there is no convincing reason for supposing that it seriously misrepresents the kind of synthesis towards which Saussure himself was working when he died. That synthesis is necessarily hypothetical, a projection of what might have happened had Saussure lived. But if its validity is questioned on quite basic points, then we are driven to one or other of two equally unlikely conclusions. Either Saussure's closest colleagues and sympathisers were not able fully to understand his thinking on linguistic topics; or else Saussure himself had inadvertently misled them, while at the same time managing not to mislead his pupils.

One comes back in the end to the fact that, whatever its imperfections, this publication was the authoritative text of Saussurean structuralism for a whole generation of scholars, and the instrument through which an entirely new approach to linguistic analysis was established. Thereby it acquires in its own right – 'mistakes' and all – a place in the history of modern thought which cannot retrospectively be denied to it.

This is the text, therefore, which has been taken as the basis of the present translation. Published by Payot in Paris in 1916, it had a second (slightly revised) edition in 1922, a third in 1931, a fourth in 1949, and a fifth in 1955. The standard pagination, adopted since the second edition, is indicated in the text published here. Current reprintings of the Payot edition unfortunately perpetuate overlooked printers' errors from previous editions, and these have been corrected in the text here translated. A new Index replaces the incomplete one given in the Payot editions.

* * *

What Saussure thought of translators and translation does not emerge at all clearly from the pages of the *Cours*. It is arguable that if translation is taken as demanding linguistic equivalence between texts, then the Saussurean position must be that translation is impossible. But even those inclined to take a more sanguine or a more practical view of translatability must concede that Saussure has on the whole been poorly served by his English translators and commentators. To demonstrate this in detail would be both an invidious and a dreary undertaking, which will not be attempted here. Suffice it to say that the varied catalogue of mistranslations available for public inspection runs the whole gamut from the trivial to the grossly misleading (*langage* rendered as 'speech'). On crossing the Channel Saussure has been made to utter such blatantly unSaussurean pronouncements as 'language is a form, not a substance'. Surprisingly few have seen that it is not at all necessary to make heavy weather of the distinction between *langage* and *langue* provided one respects the important semantic difference in English between using the word *language* with and without an article. It is small wonder that even Saussure's major theses on the subject of language are poorly understood in the English-speaking academic world. In particular, one is led to wonder whether this may not have played some part in the patently ill-informed view taken by those American generativists who dismiss Saussure's view of language structure as 'naive' (Chomsky) and lacking in any conception of 'rule-governed creativity'.

The new English translation presented here is intended primarily for the reader who is not a specialist in linguistics, but who wishes to acquaint himself in detail with a text which stands as one of the landmarks in the intellectual history of modern times. It is a text which is hard going for the non-specialist, for the lectures on which it is based were given to students who already had an extensive knowledge of Indo-European languages and comparative philology, as well as being able to speak French. The examples the *Cours* uses constantly presuppose this background. To have added footnotes explaining in detail the relevance of each example would have been a Herculean task, resulting in a corpus of notes longer than the text itself. Fortunately, most of Saussure's examples are merely illustrative: few are actually essential to the points he makes. This has made it possible to reduce glosses and comments upon examples to a minimum, on the assumption that a reader who will find this translation useful is not likely to be interested in a critical examination of Saussure's exemplificatory material.

However, a few comments on the problems involved in translating Saussure's technical terminology may be in order here. Some relate to changes in usage since Saussure's day. For example, it would nowadays be misleading to translate *phonème* by *phoneme*, since in the terminology currently accepted in Anglo-American linguistics the term *phoneme* designates a structural unit, whereas it is clear that for Saussure the term *phonème* designates in the first instance a unit belonging to *la parole* (whatever his editors may have thought, and in spite of remarks in the *Cours* which – rightly or wrongly – are held to have been influential in establishing the modern theory of phonemes). Similarly, Saussure's *phonologie* does not correspond to what is nowadays termed *phonology*, nor his *phonétique* to *phonetics*.

Again, *acoustique* no longer matches *acoustic* in its technical use in phonetics. Saussure was teaching long before the invention of the sound spectrograph. The term *acoustique* in the *Cours* appears to relate primarily to that section of the 'speech circuit' where the hearer's perception of sounds occurs. Consequently, *auditory* is preferable as a general equivalent. But this does not automatically resolve all the problems connected with translating *acoustique*.

In particular, there is the expression *image acoustique*, perhaps the most unhappy choice in the whole range of Saussurean terminology. In practice, as teachers of linguistics are well aware, it is a serious obstacle to students in their initial attempts to understand Saussure's thought. The editors of the *Cours* themselves express serious reservations about it (p. [98] footnote). In an English translation, the problems increase. For 'acoustic image' is more or less nonsense by present-day usage, while 'sound-image' unfortunately suggests some combination of the spoken and the written word (as if words were stored in the brain in quasi-graphic form). Insofar as it is clear exactly what is meant by *image acoustique*, it appears to refer to a unit which supposedly plays a part in our capacity to identify auditory impressions (e.g. of sounds, tunes) and to rehearse them mentally (as in interior monologue, humming a tune silently, etc.). It is thus an auditory generalisation which the mind is able to construct and retain, just as it is able to construct and retain visual images of things seen or imagined. The English expression which seems best to designate this is 'sound pattern'.

Finally, some of the central problems of interpretation of the *Cours de linguistique générale* hinge upon the fact that the word *langue* seems to be used in a variety of ways. Critics of Saussure may take this variation as evidence that Saussure had not properly sorted out in his own mind various possible ways of conceptualising linguistic phenomena. They thus see the term *langue* as conflating important distinctions which should have been more carefully drawn and might have been if Saussure had lived longer. How to translate *langue* is consequently a question which cannot be kept altogether separate from one's analysis of the theorising underlying the *Cours* as published.

Engler's *Lexique de la terminologie saussurienne* distinguishes uses of *langue* under no less than ten different headings; but they fall into two main types. One type comprises those instances where *langue* appears to have its usual everyday meaning (*la langue française* 'the French language'). The other comprises those instances in which *langue* clearly has the status of a special technical term in Saussurean linguistics. To have at least that distinction clearly drawn in a translation would doubtless be particularly helpful to readers making their first acquaintance with Saussure's theories. Unfortunately, there are two difficulties in the way. One is that it is not always obvious whether we are dealing with a technical or a non-technical use of *langue*. The other is that in some passages of the text a more abstract view is taken of linguistic phenomena than is taken in other passages. The result is that even the technical uses of the term *langue* sometimes seem to be at odds with one another. To what extent this is due to unwitting vacillation on the part of Saussure or his editors is a matter for debate.

In view of these problems, an easy way out for the translator – and perhaps a justifiable way in the circumstances – would be to fix upon a single all-purpose translation of the word *langue* and stick to it throughout, leaving the reader to cope with the complexities of interpretation for himself. That is not, however, the course which has been followed here, since the effect seemed to be to render Saussure's ideas more difficult of access to a non-specialist English reader than they need be; and that would have defeated the basic purpose of this translation.

Instead, an attempt has been made to indicate the full range of implications associated with the term *langue* by using different renderings in different contexts. While *the language* or *a language* are often perfectly adequate English translations, there are also many instances where expressions such as *linguistic structure* and *linguistic system* bring out much more clearly in English the particular point that is being made.

Varying the translation of a key theoretical term may perhaps be objected to in principle on grounds of inconsistency. But the inconsistency in this case is superficial; whereas in compensation one gains the possibility of expressing nuances and emphases in Saussure's thought which would otherwise risk being lost to the English reader.

* * *

I owe a debt of gratitude to a number of Oxford colleagues who have willingly answered queries on particular points arising from the text of the *Cours*, or discussed more general questions of interpretation of Saussure's views. They include Mr E. Ardener, Mr R. A. W. Bladon, Professor A. E. Davies, Professor P. F. Ganz, Mr H. R. Harré, Dr P. Mühlhäusler and Dr L. Seiffert. Without their help, my attempt to make Saussure available to present-day English readers would have had even more flaws than doubtless remain. It might well have had less if I had always taken their advice.

R. H.

Preface to the First Edition

Ferdinand de Saussure's criticisms of the inadequate tenets and methods characteristic of the linguistics which prevailed during the period of his own intellectual development we heard from his own lips on many occasions. All his life he pursued a determined search for guiding principles to direct the course of his thinking through that chaos. But it was not until 1906, when he had succeeded Joseph Wertheimer at the University of Geneva, that he was able to expound his own views. They were the mature product of many years' reflexion. He gave three courses of lectures on general linguistics, in 1906–1907, 1908–1909 and 1910–1911. The requirements of the curriculum, however, obliged him to devote half of each course to a historical and descriptive survey of the Indo-European languages, and the essential core of his subject was thus considerably reduced.

All those fortunate enough to attend these seminal lectures were disappointed when no book subsequently appeared. After his death, when Mme de Saussure kindly made her husband's papers available to us, we hoped to find something which gave a faithful or at least adequate reflexion of those masterly courses. We envisaged the possibility of a publication based upon a straightforward collation of Saussure's own notes, together with those taken by his students. This expectation was to be frustrated. We found hardly anything which corresponded to what his pupils had taken down. Saussure never kept the rough notes he used for delivering his lectures. In his desk drawers we found only old jottings which, although not without value, could not be put together and integrated with the subject matter of the three lecture courses.

This came as an even greater disappointment to us inasmuch as we had been almost entirely prevented by our own academic duties from attending these last courses of lectures, which marked a phase in Ferdinand de Saussure's career no less brilliant than the already far off days of his *Mémoire sur les voyelles*.[1]

There was thus no alternative but to rely on the notes taken by the students who had attended the three courses of lectures. We were

[1] Saussure first made his mark in the philological world at the age of 21 with the publication of a study entitled *Mémoire sur le système primitif des voyelles dans les langues indo-européennes* (*Dissertation upon the original vowel system of the Indo-European languages*). (Translator's note)

given very full notes on the first two courses by Messrs. Louis Caille, Léopold Gautier, Paul Regard and Albert Riedlinger; and on the third and most important by Mme Albert Sechehaye and Messrs. George Dégallier and Francis Joseph. From M. Louis Brütsch we had notes on one special point. To all those mentioned we owe a debt of sincere gratitude. We should also like to express our warmest thanks to the eminent Romance scholar M. Jules Ronjat, who was kind enough to go through the manuscript before it went to the printer, and give us the benefit of his valuable advice.

What was to be done with the material available? A preliminary critical analysis was indispensable. For each course of lectures and every individual point, a comparison of all the versions was necessary in order to establish what Saussure's views had been. The notes gave us no more than echoes of his thought, and these were not always in unison. For the first two courses we enlisted the collaboration of one of Saussure's pupils who had followed his thinking most closely, M. A. Riedlinger. His help was of great assistance to us. For the third course, the same detailed work of collating and putting the material in order was undertaken by one of us, A. Sechehaye.

But what was the next move to be? The form of oral delivery is often difficult to reconcile with the requirements of a book, and this posed serious problems. Furthermore, Saussure was one of those thinkers for whom thinking is a constant process of intellectual renewal. His ideas developed in all kinds of ways and yet managed to avoid inconsistency. To publish everything we had as it stood would have been impossible. The inevitable repetitions which resulted from extemporisation, the overlaps and the variations of wording would have made such a publication a hotchpotch. On the other hand, to publish only one (but which?) of the three courses would have meant sacrificing the valuable material contained in the other two. Even the third course of lectures, although more definitive than its predecessors, would not in itself have given a complete picture of Saussure's theories and methods.

One suggestion was that we should simply publish without emendating certain excerpts of particular importance. We found the idea attractive at first; but it soon became evident that this would fail to do justice to Saussure's thought. It would have dismembered a system which needed to be seen as a whole in order to be appreciated.

We eventually hit upon a bolder solution which was also, in our view, a more rational one. We would attempt a reconstruction, a synthesis. It would be based upon the third course of lectures, but make use of all the material we had, including Saussure's own notes. This would involve a task of re-creation. It would be by no means a straightforward one, since complete objectivity was essential. We should need to identify every essential idea by reference to the system as a whole, analyse it in depth, and express it in a definitive form, unobscured by the variations and hesitations which naturally accompany oral delivery. We should then need to put each idea in its proper place, and present all the various parts in an order corresponding to the author's intentions, even if the intentions were not apparent but could only be inferred.

The book we now offer with all due diffidence to the academic world and to everyone interested in linguistics is the result of this attempt at synthesis and reconstitution.

Our main aim has been to present an organic whole, omitting nothing which could contribute to the sense of unity. But in that very respect we lay ourselves open to criticism on two different counts.

In the first place, we may be told that this 'unity' is not complete. Saussure in his teaching never claimed to cover the whole of linguistics, or to throw equal light on every aspect of the subject. In practical terms this would have been an impossibility, and in any case his interests lay elsewhere. His main concern was with the fundamentals of the subject, to which he applied certain basic principles of his own. They are present throughout his work, running through it like the warp of a well woven cloth of varied texture. He does not attempt to cover wide areas of linguistics, but chooses topics where he can either provide his principles with particularly striking applications, or else test them against some rival theory.

This is why certain disciplines are scarcely mentioned – semantics, for example. But we do not feel that such gaps weaken the architecture of the whole. The absence of a 'linguistics of speech' is more serious. This had been promised to those who attended the third course of lectures, and it would doubtless have occupied a prominent place in later series. The reason why that promise was never kept is only too well known. Here, we confined ourselves to collecting together Saussure's elusive hints concerning this barely outlined project, and putting them in their natural place in the scheme. We felt we had no brief to go further.

On the other hand, we may perhaps be criticised for including parts which deal with ground already covered before Saussure's day. But in a survey of such scope as this, not everything can be expected to be new; and since principles already familiar are necessary for an understanding of the whole, it is questionable whether it would have been right for us to omit them. Thus the chapter on sound changes includes points already made elsewhere, and perhaps in a more definitive form. None the less, this section contains quite a number of original and valuable details. Moreover, it is evident even from a superficial reading that omitting it would have meant losing the contrast which is essential for an understanding of the principles on which Saussure based his system of static linguistics.

Preface to the First Edition

We are fully aware of the responsibility we owe not only to our readers but also to Saussure himself, who perhaps might not have authorised the publication of this text.

We accept this responsibility, and it is ours alone. Will critics be able to distinguish between Saussure and our interpretation of Saussure? We hope that any blame may be laid at our door, rather than reflect upon the reputation of someone whose memory we cherish.

Geneva, July 1915 Charles BALLY, Albert SECHEHAYE.

Preface to the Second Edition

This second edition does not depart in any essential respect from the text of the first. The editors have confined their attention to certain points of detail, which have been altered in the interests of clarity and precision.

Ch. B. A.S.

Preface to the Third Edition

Apart from a few minor corrections, this edition does not differ from the second.

Ch. B. A.S.

INTRODUCTION [13]

CHAPTER I

A Brief Survey of the History of Linguistics

The science which has grown up around linguistic facts passed through three successive phases before coming to terms with its one and only true object of study.

First of all came what was called 'grammar'. This discipline, first instituted by the Greeks and continued mainly by the French, is based on logic. It offers no scientific or objective approach to a language as such. Grammar aims solely at providing rules which distinguish between correct and incorrect forms. It is a prescriptive discipline, far removed from any concern with impartial observation, and its outlook is inevitably a narrow one.

Next came philology. At Alexandria there had been a 'philological' school, but the term is chiefly applied to the scientific movement inaugurated by Friedrich August Wolf in 1777, which still thrives today. Linguistic structure, however, is not the central concern of philology. Philology seeks primarily to establish, interpret and comment upon texts. This main preoccupation leads to a concern with literary history, customs, institutions, etc. In all these areas, philology applies its own method, which is that of criticism. Insofar as it touches
upon linguistic questions, these arise principally in the comparison of [14]
texts of different periods, in establishing the language characteristic of each writer, and in deciphering and interpreting inscriptions couched in some archaic or problematic language. Such research undoubtedly paved the way for historical linguistics: Ritschl's work on Plautus may be described as 'linguistic'. But in this field philological criticism has one failing: it is too slavishly subservient to the written language, and so neglects the living language. Furthermore, its concern is almost exclusively with Greek and Roman antiquity.

The third period began when it was discovered that languages could be compared with one another. That discovery ushered in comparative philology, or 'comparative grammar'. In 1816, in a work entitled *The Sanskrit Conjugation System*, Franz Bopp studied the connexions between Sanskrit, Germanic, Greek, Latin, etc. Bopp was not the first to observe these affinities or to consider that all these languages belonged to the same family. In that respect Bopp had been forestalled, notably by the English orientalist W. Jones (d. 1794). But isolated statements here and there do not prove that in 1816 there was already a general understanding of the significance and importance of the facts in question. Although Bopp cannot be credited with having discovered the relationship between Sanskrit and various languages of Europe and Asia, he did see that connexions between related languages could furnish the data for an autonomous science. What was new was the elucidation of one language by reference to a related language, explaining the forms of one by appeal to the forms of the other.

It is doubtful whether Bopp would have been able to inaugurate his science – or at least to inaugurate it so quickly – without the discovery of Sanskrit. Sanskrit, as a third source of evidence beside Greek and Latin, provided a broader and sounder basis for study. In addition, as
[15] luck would have it, Sanskrit happens to be exceptionally well situated to provide illuminating linguistic comparisons.

For example, suppose we take the paradigms of Latin *genus* and Greek *génos*:

genus, *generis*, *genere*, *genera*, *generum*, etc.
génos, *géneos*, *géneï*, *génea*, *genéōn*, etc.

These series of forms tell us little, either on their own or when compared with one another. But they tell us a great deal as soon as we set beside them the corresponding Sanskrit forms:

ǵanas, *ǵanasas*, *ǵanasi*, *ǵanassu*, *ǵanasām*, etc.

At a glance we now can see the relationship between the Greek and Latin paradigms. On the hypothesis – which seems explanatorily a productive one – that Sanskrit *ǵanas* represents the primitive form, one concludes that *s* fell in the Greek forms *géne(s)os* etc. wherever it occurred between vowels. A further conclusion is that under the same conditions *s* became *r* in Latin. Moreover, as regards grammatical analysis, the Sanskrit paradigm makes it evident that the stem of these forms is the stable and clearly isolable element *ǵanas*-. Only early Latin and early Greek ever had the primitive system preserved in Sanskrit. So it emerges that the maintenance of Proto-Indo-European *s* in all cases is what makes Sanskrit illuminating in this instance. It is true that in other respects Sanskrit remains less faithful to the original prototype forms: it plays havoc with the original vowel system, for example. But in general the primitive elements which it maintains are vital for purposes of reconstruction. By chance it happens to be a language which is remarkably useful in throwing light on those languages related to it.

Along with Bopp there emerged straight away a number of linguists of distinction: Jacob Grimm, the founder of Germanic studies (his *German Grammar* was published 1822 – 1836); Pott, whose etymological researches provided linguists with a great deal of material; Kuhn, who worked both in linguistics and in comparative mythology, the [16]
Sanskritists Benfey and Aufrecht, and others.

Finally, among the later representatives of that school, special mention must be made of Max Müller, G. Curtius and A. Schleicher. All three, in various ways, made important contributions to comparative studies. Max Müller popularised the subject in a series of brilliant if somewhat superficial lectures (*Lectures on the Science of Language*, 1861). Curtius, a distinguished philologist, known principally as the author of *Principles of Greek Etymology* (1879), was one of the first to reconcile comparative grammar with classical philology. Classical philologists had looked upon the progress made by the comparativists with less than enthusiasm, and the feeling had become mutual. Schleicher, finally, was the first to attempt a codification of the results of research on points of detail. His *Concise Comparative Grammar of the Indo-Germanic Languages* (1861) represents a systematisation of the science founded by Bopp. It is a volume which has remained of great value for many years, and it gives a better idea than any other book of what the comparativist school which dominated this first period of Indo-European linguistics stood for.

But although no one would deny that the comparativists succeeded in opening up a new and profitable field of investigation, they did not manage to found a true science of linguistics. For they never took very great care to define exactly what it was they were studying. And until this elementary step is taken, no science can hope to establish its own methods.

The first mistake made by the comparative philologists was one which contains the seeds of all their other mistakes. Their investigations, which were in any case limited to the Indo-European languages, show a failure to inquire into the significance of the linguistic comparisons they established and the connexions they discovered. Comparative grammar was exclusively comparative, instead of being historical. Comparison is no doubt essential for all historical recon- [17]
struction. But in itself comparison does not warrant drawing conclusions. And the right conclusion was all the more likely to elude the comparativists because they looked upon the development of two languages much as a naturalist might look upon the growth of two

plants. Schleicher, for example, always starts from Proto-Indo-European, which seems at first sight a strictly historical approach; but he does not hesitate to treat Greek *e* and *o* as two 'grades' (*Stufen*) of the same vowel. This is because Sanskrit has a system of vowel alternations which suggests this notion of grades. So Schleicher takes Greek *o* as a reinforced vocalic grade of *e*, in the same way as he takes Sanskrit *ā* to be a reinforced grade of *ă*; rather as if these grades were stages that vowels would go through separately but in parallel development in each language, like plants of the same species passing through the same phases of growth. Whereas in fact we are dealing here with a Proto-Indo-European alternation which has different reflexes in Greek and Sanskrit. There is no necessary parity between the results in the grammars of these two languages (cf. p. [217] ff.).

An exclusively comparative approach of this kind brings with it a whole series of mistaken notions. They have no basis in reality and fail to reflect the conditions which do obtain in language everywhere. At that time languages were looked upon as belonging to a province of their own, a fourth realm of nature. Hence forms of reasoning were permissible which would have shocked any other science. Nowadays, one cannot read even a few lines of what was written by the linguists of that period without being struck by their bizarre ways of thinking about language and the bizarre terms they used in order to validate them.

From a methodological point of view, however, it is of some interest to be acquainted with these errors. The mistakes a science makes in its initial stages present a magnified picture of the mistakes made by
[18] individuals starting out on scientific research. We shall have occasion to point out various instances of this later.

Not until about 1870 did anyone begin to inquire into the conditions governing the life of languages. It was then realised that correspondences between languages reflect only one aspect of language, and that comparison is only a tool, a method to be employed for reconstructing the facts.

Linguistics properly so called, in which comparison was relegated to its proper place, emerged from the study of the Romance and Germanic languages. Romance studies, founded by Diez, whose *Grammar of the Romance languages* dates from 1836–1838, contributed in particular to bringing linguistics nearer to its true object of study. The fact is that Romance scholars found themselves in a privileged position not enjoyed by their Indo-European colleagues. Latin, the prototype of the Romance languages, was itself an attested language. Furthermore, the wealth of available texts made it possible to follow the evolution of the different varieties of Romance in some detail. These two circumstances restricted the scope of speculation and gave Romance studies a particularly matter-of-fact approach. Germanic scholars were in a similar position. Although Proto-Germanic is not itself attested, the evolution of those languages descended from it can be followed over the course of many centuries through copious documentary evidence. So those who studied Germanic, being in more direct contact with reality, came to look at language in a different way from the early Indo-European scholars.

Some first steps in the right direction were taken by the American scholar Whitney, author of *The Life of Language* (1875). Shortly afterwards a new school arose, the Neogrammarians (*Junggrammatiker*), whose leading figures were all Germans: K. Brugmann, H. Osthoff, the Germanic specialists W. Braune, E. Sievers, H. Paul, and the Slavist Leskien, and others. The achievement of the Neogrammarians was to place all the results of comparative philology in a historical perspective, so that linguistic facts were connected in their natural [19]
sequence. The Neogrammarians no longer looked upon a language as an organism developing of its own accord, but saw it as a product of the collective mind of a linguistic community. At the same time, there emerged a realisation of the errors and inadequacies of the concepts associated with philology and comparative grammar.[1] However, great as were the advances made by the Neogrammarians, it cannot be said that they shed light upon the fundamental problems of general linguistics, which still await a solution today.

[1] The Neogrammarians, being more down-to-earth than the comparativists, attacked the comparativists' terminology, especially its illogical metaphors. From then on it became unacceptable to say 'the language does this or does that', to speak of the 'life of the language', and so on, because a language is not an entity, and exists only in its users. However, such an attitude must not be carried too far. What matters is that people should not be misled. There are certain figurative ways of speaking which are indispensable. To require that one should restrict oneself to a linguistic terminology corresponding to linguistic realities is to presuppose that we have already solved the mysteries surrounding these realities. But this is far from being the case. So in what follows we shall not hesitate occasionally to use expressions which were formerly censured as inappropriate.

[20]

CHAPTER II

Data and Aims of Linguistics: Connexions with Related Sciences

Linguistics takes for its data in the first instance all manifestations of human language. Primitive peoples and civilised nations, early periods, classical periods, and periods of decadence, are all to be included. In each case due account must be taken not only of what is considered linguistically correct and 'elegant', but of all forms of expression. Furthermore, since the linguist is very often in no position to make his own linguistic observations at first hand, he cannot afford to neglect written texts, for these alone will acquaint him with the languages of far-off times or places.

The aims of linguistics will be:

(*a*) to describe all known languages and record their history. This involves tracing the history of language families and, as far as possible, reconstructing the parent languages of each family;

(*b*) to determine the forces operating permanently and universally in all languages, and to formulate general laws which account for all particular linguistic phenomena historically attested;

(*c*) to delimit and define linguistics itself.

Linguistics has very close connexions with other sciences. Sometimes they provide linguistics with data and sometimes linguistics provides them with data. The boundaries between linguistics and its neigh-
[21] bouring sciences are not always clearly drawn. For example, linguistics must be carefully distinguished from ethnography and prehistory; both of them disciplines in which linguistic facts may be utilised as evidence. It must likewise be distinguished from anthropology, which studies mankind as a species; whereas language is a social phenomenon. But ought linguistics on that account to be incorporated in sociology? What are the relations between linguistics and social

psychology? In the final analysis, where languages are concerned everything has its psychological aspect, including the physical and mechanical processes, such as sound change. And since linguistics supplies social psychology with such essential data, are not the two indissolubly linked? These are questions which will be given only brief answers here, but we shall return to them later.

The connexions between linguistics and physiology are less difficult to unravel. The relation is unilateral, in that the study of languages requires information about the physiological aspects of sound, but can supply physiology with no information in return. In any case, confusion between the two disciplines is impossible. The essence of a language, as we shall see, has nothing to do with the phonic nature of the linguistic sign.

The position of philology has already been clarified: it is clearly separate from linguistics, although there are points of contact between the two sciences, and they can be of mutual service.

Finally, we may ask, of what use is linguistics? Very few people have clear ideas on the subject, and this is not the place to give a detailed answer. However, what can be said is that for obvious reasons linguistic questions are of interest to all those, including historians, philologists and others, who need to deal with texts. Even more obvious is the importance of linguistics for culture in general. In the lives of individuals and of societies, language is a factor of greater importance than any other. For the study of language to remain solely the business of a handful of specialists would be a quite unacceptable state of affairs. In practice, the study of language is in some degree or [22]
other the concern of everyone. But a paradoxical consequence of this general interest is that no other subject has fostered more absurd notions, more prejudices, more illusions, or more fantasies. From a psychological point of view, these errors are of interest in themselves. But it is the primary task of the linguist to denounce them, and to eradicate them as completely as possible.

[23]

CHAPTER III

The Object of Study

§1. On defining a language

What is it that linguistics sets out to analyse? What is the actual object of study in its entirety? The question is a particularly difficult one. We shall see why later. First, let us simply try to grasp the nature of the difficulty.

Other sciences are provided with objects of study given in advance, which are then examined from different points of view. Nothing like that is the case in linguistics. Suppose someone pronounces the French word *nu* ('naked'). At first sight, one might think this would be an example of an independently given linguistic object. But more careful consideration reveals a series of three or four quite different things, depending on the viewpoint adopted. There is a sound; there is the expression of an idea; there is a derivative of Latin *nūdum*, and so on. The object is not given in advance of the viewpoint: far from it. Rather, one might say that it is the viewpoint adopted which creates the object. Furthermore, there is nothing to tell us in advance whether one of these ways of looking at it is prior to or superior to any of the others.

Whichever viewpoint is adopted, moreover, linguistic phenomena always present two complementary facets, each depending on the other. For example:

(1) The ear perceives articulated syllables as auditory impressions. But the sounds in question would not exist without the vocal organs.
[24] There would be no *n*, for instance, without these two complementary aspects to it. So one cannot equate the language simply with what the ear hears. One cannot divorce what is heard from oral articulation. Nor, on the other hand, can one specify the relevant movements of the

vocal organs without reference to the corresponding auditory impression (cf. p. [63] ff.).

(2) But even if we ignored this phonetic duality, would language then be reducible to phonetic facts? No. Speech sounds are only the instrument of thought, and have no independent existence. Here another complementarity emerges, and one of great importance. A sound, itself a complex auditory-articulatory unit, in turn combines with an idea to form another complex unit, both physiologically and psychologically. Nor is this all.

(3) Language has an individual aspect and a social aspect. One is not conceivable without the other. Furthermore:

(4) Language at any given time involves an established system and an evolution. At any given time, it is an institution in the present and a product of the past. At first sight, it looks very easy to distinguish between the system and its history, between what it is and what it was. In reality, the connexion between the two is so close that it is hard to separate them. Would matters be simplified if one considered the ontogenesis of linguistic phenomena, beginning with a study of children's language, for example? No. It is quite illusory to believe that where language is concerned the problem of origins is any different from the problem of permanent conditions. There is no way out of the circle.

So however we approach the question, no one object of linguistic study emerges of its own accord. Whichever way we turn, the same dilemma confronts us. Either we tackle each problem on one front only, and risk failing to take into account the dualities mentioned above: or else we seem committed to trying to study language in several ways simultaneously, in which case the object of study becomes a muddle of disparate, unconnected things. By proceeding thus one opens the door to various sciences – psychology, anthropology, prescriptive grammar, philology, and so on – which are to be distinguish- [25]
ed from linguistics. These sciences could lay claim to language as falling in their domain; but their methods are not the ones that are needed.

One solution only, in our view, resolves all these difficulties. *The linguist must take the study of linguistic structure as his primary concern, and relate all other manifestations of language to it.* Indeed, amid so many dualities, linguistic structure seems to be the one thing that is independently definable and provides something our minds can satisfactorily grasp.

What, then, is linguistic structure? It is not, in our opinion, simply the same thing as language. Linguistic structure is only one part of language, even though it is an essential part. The structure of a language is a social product of our language faculty. At the same time, it is also a body of necessary conventions adopted by society to enable members of society to use their language faculty. Language in its entirety has many different and disparate aspects. It lies astride the boundaries separating various domains. It is at the same time physical, physiological and psychological. It belongs both to the individual and to society. No classification of human phenomena provides any single place for it, because language as such has no discernible unity.

A language as a structured system, on the contrary, is both a self-contained whole and a principle of classification. As soon as we give linguistic structure pride of place among the facts of language, we introduce a natural order into an aggregate which lends itself to no other classification.

It might be objected to this principle of classification that our use of language depends on a faculty endowed by nature: whereas language systems are acquired and conventional, and so ought to be subordinated to – instead of being given priority over – our natural ability.

To this objection one might reply as follows.

First, it has not been established that the function of language, as manifested in speech, is entirely natural: that is to say, it is not clear that our vocal apparatus is made for speaking as our legs for walking.
[26] Linguists are by no means in agreement on this issue. Whitney, for instance, who regards languages as social institutions on exactly the same footing as all other social institutions, holds it to be a matter of chance or mere convenience that it is our vocal apparatus we use for linguistic purposes. Man, in his view, might well have chosen to use gestures, thus substituting visual images for sound patterns. Whitney's is doubtless too extreme a position. For languages are not in all respects similar to other social institutions (cf. p.[107] ff., p.[110]). Moreover, Whitney goes too far when he says that the selection of the vocal apparatus for language was accidental. For it was in some measure imposed upon us by Nature. But the American linguist is right about the essential point: the language we use is a convention, and it makes no difference what exactly the nature of the agreed sign is. The question of the vocal apparatus is thus a secondary one as far as the problem of language is concerned.

This idea gains support from the notion of *language articulation*. In Latin, the word *articulus* means 'member, part, subdivision in a sequence of things'. As regards language, articulation may refer to the division of the chain of speech into syllables, or to the division of the chain of meanings into meaningful units. It is in this sense that one speaks in German of *gegliederte Sprache*. On the basis of this second interpretation, one may say that it is not spoken language which is natural to man, but the faculty of constructing a language, i.e. a system of distinct signs corresponding to distinct ideas.

Broca discovered that the faculty of speech is localised in the third

frontal convolution of the left hemisphere of the brain. This fact has been seized upon to justify regarding language as a natural endowment. But the same localisation is known to hold for *everything* connected with language, including writing. Thus what seems to be indicated, when we take into consideration also the evidence from various forms of aphasia due to lesions in the centres of localisation [27]
is: (1) that the various disorders which affect spoken language are interconnected in many ways with disorders affecting written language, and (2) that in all cases of aphasia or agraphia what is affected is not so much the ability to utter or inscribe this or that, but the ability to produce in any given mode signs corresponding to normal language. All this leads us to believe that, over and above the functioning of the various organs, there exists a more general faculty governing signs, which may be regarded as the linguistic faculty *par excellence*. So by a different route we are once again led to the same conclusion.

Finally, in support of giving linguistic structure pride of place in our study of language, there is this argument: that, whether natural or not, the faculty of articulating words is put to use only by means of the linguistic instrument created and provided by society. Therefore it is no absurdity to say that it is linguistic structure which gives language what unity it has.

§2. Linguistic structure: its place among the facts of language

In order to identify what role linguistic structure plays within the totality of language, we must consider the individual act of speech and trace what takes place in the speech circuit. This act requires at least two individuals: without this minimum the circuit would not be complete. Suppose, then, we have two people, *A* and *B*, talking to each other:

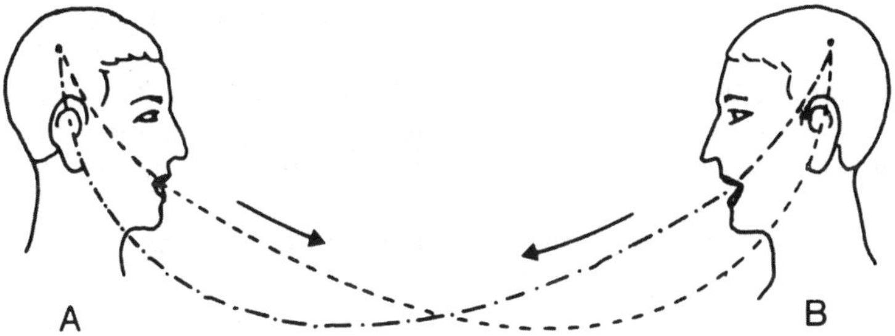

The starting point of the circuit is in the brain of one individual, for [28]
instance *A*, where facts of consciousness which we shall call concepts

are associated with representations of linguistic signs or sound patterns by means of which they may be expressed. Let us suppose that a given concept triggers in the brain a corresponding sound pattern. This is an entirely *psychological* phenomenon, followed in turn by a *physiological* process: the brain transmits to the organs of phonation an impulse corresponding to the pattern. Then sound waves are sent from *A*'s mouth to *B*'s ear: a purely *physical* process. Next, the circuit continues in *B* in the opposite order: from ear to brain, the physiological transmission of the sound pattern; in the brain, the psychological association of this pattern with the corresponding concept. If *B* speaks in turn, this new act will pursue – from his brain to *A*'s – exactly the same course as the first, passing through the same successive phases, which we may represent as follows:

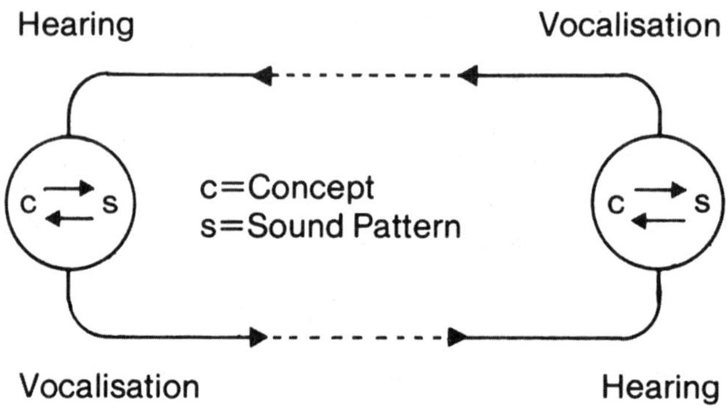

This analysis makes no claim to be complete. One could go on to distinguish the auditory sensation itself, the identification of that sensation with the latent sound pattern, the patterns of muscular movement associated with phonation, and so on. We have included only those elements considered essential; but our schematisation enables us straight away to separate the parts which are physical (sound
[29] waves) from those which are physiological (phonation and hearing) and those which are psychological (the sound patterns of words and the concepts). It is particularly important to note that the sound patterns of the words are not to be confused with actual sounds. The word patterns are psychological, just as the concepts associated with them are.

The circuit as here represented may be further divided:

(a) into an external part (sound vibrations passing from mouth to ear) and an internal part (comprising all the rest);

(b) into a psychological and a non-psychological part, the latter comprising both the physiological facts localised in the organs and the physical facts external to the individual; and

(c) into an active part and a passive part, the former comprising everything which goes from the association centre of one individual to the ear of the other, and the latter comprising everything which goes from an individual's ear to his own association centre.

Finally, in the psychological part localised in the brain, one may call everything which is active 'executive' ($c \rightarrow s$), and everything which is passive 'receptive' ($s \rightarrow c$).

In addition, one must allow for a faculty of association and co-ordination which comes into operation as soon as one goes beyond individual signs in isolation. It is this faculty which plays the major role in the organisation of the language as a system (cf. p.[170] ff.).

But in order to understand this role, one must leave the individual act, which is merely language in embryo, and proceed to consider the social phenomenon.

All the individuals linguistically linked in this manner will establish among themselves a kind of mean; all of them will reproduce – doubtless not exactly, but approximately – the same signs linked to the same concepts.

What is the origin of this social crystallisation? Which of the parts of the circuit is involved? For it is very probable that not all of them [30]
are equally relevant.

The physical part of the circuit can be dismissed from consideration straight away. When we hear a language we do not know being spoken, we hear the sounds but we cannot enter into the social reality of what is happening, because of our failure to comprehend.

The psychological part of the circuit is not involved in its entirety either. The executive side of it plays no part, for execution is never carried out by the collectivity: it is always individual, and the individual is always master of it. This is what we shall designate by the term *speech*.

The individual's receptive and co-ordinating faculties build up a stock of imprints which turn out to be for all practical purposes the same as the next person's. How must we envisage this social product, so that the language itself can be seen to be clearly distinct from the rest? If we could collect the totality of word patterns stored in all those individuals, we should have the social bond which constitutes their language. It is a fund accumulated by the members of the community through the practice of speech, a grammatical system existing potentially in every brain, or more exactly in the brains of a group of individuals; for the language is never complete in any single individual, but exists perfectly only in the collectivity.

By distinguishing between the language itself and speech, we distinguish at the same time: (1) what is social from what is individual, and (2) what is essential from what is ancillary and more or less accidental.

The language itself is not a function of the speaker. It is the product passively registered by the individual. It never requires premeditation, and reflexion enters into it only for the activity of classifying to be discussed below (p.[170] ff.).

Speech, on the contrary, is an individual act of the will and the
[31] intelligence, in which one must distinguish: (1) the combinations through which the speaker uses the code provided by the language in order to express his own thought, and (2) the psycho-physical mechanism which enables him to externalise these combinations.

It should be noted that we have defined things, not words. Consequently the distinctions established are not affected by the fact that certain ambiguous terms have no exact equivalents in other languages. Thus in German the word *Sprache* covers individual languages as well as language in general, while *Rede* answers more or less to 'speech', but also has the special sense of 'discourse'. In Latin the word *sermo* covers language in general and also speech, while *lingua* is the word for 'a language'; and so on. No word corresponds precisely to any one of the notions we have tried to specify above. That is why all definitions based on words are vain. It is an error of method to proceed from words in order to give definitions of things.

To summarise, then, a language as a structured system may be characterised as follows:

1. Amid the disparate mass of facts involved in language, it stands out as a well defined entity. It can be localised in that particular section of the speech circuit where sound patterns are associated with concepts. It is the social part of language, external to the individual, who by himself is powerless either to create it or to modify it. It exists only in virtue of a kind of contract agreed between the members of a community. On the other hand, the individual needs an apprenticeship in order to acquaint himself with its workings: as a child, he assimilates it only gradually. It is quite separate from speech: a man who loses the ability to speak none the less retains his grasp of the language system, provided he understands the vocal signs he hears.

2. A language system, as distinct from speech, is an object that may be studied independently. Dead languages are no longer spoken, but we can perfectly well acquaint ourselves with their linguistic structure. A science which studies linguistic structure is not only able to dispense with other elements of language, but is possible only if those other elements are kept separate.

[32] 3. While language in general is heterogeneous, a language system is homogeneous in nature. It is a system of signs in which the one essential is the union of sense and sound pattern, both parts of the

sign being psychological.

4. Linguistic structure is no less real than speech, and no less amenable to study. Linguistic signs, although essentially psychological, are not abstractions. The associations, ratified by collective agreement, which go to make up the language are realities localised in the brain. Moreover, linguistic signs are, so to speak, tangible: writing can fix them in conventional images, whereas it would be impossible to photograph acts of speech in all their details. The utterance of a word, however small, involves an infinite number of muscular movements extremely difficult to examine and to represent. In linguistic structure, on the contrary, there is only the sound pattern, and this can be represented by one constant visual image. For if one leaves out of account that multitude of movements required to actualise it in speech, each sound pattern, as we shall see, is only the sum of a limited number of elements or speech sounds, and these can in turn be represented by a corresponding number of symbols in writing. Our ability to identify elements of linguistic structure in this way is what makes it possible for dictionaries and grammars to give us a faithful representation of a language. A language is a repository of sound patterns, and writing is their tangible form.

§3. Languages and their place in human affairs. Semiology

The above characteristics lead us to realise another, which is more important. A language, defined in this way from among the totality of facts of language, has a particular place in the realm of human [33]
affairs, whereas language does not.

A language, as we have just seen, is a social institution. But it is in various respects distinct from political, juridical and other institutions. Its special nature emerges when we bring into consideration a different order of facts.

A language is a system of signs expressing ideas, and hence comparable to writing, the deaf-and-dumb alphabet, symbolic rites, forms of politeness, military signals, and so on. It is simply the most important of such systems.

It is therefore possible to conceive of a science *which studies the role of signs as part of social life*. It would form part of social psychology, and hence of general psychology. We shall call it *semiology*[1] (from the Greek *sēmeîon*, 'sign'). It would investigate the nature of signs and the laws governing them. Since it does not yet exist, one cannot say for certain that it will exist. But it has a right to exist, a place ready

[1] Not to be confused with *semantics*, which studies changes of meaning. Saussure gave no detailed exposition of semantics, but the basic principle to be applied is stated on p.[109]. (Editorial note)

for it in advance. Linguistics is only one branch of this general science. The laws which semiology will discover will be laws applicable in linguistics, and linguistics will thus be assigned to a clearly defined place in the field of human knowledge.

It is for the psychologist to determine the exact place of semiology.[1] The linguist's task is to define what makes languages a special type of system within the totality of semiological facts. The question will be taken up later on: here we shall make just one point, which is that if we have now for the first time succeeded in assigning linguistics its
[34] place among the sciences, that is because we have grouped it with semiology.

Why is it that semiology is not yet recognised as an autonomous science with its own object of study, like other sciences? The fact is that here we go round in a circle. On the one hand, nothing is more appropriate than the study of languages to bring out the nature of the semiological problem. But to formulate the problem suitably, it would be necessary to study what a language is in itself: whereas hitherto a language has usually been considered as a function of something else, from other points of view.

In the first place, there is the superficial view taken by the general public, which sees a language merely as a nomenclature (cf. p. [97]). This is a view which stifles any inquiry into the true nature of linguistic structure.

Then there is the viewpoint of the psychologist, who studies the mechanism of the sign in the individual. This is the most straightforward approach, but it takes us no further than individual execution. It does not even take us as far as the linguistic sign itself, which is social by nature.

Even when due recognition is given to the fact that the sign must be studied as a social phenomenon, attention is restricted to those features of languages which they share with institutions mainly established by voluntary decision. In this way, the investigation is diverted from its goal. It neglects those characteristics which belong only to semiological systems in general, and to languages in particular. For the sign always to some extent eludes control by the will, whether of the individual or of society: that is its essential nature, even though it may be by no means obvious at first sight.

So this characteristic emerges clearly only in languages, but its manifestations appear in features to which least attention is paid. All of which contributes to a failure to appreciate either the necessity or the particular utility of a science of semiology. As far as we are concerned, on the other hand, the linguistic problem is first and fore-
[35] most semiological. All our proposals derive their rationale from this

[1] Cf. A. Naville, *Classification des sciences*, 2nd ed., p.104. (Editorial note)

basic fact. If one wishes to discover the true nature of language systems, one must first consider what they have in common with all other systems of the same kind. Linguistic factors which at first seem central (for example, the workings of the vocal apparatus) must be relegated to a place of secondary importance if it is found that they merely differentiate languages from other such systems. In this way, light will be thrown not only upon the linguistic problem. By considering rites, customs, etc., as signs, it will be possible, we believe, to see them in a new perspective. The need will be felt to consider them as semiological phenomena and to explain them in terms of the laws of semiology.

[36] CHAPTER IV

Linguistics of Language Structure and Linguistics of Speech

In allocating to a science of linguistic structure its essential role within the study of language in general, we have at the same time mapped out linguistics in its entirety. The other elements of language, which go to make up speech, are automatically subordinated to this first science. In this way all the parts of linguistics fall into their proper place.

Take, for example, the production of sounds necessary to speech. The vocal organs are as external to the language system as the electrical apparatus which is used to tap out the Morse code is external to that code. Phonation, that is to say the execution of sound patterns, in no way affects the system itself. In this respect one may compare a language to a symphony. The symphony has a reality of its own, which is independent of the way in which it is performed. The mistakes which musicians may make in performance in no way compromise that reality.

One may perhaps object to regarding phonation as separate from the language system. What about the evidence provided by phonetic changes, coming from alterations in sounds as produced in speech? Do not these have a profound influence upon the destiny of the language itself? Do we really have the right to claim that a language exists inde-
[37] pendently of such phenomena? Yes, for they affect only the material substance of words. The language itself as a system of signs is affected only indirectly, through the change of interpretation which results. But that has nothing to do with phonetic change as such (cf. p. [121]). It may be of interest to investigate the causes of such changes, and the study of sounds may be of assistance. But it is not essential. For a science which deals with linguistic structure, it will always suffice to take note of sound changes and to examine what effects they have on the system.

What applies to phonation will apply also to all other elements of speech. The activity of the speaker must be studied in a variety of disciplines, which are of concern to linguistics only through their connexions with linguistic structure.

The study of language thus comprises two parts. The essential part takes for its object the language itself, which is social in its essence and independent of the individual. This is a purely psychological study. The subsidiary part takes as its object of study the individual part of language, which means speech, including phonation. This is a psycho-physical study.

These two objects of study are doubtless closely linked and each presupposes the other. A language is necessary in order that speech should be intelligible and produce all its effects. But speech also is necessary in order that a language may be established. Historically, speech always takes precedence. How would we ever come to associate an idea with a verbal sound pattern, if we did not first of all grasp this association in an act of speech? Furthermore, it is by listening to others that we learn our native language. A language accumulates in our brain only as the result of countless experiences. Finally, it is speech which causes a language to evolve. The impressions received from listening to others modify our own linguistic habits. Thus there is an interdependence between the language itself and speech. The former is at the same time the instrument and the product of the latter. But none of this compromises the absolute nature of the dis- [38]
tinction between the two.

A language, as a collective phenomenon, takes the form of a totality of imprints in everyone's brain, rather like a dictionary of which each individual has an identical copy (cf. p. [30]). Thus it is something which is in each individual, but is none the less common to all. At the same time it is out of the reach of any deliberate interference by individuals. This mode of existence of a language may be represented by the following formula:

1 + 1 + 1 + 1 . . . = I (collective model).

In what way is speech present in this same collectivity? Speech is the sum total of what people say, and it comprises (*a*) individual combinations of words, depending on the will of the speakers, and (*b*) acts of phonation, which are also voluntary and are necessary for the execution of the speakers' combinations of words.

Thus there is nothing collective about speech. Its manifestations are individual and ephemeral. It is no more than an aggregate of particular cases, which may be represented by the following formula:

$(1 + 1' + 1'' + 1''' \ldots)$.

For all these reasons, it would be impossible to consider language systems and speech from one and the same point of view. Language in its totality is unknowable, for it lacks homogeneity. But the distinction drawn above and the priority it implies make it possible to clarify everything.

That is the first parting of the ways that we come to when endeavouring to construct a theory of language. It is necessary to choose between two routes which cannot both be taken simultaneously. Each must be followed separately.

It would be possible to keep the name *linguistics* for each of these two disciplines. We would then have a linguistics of speech. But it would be essential not to confuse the linguistics of speech with lin-
[39] guistics properly so called. The latter has linguistic structure as its sole object of study.

We shall here concern ourselves strictly with linguistics proper, and although in the course of our discussion we may draw upon what the study of speech can tell us, we shall endeavour never to blur the boundaries which separate the two domains.

CHAPTER V [40]

Internal and External Elements of a Language

Our definition of a language assumes that we disregard everything which does not belong to its structure as a system; in short everything that is designated by the term 'external linguistics'. External linguistics is none the less concerned with important matters, and these demand attention when one approaches the study of language.

First of all, there are all the respects in which linguistics links up with ethnology. There are all the relations which may exist between the history of a language and the history of a race or a civilisation. The two histories intermingle and are related one to another. This situation is in some measure reminiscent of the correspondences already noted between linguistic phenomena proper (cf. p. [23] ff.). A nation's way of life has an effect upon its language. At the same time, it is in great part the language which makes the nation.

Secondly, mention must be made of the relations between languages and political history. Major historical events such as the Roman Conquest are of incalculable linguistic importance in all kinds of ways. Colonisation, which is simply one form of conquest, transports a language into new environments, and this brings changes in the language. A great variety of examples could be cited in this connexion. Norway, for instance, adopted Danish on becoming politically united to Denmark, although today Norwegians are trying to shake off this [41] linguistic influence. The internal politics of a country is of no less importance for the life of a language. The governments of certain countries, such as Switzerland, allow the coexistence of several languages. Other countries, like France, aspire to linguistic unification. Advanced stages of civilisation favour the development of certain special languages (legal language, scientific terminology, etc.).

This brings us to a third point. A language has connexions with institutions of every sort: church, school, etc. These institutions in turn are intimately bound up with the literary development of a language. This is a phenomenon of general importance, since it is inseparable from political history. A literary language is by no means confined to the limits apparently imposed upon it by literature. One has only to think of the influence of salons, of the court, and of academies. In connexion with a literary language, there arises the important question of conflict with local dialects (cf. p. [267] ff.). The linguist must also examine the reciprocal relations between the language of books and the language of colloquial speech. Eventually, every literary language, as a product of culture, becomes cut off from the spoken word, which is a language's natural sphere of existence.

Finally, everything which relates to the geographical extension of languages and to their fragmentation into dialects concerns external linguistics. It is on this point, doubtless, that the distinction between external linguistics and internal linguistics appears most paradoxical. For every language in existence has its own geographical area. None the less, in fact geography has nothing to do with the internal structure of the language.

It is sometimes claimed that it is absolutely impossible to separate all these questions from the study of the language itself. That is a view which is associated especially with the insistence that science should study 'Realia'. Just as a plant has its internal structure modified by outside factors, such as soil, climate, etc., in the same way does
[42] not grammatical structure depend constantly upon external factors of linguistic change? Is it not difficult to explain technical terms and borrowings, which commonly appear in a language, if we give no consideration to their provenance? Is it possible to distinguish the natural, organic development of languages from artificial forms, such as literary languages, which are due to external factors, and consequently not organic? Do we not constantly see the development of a common language alongside local dialects?

In our opinion, the study of external linguistic phenomena can teach linguists a great deal. But it is not true to say that without taking such phenomena into account we cannot come to terms with the internal structure of the language itself. Take the borrowing of foreign words. We may note, first of all, that this is by no means a constant process in the life of a language. There are in certain remote valleys patois which have rarely if ever accepted any word of outside provenance. Are we to say that these languages do not conform to the normal conditions for language, and are therefore invalid as examples? Would such languages have to be studied as special cases of linguistic abnormality because they had never been affected by outside influences? The main point here is that a borrowed word no longer counts as borrowed as soon as it is studied in the context of a system. Then it exists only in virtue of its relation and opposition to words associated with it, just like any indigenous word. In general, it is never absolutely essential to know the circumstances in which a language has developed. In the case of certain languages, such as Zend and Old Slavonic, we do not even know exactly which peoples spoke them. But our ignorance in no way prevents us from studying their internal structure, or from understanding the developments they underwent. In any case, a separation of internal and external viewpoints is essential. The more rigorously it is observed, the better.

The best demonstration of this is that each viewpoint gives rise to [43]
a distinct method. External linguistics can accumulate detail after detail, without ever being forced to conform to the constraints of a system. For example, the facts concerning the expansion of a language outside its territorial boundaries can be presented in any way a writer decides. If a scholar is dealing with the factors which gave rise to the creation of a literary language as opposed to dialects, he can always proceed by simple enumeration. If he orders his facts in a more or less systematic fashion, that will be simply in the interests of clarity.

As far as internal linguistics is concerned, the situation is quite different. Any old order will not do. The language itself is a system which admits no other order than its own. This can be brought out by comparison with the game of chess. In the case of chess, it is relatively easy to distinguish between what is external and what is internal. The fact that chess came from Persia to Europe is an external fact, whereas everything which concerns the system and its rules is internal. If pieces made of ivory are substituted for pieces made of wood, the change makes no difference to the system. But if the number of pieces is diminished or increased, that is a change which profoundly affects the 'grammar' of the game. Care must none the less be taken when drawing distinctions of this kind. In each case, the question to be asked concerns the nature of the phenomenon. The question must be answered in accordance with the following rule. Everything is internal which alters the system in any degree whatsoever.

[44] CHAPTER VI

Representation of a Language by Writing

§1. Why it is necessary to study this topic

The actual object we are concerned to study, then, is the social product stored in the brain, the language itself. But this product differs from one linguistic community to another. What we find are languages. The linguist must endeavour to become acquainted with as many languages as possible, in order to be able to discover their universal features by studying and comparing them.

Languages are mostly known to us only through writing. Even in the case of our native language, the written form constantly intrudes. In the case of languages spoken in remote parts, it is even more necessary to have recourse to written evidence. The same is true for obvious reasons in the case of languages now dead. In order to have direct evidence available, it would have been necessary to have compiled throughout history collections of the kind currently being compiled in Vienna and in Paris, comprising recordings of spoken samples of all languages. Even then writing is necessary when it comes to publishing the texts thus recorded.

Thus although writing is in itself not part of the internal system of the language, it is impossible to ignore this way in which the language is constantly represented. We must be aware of its utility, its defects and its dangers.

[45] *§2. The prestige of writing: reasons for its ascendancy over the spoken word*

A language and its written form constitute two separate systems of signs. The sole reason for the existence of the latter is to represent the former. The object of study in linguistics is not a combination of the written word and the spoken word. The spoken word alone constitutes that object. But the written word is so intimately connected with the spoken word it represents that it manages to usurp the principal role. As much or even more importance is given to this representation of the vocal sign as to the vocal sign itself. It is rather as if people believed that in order to find out what a person looks like it is better to study his photograph than his face.

This misconception has a long history, and current views about languages are tainted with it. For instance, it is commonly held that a language alters more rapidly when it has no written form. This is quite false. In certain circumstances, writing may well retard changes in a language. But, on the other hand, linguistic stability is in no way undermined by the absence of a written form. The Lithuanian which is still spoken today in Eastern Prussia and part of Russia is attested in written documents only since 1540; but at that late period it presents on the whole as accurate a picture of Proto-Indo-European as Latin of the third century B.C. That in itself suffices to show the extent to which a language is independent of writing.

Certain very subtle linguistic features can long survive without the assistance of written notation. Throughout the Old High German period, we find the written forms *tōten*, *fuolen* and *stōzen*, but at the end of the twelfth century appear the spellings *töten*, *füelen*, whereas *stōzen* persists. What is the origin of this difference? Wherever it occurred, there had been a *y* in the following syllable: Proto-Germanic [46]
had **daupyan*, **fōlyan*, but **stautan*. On the eve of the literary period, about 800, this *y* weakened and vanished from writing for three hundred years. However, it had left a slight trace in pronunciation, with the result that about 1180, as noted above, it reappears miraculously in the form of an 'umlaut'! This nuance of pronunciation had been faithfully transmitted without any support in writing.

A language, then, has an oral tradition independent of writing, and much more stable; but the prestige of the written form prevents us from seeing this. The first linguists were misled in this way, as the humanists had been before them. Even Bopp does not distinguish clearly between letters and sounds. Reading Bopp, we might think that a language is inseparable from its alphabet. His immediate successors fell into the same trap. The spelling *th* for the fricative *þ* misled Grimm into believing not only that this was a double consonant, but also that it was an aspirate stop. Hence the place he assigns to it in his Law of Consonantal Mutation or 'Lautverschiebung' (see p. [199]). Even nowadays educated people confuse the language with its spelling: Gaston Deschamps said of Berthelot 'that he had saved the French language from ruin' because he had opposed spelling reforms.[1]

[1] The reforms in question were proposed just a few years before Saussure's lectures were given. The issue was a topical one. (Translator's note)

But what explains the prestige of writing?

1. The written form of a word strikes us as a permanent, solid object and hence more fitting than its sound to act as a linguistic unit persisting through time. Although the connexion between word and written form is superficial and establishes a purely artificial unit, it is none the less much easier to grasp than the natural and only authentic connexion, which links word and sound.

2. For most people, visual impressions are clearer and more lasting than auditory impressions. So for preference people cling to the former.
[47] The written image in the end takes over from the sound.

3. A literary language enhances even more the unwarranted importance accorded to writing. A literary language has its dictionaries and its grammars. It is taught at school from books and through books. It is a language which appears to be governed by a code, and this code is itself a written rule, itself conforming to strict norms – those of orthography. That is what confers on writing its primordial importance. In the end, the fact that we learn to speak before learning to write is forgotten, and the natural relation between the two is reversed.

4. Finally, when there is any discrepancy between a language and its spelling, the conflict is always difficult to resolve for anyone other than a linguist. Since the linguist's voice often goes unheeded, the written form almost inevitably emerges victorious, because any solution based on writing is an easier solution. In this way, writing assumes an authority to which it has no right.

§3. Systems of writing

There are only two systems of writing:

1. The ideographic system, in which a word is represented by some uniquely distinctive sign which has nothing to do with the sounds involved. This sign represents the entire word as a whole, and hence represents indirectly the idea expressed. The classic example of this system is Chinese.

2. The system often called 'phonetic', intended to represent the sequence of sounds as they occur in the word. Some phonetic writing systems are syllabic. Others are alphabetic, that is to say based upon the irreducible elements of speech.

Ideographic writing systems easily develop into mixed systems. Certain ideograms lose their original significance, and eventually come to represent isolated sounds.

The written word, as mentioned above, tends to become a substitute in our mind for the spoken word. That applies to both systems of writing, but the tendency is stronger in the case of ideographic writing. For a Chinese, the ideogram and the spoken word are of equal validity as signs for an idea. He treats writing as a second language, and when in conversation two words are identically pronounced, he sometimes refers to the written form in order to explain which he means. But this substitution, because it is a total substitution, does not give rise to the same objectionable consequences as in our Western systems of writing. Chinese words from different dialects which correspond to the same idea are represented by the same written sign. [48]

Our survey here will be restricted to the phonetic system of writing, and in particular to the system in use today, of which the prototype is the Greek alphabet.

At the time when an alphabet of this kind becomes established, it will represent the contemporary language in a more or less rational fashion, unless it is an alphabet which has been borrowed from elsewhere and is already marred by inconsistencies. As regards its logic, the Greek alphabet is particularly remarkable, as will be seen on p. [64]. But harmony between spelling and pronunciation does not last. Why not is what we must now examine.

§4. Causes of inconsistency between spelling and pronunciation

There are many causes of inconsistency: we shall be concerned here only with the most important ones.

In the first place, a language is in a constant process of evolution, whereas writing tends to remain fixed. It follows that eventually spelling no longer corresponds to the sounds it should represent. A spelling which is appropriate at one time may be absurd a century later. For a while spelling is altered in order to reflect changes in pronunciation; but then the attempt is abandoned. This is what happened in French [49]
to *oi*.[1]

	period	*pronounced*	*written*
1	11th c.	*rei, lei*	*rei, lei*
2	13th c.	*roi, loi*	*roi, loi*
3	14th c.	*roè, loè*	*roi, loi*
4	19th c.	*rwa, lwa*	*roi, loi*

In this case, spelling followed pronunciation as far as stage 2, the

[1] The examples in the table are the French words for 'king' (*roi*) and 'law' (*loi*). (Translator's note)

history of orthography keeping in step with the history of the language. But from the fourteenth century onwards, the written form remained stationary while the language continued its evolution. From that point, there has been an increasingly serious disparity between the language and its spelling. Eventually, the association of incompatible written and spoken forms had repercussions on the written system itself: the digraph *oi* acquired a phonetic value ([wa]) unrelated to those of its constituent letters.

Such examples could be cited *ad infinitum*. Why is it that in French we write *mais* and *fait*, but pronounce these words *mè* and *fè*? Why does the letter *c* in French often have the value of *s*? In both cases, French has kept spellings which no longer have any rationale.

Similar changes are going on all the time. At present our palatal *l* is changing to *y*: although we still go on writing *éveiller* and *mouiller*, we pronounce these words *éveyer* and *mouyer* (just like *essuyer* and *nettoyer*).

Another cause of discrepancy between spelling and pronunciation is the borrowing of an alphabet by one people from another. It often happens that the resources of the graphic system are poorly adapted to its new function, and it is necessary to have recourse to various expedients. Two letters, for example, will be used to designate a single sound. This is what happened in the case of *þ* (a voiceless dental
[50] fricative) in the Germanic languages. The Latin alphabet having no character to represent it, it was rendered by *th*. The Merovingian king Chilperic tried to add a special letter to the Latin alphabet to denote this sound, but the attempt did not succeed, and *th* became accepted. English in the Middle Ages had both a close *e* (for example, in *sed* 'seed') and an open *e* (for example, in *led* 'to lead'): but since the alphabet did not have distinct signs for these two sounds, recourse was had to writing *seed* and *lead*. In French, to represent the consonant *š*, the digraph *ch* was used. And so on.

Etymological preoccupations also intrude. They were particularly noticeable at certain periods, such as the Renaissance. It is not infrequently the case that a spelling is introduced through mistaken etymologising: *d* was thus introduced in the French word *poids* ('weight'), as if it came from Latin *pondus*, when in fact it comes from *pensum*. But it makes little difference whether the etymology is correct or not. It is the principal of etymological spelling itself which is mistaken.

In other cases, the reason for a discrepancy is obscure. Some bizarre spellings have not even an etymological pretext. Why in German did they write *thun* instead of *tun*? It is said that the *h* represents the aspiration following the consonant: but in that case an *h* should have been written wherever the same aspiration occurred, and yet there are very many words (*Tugend*, *Tisch*, etc.) which have never been spelt this way.

§5. *Consequences of this inconsistency*

An exhaustive list of the inconsistencies found in writing systems cannot be given here. One of the most unfortunate is having a variety of characters for the same sound. In French, for *ž* we have: *j*, *g*, *ge* (*joli*, *geler*, *geai*). For *z* we have both *z* and *s*. For *s* we have *c*, *ç* and *t* (*nation*), *ss* (*chasser*), *sc* (*acquiescer*), *sç*(*acquiesçant*), and *x* (*dix*). For *k* we have *c*, *qu*, *k*, *ch*, *cc*, *cqu* (*acquérir*). On the other hand, different sounds are sometimes represented by the same sign: we have *t* representing *t* or *s*, *g* representing *g* or *ž*, and so on.

Then there are 'indirect' spellings. In German, although there are [51] no double consonants in *Zettel*, *Teller*, etc., the words are spelt with *tt*, *ll*, simply in order to indicate that the preceding vowel is short and open. An aberration of the same kind is seen in English, which adds a silent final *e* in order to lengthen the preceding vowel, as in *made* (pronounced *mēd*) as distinct from *mad* (*măd*). This *e* gives the misleading appearance of indicating a second syllable in monosyllabic words.

Irrational spellings such as these do indeed correspond to something in the language itself: but others reflect nothing at all. French at present has no double consonants except in the future tense forms *mourrai*, *courrai*: none the less, French orthography abounds in illegitimate double consonants (*bourru*, *sottise*, *souffrir*, etc.).

It also happens sometimes that spelling fluctuates before becoming fixed, and different spellings appear, representing attempts made at earlier periods to spell certain sounds. Thus in forms like *ertha*, *erdha*, *erda*, or *thrī*, *dhrī*, *drī*, which appear in Old High German, *th*, *dh*, and *d* evidently represent the same sound; but from the spelling it is impossible to tell what that sound is. Hence we have the additional complication that when a certain form has more than one spelling, it is not always possible to tell whether in fact there were two pronunciations. Documents in neighbouring dialects spell the same word *asca* and *ascha*: if the pronunciation was identical, this is a case of fluctuating orthography; but if not, the difference is phonetic and dialectal, as in the Greek forms *paízō*, *paízdō*, *paíddō*. In other cases the problem arises with a chronological succession of spellings. In English, we find at first *hwat*, *hweel*, etc., but later *what*, *wheel*, etc., and it is unclear whether this is merely a change in spelling or a change in pronunciation.

The obvious result of all this is that writing obscures our view of the language. Writing is not a garment, but a disguise. This is de- [52] monstrated by the spelling of the French word *oiseau*, where not one of the sounds of the spoken word (*wazo*) is represented by its appropriate sign and the spelling completely obscures the linguistic facts.

Another result is that the more inadequately writing represents what it ought to represent, the stronger is the tendency to give it priority over the spoken language. Grammarians are desperately eager to draw our attention to the written form. Psychologically, this is quite understandable, but the consequences are unfortunate. The use acquired by the words 'pronounce' and 'pronunciation' confirms this abuse and reverses the true relationship obtaining between writing and the language. Thus when people say that a certain letter should be pronounced in this way or that, it is the visual image which is mistaken for the model. If *oi* can be pronounced *wa*, then it seems that *oi* must exist in its own right. Whereas the fact of the matter is that it is *wa* which is written *oi*. To explain this strange case, our attention is drawn to the fact that this is an exception to the usual pronunciation of *o* and *i*. But this explanation merely compounds the mistake, implying as it does that the language itself is subordinate to its spelling. The case is presented as contravening the spelling system, as if the orthographic sign were basic.

These misconceptions extend even to rules of grammar: for example, the rule concerning *h* in French. French has words with an unaspirated initial vowel, but which are nevertheless spelt with an initial *h*, because of the corresponding Latin form, e.g. *homme* 'man' (in former times *ome*), corresponding to Latin *homo*. But there are also French words of Germanic origin, in which the *h* was actually pronounced: *hache* ('axe'), *hareng* ('herring'), *honte* ('shame'), etc. As long as the *h* was pronounced, these words conformed to the laws governing initial consonants. You said *deu haches* ('two axes'), *le hareng* ('the herring'), whereas in accordance with the law for words beginning with a vowel you said *deu-z-hommes* ('two men'), *l'omme* ('the man'). At that period, the rule which said 'no liaison or elision before aspirate *h*' was correct. But nowadays this formulation is meaningless. For aspirate *h* no [53] longer exists, unless we apply the term to something which is not a sound at all, but before which there is neither liaison nor elision. It is a vicious circle: the aspirate *h* in question is an orthographic ghost.

The pronunciation of a word is determined not by its spelling but by its history. Its spoken form at any given time represents one stage in a phonetic evolution from which it cannot escape. This evolution is governed by strict laws. Each stage may be ascertained by referring back to the preceding stage. The only factor to consider, although it is most frequently forgotten, is the etymological derivation of the word.

The name of the town of Auch is *oš* in phonetic transcription. It is the only case in French orthography where *ch* represents *š* at the end of a word. It is no explanation to say: *ch* in final position is pronounced *š* only in this word. The only relevant question is how the Latin *Auscii* developed into *oš*: the spelling is of no importance.

Should the second vowel of the French noun *gageure* ('wager') be pronounced *ö* or *ü*? Some say *gažör*, since *heure* ('hour') is pronounced *ör*. Others say it should be pronounced *gažür*, since *ge* stands for *ž*, as in *geôle* ('jail'). The dispute is vacuous. The real question is etymological. For the noun *gageure* was formed from the verb *gager* ('to bet'), just like the noun *tournure* ('turn') from the verb *tourner* ('to turn'). Both are examples of the same type of derivation. The only defensible pronunciation is *gažür*. The pronunciation *gažör* is simply the result of ambiguous spelling.

But the tyranny of the written form extends further yet. Its influence on the linguistic community may be strong enough to affect and modify the language itself. That happens only in highly literate communities, where written documents are of considerable importance. In these cases, the written form may give rise to erroneous pronunciations. The phenomenon is strictly pathological. It occurs frequently in French. The family name *Lefèvre* (from Latin *faber*) had two spellings: the popular, straightforward spelling was *Lefèvre*, while the learned etymological spelling was *Lefèbvre*. Owing to the confusion of *v* and *u* in medieval writing, *Lefèbvre* was read as *Lefébure*, thus [54]
introducing a *b* which never really existed in the word, as well as a *u* coming from an ambiguous letter. But now this form of the name is actually pronounced.

Probably such misunderstandings will become more and more frequent. More and more dead letters will be resuscitated in pronunciation. In Paris, one already hears *sept femmes* ('seven women') with the *t* pronounced. Darmesteter foresees the day when even the two final letters of *vingt* ('twenty') will be pronounced: a genuine orthographic monstrosity.

These phonetic distortions do indeed belong to the language but they are not the result of its natural evolution. They are due to an external factor. Linguistics should keep them under observation in a special compartment: they are cases of abnormal development.

[55]

CHAPTER VII

Physiological Phonetics

§1. Definition of the subject

If we try to dismiss the written form from our mind, and do away with any visual image altogether, we run the risk of being left with an amorphous object which is difficult to grasp. It is as if someone learning to swim had suddenly had his cork float taken away.

What is needed is to provide a natural substitute for the artificial aid. But that is impossible unless we have studied the sounds of the language. For without its orthographic sign a sound is something very vague. We find ourselves at a loss without a system of writing, even if its assistance is misleading. That is why the first linguists, who knew nothing about the physiology of articulated sound, constantly fell into these pitfalls. For them, letting go of the letter meant losing their footing. For us, it means taking a first step towards the truth. For the study of sounds will provide us with the help we need. In recent times linguists have at last learned that lesson. Turning to their own account the investigations begun by others (including physiologists and singing teachers), they have provided linguistics with an auxiliary science which sets it free from the written word.

The physiology of sounds (German *Lautphysiologie* or *Sprachphysiologie*) is often called simply 'phonetics' (French *phonétique*, German *Phonetik*, English *phonetics*). But this is inappropriate. We prefer to call it *physiological phonetics*. For the word *phonetics* originally de-
[56] signated the study of the evolution of sounds, and should continue to do so. But it would be misleading to have only one term for two entirely different branches of study. Phonetics as a historical science analyses events and changes: it is concerned with the passage of time. Whereas physiological phonetics is indifferent to the passage of time, for the mechanism of articulation itself remains unchanged.

These two branches of study are not to be confused, but they are in no way incompatible. Historical phonetics is one of the essential parts of a science which concerns itself with languages; whereas physiological phonetics, it must be stressed, is only an auxiliary discipline and is concerned simply with speech (see p. [36]). It is true that if no language existed the movements of the vocal apparatus would be pointless. None the less, these movements are not part of any language, and an exhaustive analysis of the processes of phonation required to produce every auditory impression tells us nothing about what a language is. A language is a system based upon psychological contrasts between these auditory impressions, just as a tapestry is a work of art based upon the visual contrast between strands of different colours. What is important for an analysis is the effect of these contrasts, and not the processes by which the colours were obtained in the first place.

An outline of a system of physiological phonetics will be found in the Appendix, p. [63] ff. Here we shall be concerned simply with how such a study can serve to free linguistics from the illusions created by systems of writing.

§2. *Transcription*

The primary requirement of the linguist is that writing should provide him with a system for representing sounds which is free from ambiguity. Very many systems have in fact been proposed.

What are the principles underlying an adequate system of transcrip- [57]
tion? It should provide one symbol for each unit in the sequence of spoken sounds. But this requirement is not always given due weight. English phoneticians, for example, have been more concerned with classification than with analysis, and consequently represent some sounds by combinations of two or even three letters. Another requirement is to draw a strict distinction between abductive and adductive sounds, as will be explained below (cf. p. [77] ff.).

Is there a case for replacing conventional orthography by a phonetic alphabet? This is an interesting question, but it cannot be pursued here. In our opinion, any such alphabet is destined to remain a tool for linguists. There is little hope of persuading the English, the Germans, the French, etc. all to adopt one uniform system! In any case, an alphabet applicable to all languages would very probably have to employ a large number of diacritics. It would make for a dismal-looking printed page, obscuring what it was supposed to make clear, and confusing the reader. These drawbacks would not be counterbalanced by sufficient advantages. Except for purposes of linguistic science, exact phonetic precision is not particularly desirable.

There is also the question of reading. We read in two ways. A new or unknown word is scanned letter by letter. But a common, familiar word is taken in at a glance, without bothering about the individual letters: its visual shape functions like an ideogram. Here, traditional spelling has something to be said for it: for it is useful to separate *tant* from *temps*, *et* from *est* and *ait*, *du* from *dû*, *il devait* from *ils devaient*, etc.[1] One could wish, none the less, that traditional spelling might be relieved of some of its most conspicuous absurdities. A phonetic alphabet may be of use in language teaching, but is hardly likely to become general.

[58] *§3. Writing as evidence*

It does not follow, then, that because systems of writing are manifestly misleading one should rush to reform spelling. The true value of physiological phonetics is that it induces caution about reaching conclusions concerning the language based upon its written form. The evidence of orthography requires careful interpretation. In each case, it is necessary to establish the *sound system* of the language in question, i.e. the inventory of sounds it employs. For each language uses a fixed number of distinct speech sounds and this is the only sound system which has any reality as far as the linguist is concerned.[2] Orthographic symbols reflect this system, but how accurately is another question. The answer may be difficult to determine, depending on the circumstances of the case.

When the language in question is no longer spoken, we must have recourse to indirect evidence. How can we establish what the sound system was in such cases?

1. First of all, we may have *external evidence*. In particular, we may have evidence from contemporary writers who described the sounds and pronunciation of their day. For example, French grammarians of the sixteenth and seventeenth centuries, especially those writing for the benefit of foreigners, have left us much interesting material. However, it is far from reliable, for want of any articulatory systematisation in those descriptions. They utilise whatever terms come to hand, with no scientific rigour at all. Their evidence consequently requires interpretation. Sounds are often described in terms which are far from clear: Greek grammarians called voiced sounds like *b*, *d* and *g* 'medial'

[1] Comparable English examples to illustrate the same point would be *pear*, *pair* and *pare*, or *your* and *you're*. (Translator's note)

[2] Cf. pp. [164–5], [180]. This passage as it stands appears to run counter to one of the key Saussurean doctrines. It is difficult fully to reconcile acknowledgment of language-specific sound systems or inventories with the claim that sounds as such belong to speech. The *Cours* proposes no explicit distinction between sounds on the one hand and functionally equivalent classes of sounds on the other. (Translator's note)

consonants (*mésai*), and their voiceless counterparts *p*, *t* and *k* they [59]
called *psīlaí*, which the Romans translated as *tenuēs*.[1]

2. More reliable information can be obtained by combining evidence of the above kind with *internal evidence*. This may be considered under two heads.

(*a*) Evidence from the regularity of sound changes.

When the linguist needs to determine what sound a letter represents at a given period, it is very important to know the previous history of that sound. For the current phonetic value of a letter is always the product of an evolutionary process. This allows us to eliminate certain hypotheses straight away. Although we do not know the exact value of the letter *ç* in Sanskrit, for instance, we do know that it is a continuation of Proto-Indo-European palatal *k*, and this fact clearly reduces the number of possibilities available.

If, in addition to the point of departure of a phonetic evolution, the linguist has information about the related development of similar sounds in the same language at the same period, he is able to reason by analogy and establish parallels.

The problem is evidently easier if he needs to determine the pronunciation of an intermediate stage of evolution, knowing already the point of departure and the final outcome. In French, *au* (as e.g. in *sauter*) must have been a diphthong in the Middle Ages, since it is intermediate between an earlier *al* and the *o* of modern French. If we discover in this case that the diphthong *au* still existed at a certain period, then it must certainly have existed in the preceding period.[2] Similarly, we do not know exactly what the *z* stands for in a word like the Old High German *wazer*. But clues are given by the earlier form *water* and the modern form *wasser*. So the *z* must be a sound intermediate between *t* and *s*. We can reject any hypothesis which would fit in only with the *t* or only with the *s*: for example, we can dismiss the possibility that it was a palatal consonant, since a sound intermediate between two dental consonants must be assumed to be itself [60]
a dental consonant.[3]

[1] Literally, 'smooth'. (Translator's note)

[2] This does not follow. It does not even follow that no reduction of the diphthong to *o* had yet occurred, unless one can be sure that there was no overlap between the phases of sound change. The point this example was intended to illustrate is clear enough, but the reasoning has been blurred by omitting the necessary qualifications. (Translator's note)

[3] As it stands, this is equally bad reasoning. For palatalisation is by no means impossible as an intermediate stage between *t* and *s*. This occurs, for instance, in the history of French, as Saussure and his editors must have been well aware. Again, the point of the example has been spoilt by oversimplification, although Saussure's lecture audience would have followed it without difficulty. (Translator's note)

(*b*) Contemporary evidence. This may be of various kinds.

Variations of spelling may be informative. At a certain period in Old High German, for instance, one finds the spellings *wazer*, *zehan*, *ezan*, but never *wacer*, *cehan*, etc. If at the same period such spellings as *esan*, *essan*, *waser* and *wasser* are also found, the conclusion can be drawn that this *z* represents a sound very close to *s*, but distinct from the sound represented by *c* at this period. When later forms like *wacer* begin to appear, they provide evidence that the two formerly distinct sounds are now more or less identically pronounced.

Poetic texts are valuable documents as evidence about pronunciation. The information to be gleaned from them will depend on whether the system of versification is based on the number of syllables, or on syllable length, or on likeness of sounds (alliteration, assonance, rhyme). Greek, for example, distinguishes long from short vowels in certain cases (e.g. *ō*, which is represented as *ω*), but not in others: it is the evidence of Greek poetry which must be examined in order to determine the vowel quantity of *a*, *i* and *u*. In Old French, rhymes allow us to work out how long the final consonants of *gras* and *faz* (from Latin *faciō*, 'I make') remained distinct in pronunciation, and at what period they began to fall together. Rhymes and assonances also tell us that in Old French the *e* which came from a Latin *a* (for example, *père* from *patrem*, *tel* from *talem*, *mer* from *mare*) had a sound which was unlike that of any other *e*: for these words never rhyme or assonate with *elle* (from *illa*), *vert* (from *viridem*), *belle* (from *bella*), etc.

Mention must be made, finally, of the spelling of words borrowed from other languages, of puns, of parodies, and similar evidence. The Gothic form *kawtsjo*, for instance, tells us something about the pronunciation of *cautio* in Late Latin. The pronunciation *rwè* for *roi*
[61] ('king') is attested in the late eighteenth century by the following anecdote, cited by Nyrop, *Grammaire historique de la langue française*, I, 3, p. 178. A woman was asked by the revolutionary tribunal if she had not said in front of witnesses that it was essential to have a king (*roi*). She replied that she had not been talking about a king (*roi*), but about a spinning-wheel (*rouet*).

All these sources of information are useful up to a point in helping us to reconstruct the sound system of a given period, and in assessing the value of orthography, while at the same time using orthography as evidence.

In the case of a contemporary language, the only rational procedure is: (*a*) to establish the system of sounds by direct observation, and then (*b*) to compare this with the system of letters used – inexactly – to represent them. Many grammarians still keep to the old method, criticised above, and describe how each letter is pronounced in the language they are describing. By such a method it is impossible to set out the sound system of a language clearly.

It is certain, however, that considerable progress has been made in this area. Physiological phonetics has made an important contribution to the revision of ideas about writing and spelling.

Appendix [63]

Principles of Physiological Phonetics

CHAPTER I

Sound Types

§1. On defining speech sounds

[For this section we were able to make use of shorthand notes taken at three lectures Saussure gave in 1897 on *The Theory of the Syllable*, in which he also touched upon general principles relating to the subject matter of this chapter. Much of the material in his personal notes deals with physiological phonetics, clarifying and amplifying the points made in his first and third courses of lectures. (Editorial note)]

Many authorities on the physiology of speech concern themselves almost exclusively with the act of phonation; that is, with the production of sounds by the organs of speech (the larynx, mouth, etc.). They neglect the auditory aspect of speech. This is a mistake; for the impression produced on the ear is not only given to us as directly as that of the movements of the speech organs, but also provides the more natural basis for a theory of speech sounds.

Our recognition of sound units has an auditory basis. The ear is what
tells us that a particular sound is a *b*, or a *t*, etc. If it were possible to [64]
film every movement of mouth and larynx involved in articulating a sequence of sounds, it would be impossible to detect subdivisions in that series of articulatory movements. We cannot tell articulatorily where one sound ends and another begins. If it were not for the auditory impression, it would be impossible to say whether the sequence *fāl* consists of three units rather than two or four. It is the sequence the ear hears that enables us immediately to detect when

one sound is replaced by another: the impression of auditory similarity is what tells us that we are still dealing with the same sound. What matters is not the duration (it may be *făl* or *fāl*) measured strictly in quavers or semiquavers, but the character of the auditory impression. The sequence of sounds we hear is not divided into segments of equal duration, but into segments identifiable as auditory units. This fact provides us with a natural starting point for the study of speech sounds.

From this point of view, one cannot fail to admire the Greek alphabet in its most primitive form. Each sound unit is represented by one symbol, and conversely each symbol invariably corresponds to a single sound. It was a system of brilliant simplicity, later taken over by the Romans. In the spelling of the word *bárbaros* ('barbarian'), each of the letters

ΒΑΡΒΑΡΟΣ

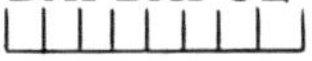

stands for a single segment. In the diagram given here, the horizontal line represents the sequence of sounds, while the vertical strokes indicate the transitions between each sound and the next. In the primitive Greek alphabet, there are no combinations like our modern French *ch* for *š*. Nor are there variable representations of a single sound, like our *c* and *s* for the sound *s*. Nor are there single characters representing a combination of sounds, like our *x* for *ks*. This principle, which is both a necessary and a sufficient condition for good transcription, was adopted almost without exception by the Greeks.[1]

[65] The principle was not grasped by other nations, and consequently their alphabets do not analyse sound sequences into constituent auditory units. The Cypriot system, for example, went no further than complex segments of the type *pa*, *ti*, *ko*, etc. This is usually referred to as 'syllabic' notation, although the term is not very accurate inasmuch as there are other syllabic patterns, e.g. *pak*, *tra*, etc. The Semitic system simply indicated consonants; so a word like *bárbaros* would have been written BRBRS.

The identification of sounds in a spoken sequence thus rests solely on auditory impressions. But their description is a different matter.

[1] It is true that they used Χ, Θ and Φ for *kh*, *th* and *ph*, so that ΦΕΡΩ represents *phérō*. But this is a later innovation. Archaic inscriptions have ΚΗΑΡΙΣ, and not ΧΑΡΙΣ. These inscriptions also have two symbols for *k*, the *kappa* and the *koppa*; but rightly so. For these two symbols corresponded to two different pronunciations, the *k* being sometimes palatal and sometimes velar. The *koppa* was later dropped. However, early Greek and Latin inscriptions often represent a double consonant by a single letter, as when Latin *fuisse* is written FUISE. This is an infringement of the rule, inasmuch as the sibilant has two parts which are auditorily distinguishable. None the less, the mistake is understandable, because these two sounds share a common feature (cf. p. [79] ff.).

This must be based upon articulatory considerations, since the units of an auditory sequence as such are unanalysable. We need to appeal to the corresponding sequence of movements in phonation. It then emerges that the same sound corresponds to the same movement: *b* (the auditory segment) = *b′* (the articulatory segment). The first units obtained as the result of segmenting the spoken sequence will comprise *b* plus *b′*. These units may be termed *speech sounds*. The speech sound is an aggregate of auditory impressions and articulatory movements, comprising what is heard and what is spoken, one delimiting the other. It is thus a complex unit, with a foot in each camp.

These elements determined by analysing the chain of speech are the links comprising that chain. Each is an indivisible moment in speech-time, which cannot be separated from that temporal sequence. [66]
A combination such as *ta* will always comprise two units, each occupying a certain temporal segment. Whereas the single, irreducible unit *t* may be isolated and considered *in abstracto* as having no place in any temporal sequence. In this sense one can speak of *t* in general as belonging to the type *T* (which we can represent by a capital to indicate the type in question), or of *i* as belonging to the type *I*, disregarding any feature of the sound which relates to sequence in time. In just the same way the musical phrase *doh, re, mi* must be treated as constituting a temporal sequence: but that does not prevent us from taking any one of these irreducible musical elements and considering it *in abstracto*.

After analysing a considerable number of sound sequences from a variety of languages, the linguist is able to recognise and classify the units involved. It emerges that, if we leave out of consideration those minutiae which do not affect auditory discrimination, the number of sound types is limited. Lists and detailed descriptions of them can be found in works on physiological phonetics.[1] Here we shall be concerned with the basic general principles on which classifications of this kind rest.

But first it is necessary to discuss briefly the vocal apparatus itself, the movements of the organs of speech, and their role in the production of sounds.

§2. *The vocal apparatus and how it works*[2]

In order to describe the vocal apparatus, we shall use a schematic

[1] Cf. Sievers, *Grundzüge der Phonetik*, 5th ed. 1902; Jespersen, *Lehrbuch der Phonetik*, 2nd ed. 1913; Roudet, *Eléments de phonétique générale*, 1910. (Editorial note)

[2] We have here drawn upon Jespersen's *Lehrbuch der Phonetik* to supplement Saussure's rather brief description. The system of formulae for speech sounds is Jespersen's; but this is simply a matter of presentation, which in no way affects Saussure's position. (Editorial note)

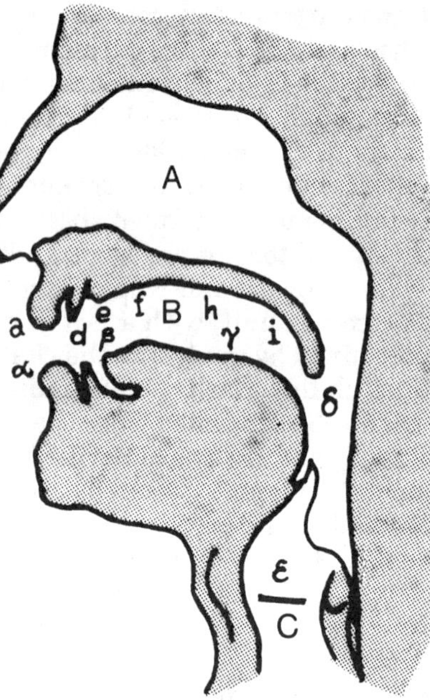

[67] diagram, in which *A* indicates the nasal cavity, *B* the oral cavity, and *C* the larynx, with the glottis ϵ between the two vocal cords.

In the mouth, α and *a* indicate the two lips; β the tip of the tongue and γ the rest of the tongue; *d* the upper teeth; *f-h* the hard palate, which is rigid and inert; *i* the soft palate, which is further back in the mouth and flexible; and δ the uvula.

In this diagram, Greek letters have been used to mark those articulators which are active, and Latin letters to mark those which are passive.[1]

The glottis ϵ is open when the two parallel muscles forming the vocal cords are drawn apart, and closed when they come together. Complete closure may for all practical purposes be left out of consideration. The opening involved varies in width. When the opening is broad, the air passes through freely and the vocal cords do not vibrate. When the opening is narrow, the passage of air produces audible vibrations. These positions exhaust the range of possibilities in normal phonation.

The nasal cavity is a completely immobile organ. The passage of air through it may be blocked by raising the uvula, δ. The uvula thus acts as a door to the nasal cavity, which may be open or shut.

[1] Unfortunately, this is an awkward and potentially confusing system, especially with respect to the symbols α, *a* and *i*. (Translator's note)

The oral cavity presents a greater range of variation. Its length may [68]
be increased by protrusion of the lips; it may be broadened or narrowed by control of the cheek muscles; while the movements of lips and tongue provide a whole gamut of possibilities, including complete closure.

The role of the different organs in sound production depends directly on mobility, the functions of the larynx and the nasal cavity being very restricted, and those of the oral cavity very diverse.

The air expelled from the lungs passes first of all through the glottis. A laryngeal sound may be produced by narrowing the vocal cord aperture. But the movement of the larynx is incapable of producing enough phonetic variation to supply all the clearly distinguishable sounds of a language. In this respect, laryngeal sound is uniform. If heard as produced directly by the glottis, it would seem to be of more or less uniform quality.

The nasal cavity serves merely as a resonator for the vocal vibrations passing through it. Consequently it plays no productive role in phonation.

The oral cavity, on the other hand, acts as both a generator of sound and a resonator. If the glottis is wide open, no laryngeal vibration is produced, and any sound heard will originate in the oral cavity. (We may leave it to the physicist to decide in this case whether it is a sound or merely a noise.) But if a narrowing of the vocal cord aperture causes the glottis to vibrate, the role of the mouth is principally to modify the laryngeal sound.

In sound production, then, the relevant factors are expiration, oral articulation, laryngeal vibration and nasal resonance.

But listing the various factors involved in sound production does not explain how different speech sounds are distinguished. In order to
classify speech sounds, it is less important to know what they consist [69]
of than to know how they are differentiated one from another. Negative factors may in this respect have more weight than positive factors. Expiration, for instance, is a positive factor; but since it occurs in every act of phonation it has no contrastive value. Whereas a negative factor, such as absence of nasal resonance, is just as effective as the presence of nasal resonance in identifying a speech sound. Essentially, then, two of the factors listed above are constant, and are both necessary and sufficient for sound production:

(*a*) expiration,
and (*b*) oral articulation.

The other two may accompany or fail to accompany the first two. These are:

(*c*) vibration of the larynx
and (*d*) nasal resonance.

As already noted, *a*, *c* and *d* are uniform in character, whereas *b* varies over an extremely wide range.

Furthermore, we must bear in mind that a speech sound is identified once the act of phonation involved is identified. By the same token, the inventory of sound types is established by determining the inventory of acts of phonation. Now acts of phonation, as is evident from our classification of the factors involved in sound production, are differentiated only in respect of *b*, *c* and *d*. So for each speech sound, it is necessary to establish three things: what its oral articulation is; whether it involves laryngeal vibration (〰) or not ([]); and whether it involves nasal vibration (....) or not ([]). As long as any of these three elements is unknown, the speech sound is not fully identified. But as long as all three are known, the various possible combinations determine all the essential types of acts of phonation.

[70] Thus one arrives at the following schema of possible varieties.

	I	II	III	IV
a	Expiration	Expiration	Expiration	Expiration
b	Oral art.	Oral art.	Oral art.	Oral art.
c	[]	〰	[]	〰
d	[]	[]	....	....

Column I comprises *voiceless* sounds. Column II comprises *voiced* sounds. Column III comprises voiceless nasal sounds. Column IV comprises voiced nasal sounds.

There remains one unknown element: the nature of the oral articulation. We must now proceed, therefore, to examine the possible varieties of oral articulation.

§3. *Classification of sounds by oral articulation*

Sounds are generally classified according to their point of articulation. We shall adopt a different approach. Wherever the point of articulation of a sound may be, it always has a certain *aperture*, which will fall somewhere between the two extremes of complete closure and maximum opening. On this basis sounds may be classified into seven categories, for which we may adopt the numerals 0, 1, 2, 3, 4, 5, 6, going from smallest to largest aperture. Only within each category shall we distinguish between types of speech sound according to their point of articulation.

We shall follow current terminology, although in various respects it is incomplete or mistaken. Terms such as *guttural*, *palatal*, *dental* and *liquid* are all to some extent unsatisfactory. It would be more rational to divide the palate into a number of regions: in this way, taking tongue movement into account, it would always be possible to specify exactly in each case the main point of constriction. We shall [71] exploit this idea, and use the letters in the diagram on p. [67] to denote each articulation by means of a formula in which the figure for the aperture is placed between the Greek letter indicating the active organ (on the left) and the Latin letter indicating the passive organ (on the right). For example, the formula '$\beta 0 e$' will denote the articulation which has a degree of aperture corresponding to complete closure, when the tip of the tongue β is pressed against the upper alveolar ridge *e*.

Finally, in each articulation thus defined, the various types of speech sound will be distinguished by whether or not they are accompanied by laryngeal vibration and nasal resonance. Absence of these accompanying features will play as important a differentiating role as their presence.

This, then, is the system we propose to employ for the classification of sounds. It is a simple, rational system. It should not be expected to accommodate speech sounds of a complex or unusual character, however important they may be in practice. For example, it leaves out aspirates (*ph*, *dh*, etc.), affricates (*ts*, *dž*, *pf*, etc.), palatalised consonants, and weak vowels (*ə* or mute *e*, etc.). Nor, on the other hand, does it bother with simple speech sounds which happen to be of no practical significance and are not recognisably distinct.

A. ZERO APERTURE: STOPS. This class includes all speech sounds produced by complete closure; that is, by a full but momentary blockage of the oral cavity. We need not consider here whether the sound is produced at the moment of closure, or upon release of the closure: both types of case occur (see p. [79] ff.).

According to their point of articulation, three main types of stop may be distinguished: labials (*p*, *b*, *m*), dentals (*t*, *d*, *n*), and so-called gutturals (*k*, *g*, *ṅ*).

Labials are pronounced using the lips as articulators. Dentals are pronounced by bringing the extremity of the tongue in contact with the front of the palate. Gutturals are pronounced by bringing the back [72] of the tongue in contact with the rear of the palate.

In many languages, including Proto-Indo-European, two guttural articulations are clearly distinguished. One is palatal (in the *f-h* region), and the other velar (*i*). But other languages, including French, disregard this difference, and in these cases the ear assimilates a back *k* (as in *court*) to a front *k* (as in *qui*).[1]

[1] Approximate English equivalents would be the initial consonant sounds of *caught* and *key* respectively. (Translator's note)

The table below gives the formulae for the various speech sounds mentioned:

LABIAL			DENTAL			GUTTURAL		
p	*b*	(*m*)	*t*	*d*	(*n*)	*k*	*g*	(*ṅ*)
α0*a*	α0*a*	α0*a*	β0*e*	β0*e*	β0*e*	γ0*h*	γ0*h*	γ0*h*
[]	~	~	[]	~	~	[]	~	~
[]	[]	.....	[]	[]	.....	[]	[]	.....

The nasals *m*, *n* and *ṅ* are voiced nasalised stops: in the pronunciation of *amba*, the uvula is raised to block off the nasal cavity at the point of transition from *m* to *b*.

In theory, each type has a voiceless nasal with no glottal vibration. In the languages of Scandinavia, we find voiceless *m* following another voiceless consonant. In French too such pronunciations occur, but the feature is not recognised by speakers as distinctive.

The nasals are placed in parentheses in the above table. For although their articulation involves a complete oral closure, the fact that the nasal cavity remains open gives them a higher rank in terms of aperture (see class C).

B. APERTURE 1: FRICATIVES OR SPIRANTS. These are characterised by incomplete closure of the oral cavity, allowing the passage
[73] of air. The term *spirant* is a quite general one. The term *fricative*, while implying nothing about the degree of closure, alludes to the impression of friction produced by the passage of air (Latin *fricāre*).

This category cannot be restricted to three types, as Category A was. The labials proper in Category B (corresponding to the stops *p* and *b*) are rarely used, and may be left out of consideration: they are usually replaced by labio-dentals, articulated with the lower lip against the teeth (as in French *f* and *v*). The dentals divide into several groups, depending on the configuration of the tip of the tongue during the constriction: without going into details, it will suffice here to indicate these various tongue configurations by the symbols β, β' and β''. Among sounds where the palate is involved, the ear generally distinguishes between a front articulation (palatal) and a back articulation (velar).[1]

[74] Are there no fricatives corresponding to *n*, *m*, *ṅ* etc. among the stops (i.e. a nasal *v*, nasal *z*, etc.)? One may easily imagine there are. In French one hears a nasal *v* in *inventer*. But in general nasal fricatives are not recognised as distinct speech sounds.

[1] In accordance with his system of simplification, Saussure refrains from drawing this distinction for Category A, despite the importance of the distinction between the two series of guttural stops in Proto-Indo-European. The omission is intentional. (Editorial note)

LABIO-DENT		DENTAL					
f	*v*	*þ*	*đ*	*s*	*z*	*š*	*ž*
α1*d* [] []	α1*d* ~ []	β1*d* [] []	β1*d* ~ []	β′1*d* [] []	β′1*d* ~ []	β″1*d* [] []	β″1*d* ~ []

PALATAL		GUTTURAL	
χ′	γ′	χ	γ
γ1*f* [] []	γ1*f* ~ []	γ1*i* [] []	γ1*i* ~ []

þ	=	English	*th*	in	*thing*
đ	=	"	*th*	"	*then*
s	=	French	*s*	"	*si*
z	=	"	*s*	"	*rose*
š	=	"	*ch*	"	*chant*
ž	=	"	*g*	"	*génie*
χ′	=	German	*ch*	"	*ich*
γ′	=	N. Germ.	*g*	"	*liegen*
χ	=	German	*ch*	"	*Bach*
γ	=	N. Germ.	*g*	"	*Tage*

C. APERTURE 2: NASALS (see above, p. [72]).

D. APERTURE 3: LIQUIDS.

Two kinds of articulation fall into this category.

(1) *Lateral* articulations, in which the tongue makes contact with the front part of the palate, but leaving an opening on either side. This position is noted by a superscript *l* in our formulae. Depending on the point of articulation, the sound may be: dental (*l*), palatal or palatalised (*l′*), guttural or velar (*ł*). In almost all languages, laterals are voiced, just like *b*, *z*, etc. However, voiceless laterals are not impossible. In French, we have a voiceless lateral when *l* following a voiceless consonant is itself pronounced without vocal cord vibration (as in *pluie*, as opposed to *bleu*): but speakers are not aware of this distinction.

Lateral nasals require little comment. They are rarely found, and are not distinctive speech sounds. None the less they exist, in particular when preceded by a nasal sound (as for example in the French word *branlant*).

(2) *Trilled* articulations, in which the tongue is less close to the palate than for *l* but vibrates. The number of vibrations involved varies. The symbol denoting this type of articulation in our formulae is a superscript *v*. The degree of aperture may be considered equivalent to that of laterals. The vibration may be produced in two ways: either with the tip of the tongue against the alveolae (the type of *r* called in

French *roulé*, 'rolled'), or else further back with the back of the tongue (the type of *r* called in French *grasséyé*, 'thickened'). The same observations as were noted above in respect of voiceless and nasal laterals apply also to voiceless and nasal trills.

[75]

l	*l'*	*ɫ*	*r*	
$\beta^{l}3e$ ~ []	$\gamma^{l}3f\text{-}h$ ~ []	$\gamma^{l}3i$ ~ []	$\beta^{v}3e$ ~ []	$\gamma 3\delta^{v}$ ~ []

Above the third degree of aperture, we enter another domain. From *consonants* we pass to *vowels*. So far, we have said nothing about this distinction. In fact, the mechanism of phonation is exactly the same for both consonants and vowels. The formula for a vowel is exactly comparable to the formula for any voiced consonant. As regards oral articulation, there is no distinction to be drawn. Only the auditory effect is different. Beyond a certain degree of aperture, the mouth functions mainly as a resonator. The timbre of the laryngeal sound comes through prominently, and any noise originating in the oral cavity is lost. Progressive closure of the mouth increases the extent to which the laryngeal sound is masked; whereas the wider the mouth opens, the less oral noise interferes with it. As a result of these purely mechanical conditions, sound predominates in the production of vowels.

E. APERTURE 4: *i*, *u*, *ü*.

By comparison with other vowels, these three involve marked closure, comparable to the closure required for consonants. This degree of closure has certain consequences, to be examined below, which justify the term *semi-vowel* usually applied to these sounds.

The sound *i* is pronounced with spread lips (denoted by the symbol ‾) and front articulation; *u* with rounded lips (denoted by the symbol °) and back articulation; *ü* with the lip position of *u* and the point of articulation of *i*.

Like all vowels, *i*, *u* and *ü* have nasalised versions; but these are rare, and can be ignored for present purposes. It should be noted that
[76] the sounds spelled *in* and *un* in French orthography are not to be confused with nasal *i* and nasal *u* (see below).

Is there not a voiceless *i*, articulated without laryngeal sound? The same question applies to *u*, *ü* and indeed all vowels. Such speech sounds do exist, and correspond to voiceless consonants: but they are not to be confused with whispered vowels, articulated with a relaxed glottis. Voiceless vowels are produced, for example, when a normally voiced vowel is preceded by *h*: thus in *hi* one hears first of all an *i* without vocal cord vibration, immediately followed by a normal *i*.

i	*u*	*ü*
¯γ4*f* ∼ []	°γ4*i* ∼ []	°γ4*f* ∼ []

F. APERTURE 5: *e*, *o*, *ö*.

The articulation of *e*, *o* and *ö* corresponds to that of *i*, *u* and *ü* respectively. Nasalised versions of these vowels are common (for example, French *ẽ*, *õ* and *ö̃* in *pin*, *pont*, *brun*). The voiceless forms occur in the aspirated *h* of *he*, *ho*, *hö*.

N.B. Many languages here distinguish various degrees of aperture. French has at least two series of vowels: one called 'closed' (*ẹ*, *ọ*, *ö̩* in *dé*, *dos*, *deux*) and the other 'open' (*ę*, *ǫ*, *ǫ̈* in *mer*, *mort*, *meurt*).

e	*o*	*ö*	*ẽ*	*õ*	*ö̃*
¯γ5*f* ∼ []	°γ5*i* ∼ []	¯γ5*f* ∼ []	¯γ5*f* ∼	°γ5*i* ∼	°γ5*f* ∼ .....

G. APERTURE 6: *a*.

This vowel has the maximum aperture. It has a nasalised version which is, however, slightly less open (*ã* in French *grand*). It also has a voiceless version (*h* in *ha*).

a	*ã*
γ6*h* ∼ []	γ6*h* ∼ .....

[77]

CHAPTER II

Sounds in Spoken Sequences

§1. Necessity of studying sounds in spoken sequences

There are special treatises, particularly by English phoneticians, devoted to minute descriptions of the sounds of language.

Are these adequate to enable physiological phonetics to fulfil its role as an ancillary science to linguistics? The accumulation of all these details is of no importance in itself: what matters is their synthesis. The linguist need not be an expert in these matters. All he requires is to be supplied with certain data for studying language structure.

The approach represented by these descriptions has one serious methodological defect: it tends to overlook the fact that in a language we have not just sounds, but sequences of spoken sounds.[1] Too little attention is paid to the sequential relations between sounds, in spite of the fact that it is the syllable which is the directly observable unit of speech, rather than the individual sounds of which it is composed. Syllabic units, as has already been noted, are the basis of certain primitive writing systems, whereas alphabetic writing is a later development.

Furthermore, in linguistics simple units generally present no problems. If, for instance, at a given period in a given language, every *a* changes to *o*, that offers no difficulty: the phenomenon can be noted,
[78] without our having to look for any general explanation. A science of sounds assumes importance for us only when two or more sounds are structurally interconnected; for then there is a limit to the ways in which the one can vary in relation to the other. The very fact that two units are involved means that we are dealing with relationships and rules, which is a quite different matter. A search for linguistic principles based on the examination of isolated sounds is thus looking in

[1] Another injudicious formulation: cf. footnote p.[58]. (Translator's note)

the wrong direction. For the moment two speech sounds are involved, we are lost. In Old High German, for example, *halg*, *balg*, *wagn*, *lang*, *donr*, *dorn* eventually became *hagal*, *balg*, *wagan*, *lang*, *donnar*, *dorn*. In other words, the result varies according to the nature and sequence of sounds in question. Sometimes a vowel develops between two consonants, but sometimes the consonant group remains unsplit. But how do we state the rule? Where do the differences come from? Doubtless from the different consonant combinations (*gl*, *lg*, *gn*, etc.). These combinations obviously comprise a stop which is in some cases preceded, and in other cases followed, by a liquid or a nasal. But what of the results? As long as *g* and *n* are treated as the same two sounds in all cases, it is impossible to explain why *g* followed by *n* should produce any different result from *n* followed by *g*.

In addition to a study of sound types, therefore, we need a science which starts from binary groups and sequences of speech sounds, which will be something quite different. In studying isolated sounds, it is sufficient to note the positions of the vocal organs. The auditory quality of the sound is not open to question: it is determined by the ear. And as for articulation, the speaker is free to produce that sound by any means he can. But matters are not so simple the moment we consider the pronunciation of two sounds in combination. We find ourselves obliged to take into account the possibility of discrepancy between the pronunciation intended and the effect produced. For it is not always within our power to pronounce as we had intended. Freedom to link sound types in succession is limited by the possibility of [79] combining the right articulatory movements. To account for what happens in these combinations, we need a science which treats combinations rather like algebraic equations. A binary group will imply a certain number of articulatory and auditory features imposing conditions upon each other, in such a way that when one of them varies there will be a necessary alteration of the others which can be calculated.

If phonation presents anything of a universal nature, which takes priority over local variations in speech sounds, it is undoubtedly a rule-governed mechanism of the type just mentioned. That is why the study of combinations of sounds is of such importance for general linguistics. Whereas the rules usually formulated are limited to specifying the articulation of the various individual sounds which fortuitously occur in different languages, a combinatory phonetics would be able to limit possibilities and establish constant relations obtaining between interdependent speech sounds. Thus the case of *hagl*, *balg*, etc. (p. [78]) raises the much discussed question of Proto-Indo-European sonants: this is an area in which one can least of all afford to do without a combinatory phonetics conceived along these lines. For syllabification is virtually the only phenomenon involved from start to finish. And that is not the only problem which needs to be tackled in this way. In any case, one fact is beyond doubt: it is almost impossible to discuss the question of sonants without a detailed appreciation of the laws governing combinations of speech sounds.

§2. *Adduction and abduction*

Let us begin with an elementary observation. In the pronunciation of the sequence *appa*, we notice a difference between the first *p* and the second. The first corresponds to a closure, the second to an opening.
[80] The two impressions are sufficiently similar to allow the representation of this sequence by a single *p* (cf. p. [66], footnote). None the less, the difference justifies special signs (` ´) to mark the distinction (*ap̀ṕa*) and to note it even when one *p* is not followed by the other in a spoken sequence (cf. *ap̀ta*, *atṕa*). The same distinction applies not only to stops but to fricatives (*af̀f́a*), nasals (*am̀ḿa*), liquids (*al̀ĺa*), and in general to all speech sounds, including vowels (*aòóa*) except for *a*.

The closure is termed *adduction* and the opening *abduction*. A *p* is either adductive (*p̀*) or abductive (*ṕ*). Likewise, we may speak of *closing* and *opening* sounds.

In a sequence such as *appa*, we notice also, apart from adduction and abduction, a stable segment where the stop is held for as long as desired. If the speech sound in question is one of greater aperture, e.g. *alla*, the emission of sound continues at that point without further movement of the speech organs. In general, any spoken sequence includes such intermediary phases, which we shall call *sustainments* or *suspended articulations*. But these can be subsumed under adduction, since they have a similar effect. Consequently, in what follows we shall distinguish simply between adductive and abductive sounds.[1]

Although this assimilation would not be admissible in a detailed treatment of physiological phonetics, it is justifiable in a survey which seeks to simplify the phenomenon of syllabification as much as poss-
[81] ible, and reduce it to its essentials. We shall not claim to solve thereby all the problems connected with the division of spoken sequences into syllables, but merely to propose a rational basis for studying the matter.

[1] Theoretically, this is a moot point. Certain objections to it may be countered by pointing out that any suspended articulation, e.g. *f*, is the result of two forces: (i) air pressure against certain surfaces, and (ii) resistance from these surfaces, which are tensed to balance the pressure. The sustainment is thus only a continued adduction. That is why when adduction is followed by a sustainment of the same type, the effect is of one continued articulation throughout. Thus it is not illogical to group the two kinds of articulation together as one articulatory and auditory unit. Abduction, on the other hand, contrasts with both, involving by definition a relaxation of tension. Cf. also §6 below. (Editorial note)

One further remark is called for. The opening and closing movements necessitated by the articulation of sounds must not be confused with the various degrees of aperture of the sounds themselves. Any speech sound whatever may be pronounced either adductively or abductively. However, the aperture of the sound influences the adduction or abduction, inasmuch as the distinction between the two articulations is less clear when the aperture is larger. With *i*, *u*, and *ü*, the difference is still quite perceptible. In *aìía*, one can distinguish the closing *ì* from the opening *í*. Similarly, in *aùúa* and aǜǘa the adduction and abduction are clearly distinct; so much so that they are even occasionally distinguished in writing, contrary to normal orthographic practice. Thus in English spelling *w*, in German *j*, and often in French *y* (eg. in *yeux*) represent opening sounds (*ú*, *í*), as opposed to the letters *u* and *i*, which are used to represent *ù* and *ì*. For higher degrees of aperture (*e* and *o*), however, although adduction and abduction are theoretically distinguishable (*aèéa*, *aòóa*), the distinction is difficult to operate in practice. Finally, as already noted, at the maximum degree of aperture, the sound *a* affords no possibility of contrasting adduction with abduction, since in this case the aperture eliminates any such difference.

Our table of speech sounds, representing the inventory of minimum units, will thus show a duplication for every speech sound except *a*:

p̀ ṕ, etc.
f̀ f́, etc.
m̀ ḿ, etc.
r̀ ŕ, etc.
ì ý, etc.
è é, etc.
a.

Far from ignoring distinctions recognized in spelling (*y*, *w*), we shall [82]
take care to maintain them. The justification for so doing will be presented later (cf. §7 below).

Now for the first time we have left abstractions behind us. For the first time we are down to the concrete, irreducible elements which occupy a place and take up a certain length of time in the pronunciation of the spoken sequence. Now in retrospect *P* emerges as the abstract unit grouping together the common features linking *p̀* and *ṕ*, which are the only sounds we ever encounter in reality. In just the same way, *B*, *P* and *M* themselves may be subsumed under a higher-order abstraction, 'labials'. We may speak of *P* as we do of a zoological species: there are males and females, but no ideal exemplar of the species as such. Hitherto, then, we have been distinguishing and classifying abstractions; but now we take the necessary step of going beyond abstraction to the concrete.

It has been a great mistake in physiological phonetics to suppose that these abstractions were actually real units, without analysing the definition of a unit more attentively. The Greek alphabet succeeded in distinguishing these abstract elements, and the analysis on which it was based was, as we have already observed, a most remarkable one. However, it was an incomplete analysis, which did not go beyond a certain point.

But if we do not specify further, how can we say what a *p* is? Considered as part of a temporal event, as a unit in a spoken sequence, a *p* is neither *ṕ*, nor *p̀*, and even less the group *p̀ṕ*, which is clearly made up of two units. On the other hand, if we consider it apart from any spoken sequence, in a timeless vacuum, we are left with something which has no existence of its own, something which is quite useless. What does a combination like *l*+*k* signify in itself? Two abstractions cannot constitute any temporal unit. It is quite another matter to speak of *l̀k̀*, of *ĺḱ*, of *l̀ḱ*, or of *ĺk̀*, which are combinations of real units in speech. This is why it only takes a combination of two sounds to cause traditional physiological phonetics great embarrassment. We
[83] see immediately the impossibility of proceeding, as traditional analysis does, on the basis of abstract units.

The theory has been advanced that any speech sound, as it occurs in a spoken sequence, e.g. *p* in *pa* or *apa*, involves adduction followed by abduction (*àṕa*). Doubtless it is true that any opening must be preceded by closure: to take another example, if I say *r̀ṕ* I must, after closing the *r*, articulate an opening *r* with the uvula[1] during the labial movement of closure for the *p*. But this does not conflict with the analysis proposed here. Our analysis of the act of phonation is intended to take account only of those contrasting features which the ear picks out and which thus serve to mark the auditory units in a spoken sequence. Only these audio-motor units are to be considered. So the abduction of *r* which accompanies the abduction of *p* does not exist as far as we are concerned: it produces no perceptible sound, or at least nothing which counts in the sequence of speech sounds. This is an essential point which must be constantly borne in mind in order to understand what follows.

§3. *Combinations of adduction and abduction in the spoken sequence*

We now come to consider the results of sequences of adduction and abduction in the four theoretically possible combinations:

[1] The sound envisaged is the uvular *r* of French. (Translator's note)

1. < >
2. > <
3. < <
4. > >

1. ABDUCTION + ADDUCTION (<>). It is always possible, without interruption of a spoken sequence, to follow an abductive speech sound by an adductive one, e.g. *ḱr̀*, *ḱì*, *ým̀*, etc. (cf. Sanskrit *ḱr̀ta-*, French *ḱìte* (*quitter*), Proto-Indo-European *ým̀to-*, etc.). Although certain combinations of this type, such as *ḱt̀*, have no auditory effect of [84] any practical consequence, it is none the less true that after articulating an opening *k*, the vocal organs are in the position required for proceeding to a closure at any desired point. These two articulatory phases may occur in sequence without hindering each other.

2. ADDUCTION + ABDUCTION (><). In the same conditions, and with the same qualifications, the combination of an adduction with a following abduction is likewise possible: *ìḿ*, *k̀t́*, etc. (cf. Greek *haîma*, French *actif*, etc.)

However, this sequence of articulations is not quite as natural as in the previous case. The difference between starting with an adduction and starting with an abduction is that the abduction tends towards a neutral position of the mouth and does not affect the following sound, while the adduction results in a particular articulatory position which cannot then become the starting point for other than certain sounds. This means that a bridging movement may then be necessary in order to reach the position of the vocal organs required for the articulation of the second speech sound. Thus while pronouncing the *s* in a group *s̀ṕ*, the lips must begin to close in preparation for the opening *p* which follows. But experience teaches us that such bridging movements produce nothing audible, other than one of those fleeting sounds which we can ignore, and which do not in any case interrupt the articulation of the sequence.

3. DOUBLE ABDUCTION (<<). Two abductions may be articulated consecutively; but if the second is a speech sound of smaller aperture than the first, or of equal aperture, there will be no auditory impression of unity which otherwise accompanies the articulation of two consecutive abductions, and is also characteristic of the two types of combination considered already. Thus it is possible to pronounce *ṕḱ* (as in *ṕḱa*), but the two sounds are not linked together, the types *P* and *K* being of equal aperture. It is this rather unnatural pronunciation which would result if one introduced a pause after the first vowel

[85] of *cha-ṕḱa*.[1] The sequence *ṕŕ*, by contrast, produces an impression of continuity (cf. French *prix*). Likewise, there is no awkwardness about *ŕý* (cf. French *rien*). Why is this? Because at the moment of articulation of the first abduction the vocal organs have already been able to take up the position required to articulate the second, without interfering with the auditory effect of the first. For example, in *prix*, while the *p* is being pronounced the articulators are already in the position for *r*. But it is impossible to reverse this and pronounce *ŕṕ* smoothly as a sequence: not that it is articulatorily impossible to take up the position for *ṕ* while pronouncing an opening *ŕ*, but because the movement of that *ŕ*, encountering the smaller aperture of *ṕ*, will not be perceptible. So in order to make *ŕṕ* audible, one has to make two attempts at it, and the continuity is broken.

A sequence may contain more than two consecutive abductions, provided the aperture of each sound is less than that of its immediate successor (e.g. *ḱŕẃa*). Apart from certain special cases which cannot be examined here, it may be said that the possible number of consecutive abductions is naturally limited by the number of degrees of aperture that may be distinguished in practice.[2]

[86] 4. DOUBLE ADDUCTION (>>). Here the opposite principle operates. As long as a sound is of greater aperture than the following sound, the impression is one of continuity (e.g. *ìr̀*, *r̀t̀*). If this condition is not fulfilled, i.e. if the following sound is of greater or equal aperture, there is no impression of continuity. Thus *s̀r̀* in *às̀r̀ta* is like the group *p̀k* in *cha-pka* mentioned above (p. [85]). The phenomenon is exactly parallel to the one examined in abductive sequences: in *r̀t̀*, the *t̀* by reason of its smaller aperture automatically precludes abduction of *r̀*. Or if we take a sequence in which the two sounds do not share the same point of articulation, as in *r̀m̀*, the *m̀* does not prevent the abduction of *r̀* but, having a closer articulation, completely obscures any abduction of *r*, which comes to the same thing. Otherwise, as in

[1] In certain languages, some groups of this type are common (e.g. initial *kt* in Greek; cf. *kteínō*). But although easy to pronounce, they lack auditory unity. See the next footnote. (Editorial note)

[2] Saussure here simplifies the question by taking into account only the degree of aperture of a sound, and disregarding the place and manner of articulation (voiceless, voiced, trill, lateral, etc.). His conclusions, based solely on the degree of aperture, consequently do not cover every case in fact. In a sequence such as *trya*, it is very difficult to pronounce the first three sounds smoothly without a break (*t́ŕýá*), unless the *ý* is allowed to merge with and palatalise the preceding *ŕ*. None the less, these three sounds apparently constitute a perfect example of an abductive sequence (cf. p. [94] for cases like *meurtrier*). But *trwa*, on the other hand, presents no such difficulty. Mention might also be made of sequences like *pmla*, where it is difficult not to pronounce the nasal adductively (*ṕm̀ĺá*). These exceptions mostly involve abduction, by nature an instantaneous movement which cannot be delayed. (Editorial note)

the opposite case of *m̀ŕ*, the fleeting abduction, which is an articulatory necessity, would interrupt the sequential flow.

The adductive sequence, like the abductive sequence, may include more than two sounds, provided each has a greater degree of aperture than its immediate successor (e.g. *àr̀s̀t*).

Leaving aside now interruptions of a sequence, let us consider a normal continuous sequence of sounds of the kind we have in a French word like *particulièrement*. This we may call a 'physiological' sequence: *ṕ à r̀ t́ ì ḱ ǜ ĺ ý è r̀ ḿ ã*. Such a sequence is characterised by a succession of graduated abductions and adductions, corresponding to the opening and closing of articulators in the mouth.

A normal sequence so defined calls for the following observations, which are of fundamental importance.

§4. *Syllabic boundaries and vocalic peaks*

In any sound sequence, the passage from adduction to abduction (>|<) produces a characteristic effect which marks a *syllabic boundary*. This occurs, for example, between *ì* and *ḱ* in *particulièrement*. This regular [87] accompaniment of a given articulatory movement by a given auditory effect gives the group 'adduction + abduction' a special phonological role. It remains recognisably the same, regardless of the different types of sound involved. It constitutes a genus comprising as many species as there are possible combinations available.

A syllabic boundary may, in certain cases, occur at different points in the same sound sequence, depending on the speed of transition from adduction to abduction. In *ardra* the sequence is not interrupted, whether one pronounces it *àr̀d́ŕà* or *àr̀d̀ŕà*. For the adductive sequence *àr̀d* is as smoothly graduated as the abductive sequence *d́ŕ*. The same would apply to *ülye* in *particulièrement* (which could be either *ǜĺýè* or *ǜl̀ýè*).

Secondly, it may be observed that where the voice passes from silence to adduction (>), as in the *àrt* of the word *artiste*, or from abduction to adduction (<>), as in the *ṕàrt* of *particulièrement*, the sound where this adduction occurs produces a special effect which distinguishes that sound from its neighbours. This is the vocalic effect. It does not depend at all upon the degree of aperture as such. For *r* can produce it just as well as *a* (e.g. *ṕr̀t*). It is something inherent in the adduction, whatever its type of sound or degree of aperture. Nor does it make any difference whether it occurs after a silence or after an abduction. Any point where this effect is produced by the occurrence of a first adduction after silence or after an abduction may be termed a *vocalic peak*.

Another term used for the same unit is *sonant*, and *adsonants* are

accompanying sounds which precede or follow the sonant in the same syllable. The terms *vowel* and *consonant*, it will be recalled (cf. p. [75]), designate different sound types: whereas *sonant* and *adsonant* designate functions in the syllable. These terminological distinctions allow us to avoid a long-standing confusion. The sound type *I* is the same in
[88] the words *fidèle* and *pied*, i.e. it is a vowel; but it is a sonant in *fidèle* and an adsonant in *pied*. Analysis shows that sonants are always adductive, while adsonants are sometimes adductive (e.g. *ì* in the English word *boy*, pronounced *boì*) and sometimes abductive (e.g. *ý* in the French word *pied*, pronounced *ṕýè*). This merely confirms the validity of these distinctions. It is true that in fact *e*, *o* and *a* are regularly sonants; but that is merely coincidental. Since they have a greater aperture than other sounds, they always come at the beginning of an adductive sequence. Stops, on the contrary, having minimal aperture, are always adsonants. In practice, it is sounds having an aperture of degree 2, 3, or 4 (nasals, liquids, semi-vowels) which can adopt either role, depending on where they occur and the nature of their articulation.

§5. *Criticism of theories of syllabification*

In any given spoken sequence, the ear detects a division into syllables, and a sonant in any given syllable. These two facts are well known, but one may wonder what the reason is. Various explanations have been proposed.

1. Given that certain sounds are more sonorous than others, attempts have been made to base syllabification on sonority. But in that case, why is it that sonorous sounds like *i* and *u* do not necessarily constitute syllables? Furthermore, where does sonority stop? (For fricatives like *s* can be syllabic, as in *pst.*) If it is a question simply of the relative sonority of sounds in succession, how can one explain the fact that in groups like *ẃl* (e.g. Proto-Indo-European**wlkos* 'wolf') the less sonorous sound is syllabic?

2. Sievers was the first to establish that a sound classed as a vowel may none the less not sound like a vowel (as noted above, *y* and *w* are
[89] no different from *i* and *u*). But when we ask how this dual function comes about, or this dual auditory effect (for *function* here means the same thing), we are told that the function of a sound depends on whether or not it has a 'syllabic stress'.

But that is a vicious circle. Either I am quite free in all circumstances to assign a syllabic stress and thereby create a sonant – in which case there is no reason to call it 'syllabic stress' rather than 'sonant stress' –; or else syllabic stress, if the term means anything, has to do with laws governing syllables. But what these laws are we are not told. Worse still, the sonant quality in question is called *silbenbildend* ('syllable forming'), as if the formation of a syllable in turn depended upon that stress.

The method advocated here is quite different from either of these approaches. By analysing the syllable as it occurs in spoken sequences, we reached the irreducible units involved: opening sounds and closing sounds. Then, by considering combinations of these units, we arrived at definitions of syllabic boundaries and vocalic peaks. We now know, as a result, under what physiological conditions the auditory effects in question occur. The theories criticised above follow the reverse order. They start from types of sound in isolation, and claim to be able to deduce from these types where syllabic boundaries and sonants occur. But given any series of sounds, one way of articulating them may be more natural or easier than another: none the less, there remains to a large extent the possibility of choosing between opening and closing articulations. And it is on this choice, not directly on the types of sound involved, that syllabification depends.

It must not be supposed that this theory either exhausts or answers all the pertinent questions. Hiatus, for instance, which is common enough, is nothing other than a *broken adductive sequence*, either deliberately or involuntarily broken (e.g. $\overset{>}{\imath}$-$\overset{>}{a}$ as in *il cria*, or $\overset{>}{a}$-$\overset{>}{\imath}$ as in *ébahi*). It can be more easily produced if the sounds involved are of [90]
large aperture.

There are also *broken abductive sequences* which, while not smoothly graduated, occur in sound sequences just like normal groups: one example has already been touched on (cf. p. [85], footnote) in Greek *kteínō*. Or take the group *pzta*. Normally, this can only be pronounced $\overset{<}{p}\overset{>}{z}\overset{<}{t}\overset{>}{a}$, which means it should comprise two syllables, as indeed it does if the voicing of *z* is clearly heard. But if the *z* is devoiced, since it is a sound of very small aperture the contrast between *z* and *a* means that one then hears something like $\overset{<}{p}\overset{<}{z}\overset{<}{t}\overset{>}{a}$, which is only one syllable.

In all cases of this kind, the intervention of the speaker's deliberate effort to pronounce in a certain way may deceive our expectations and to some extent subvert natural physiological tendencies. It is often difficult to determine exactly what to attribute to one set of factors or the other. However that may be, phonation involves sequences of adduction and abduction, and that is the fundamental condition governing syllabification.

§6. Duration of adduction and abduction

Explaining syllabification in terms of adduction and abduction leads to an important observation. It is a generalisation about prosody. In

Greek and Latin words, a distinction is drawn between two kinds of long syllable. Syllables are long 'by nature' (e.g. *māter*) or 'by position' (e.g. *făctus*). Why is it that *fac* is counted long in *factus*? We are told that it is because of the consonant group *ct*. But if the consonant group itself were responsible, any syllable beginning with two consonants would also count as long, which is not the case (cf. *clĭens*, etc.).

[91] The correct explanation is that abduction and adduction are quite different in respect of duration. Abduction is always so rapid that the ear cannot measure it: that is also why abduction never gives a vocalic impression. But the ear can measure adduction, and this accounts for the feeling of longer duration associated with the vowel preceding.

Vowels before a group consisting of a stop or fricative followed by a liquid are treated in two ways in Classical prosody. In *patrem* the *a* may be long or short. This too is accounted for by the same principle. Both $\overset{<}{t}\overset{<}{r}$ and $\overset{>}{t}\overset{<}{r}$ are easy to pronounce. The former articulation allows the *a* to remain short, while the latter creates a long syllable. This dual treatment of the *a* is not possible in a word like *factus*, because $\overset{>}{c}\overset{<}{t}$ can be pronounced, whereas $\overset{<}{c}\overset{<}{t}$ cannot.

§7. Sounds of aperture 4. Diphthongs. Questions of spelling

Finally, sounds of Aperture 4 call for certain remarks. We have seen (p. [81]) that these sounds, unlike others, are represented in writing by two letters ($w=\overset{<}{u}$, $u=\overset{>}{u}$, $y=\overset{<}{\imath}$, $i=\overset{>}{\imath}$). For in groups like *aiya*, *auwa* the distinction between abduction (<) and adduction (>) is more perceptible than anywhere else: $\overset{>}{\imath}$ and $\overset{>}{u}$ sound clearly like vowels, and $\overset{<}{\imath}$ and $\overset{<}{u}$ like consonants.[1] Without claiming to give an explanation of the fact, we may point out that this 'consonantal' *i* is never found with a closing articulation. So we never have an *ai* where the $\overset{>}{\imath}$ produces the same effect as the *y* in *aiya*. (Compare the English *boy* with the French *pied*.) Thus their position is what determines that *y* is a consonant and

[92] *i* a vowel. For these two varieties of *I* cannot be identically pronounced in all positions. The same remarks apply to *u* and *w*, *ü* and *ẅ*.

This throws light upon the question of diphthongs. A diphthong is simply a special case of an adductive sequence. The groups $\overset{>}{a}\overset{>}{r}ta$ and $\overset{>}{a}\overset{>}{u}ta$ are absolutely parallel: the only difference is the aperture of the second sound. A diphthong is an adductive sequence of two sounds, in which the second is relatively open. Hence its characteristic auditory impression. We might say that in a diphthong the sonant is prolonged in the second of the two sounds. Contrariwise, a group like $\overset{<}{t}\overset{<}{y}a$ does not contrast in any respect with $\overset{<}{t}\overset{<}{r}a$, except for the aperture

[1] The *i* of Aperture 4 is not to be confused with the palatal fricative heard in the North German pronunciation of *liegen*, which indeed is a consonant and has all the characteristics of consonants.

of the second abduction. What this amounts to is that the groups commonly called 'ascending diphthongs' are not diphthongs at all, but combinations of 'abduction + adduction' with a relatively open first element: but from an auditory point of view there is nothing special about this (*t́ýà*). As for groups like *ủo*, *ỉa*, with stress on the *ủ* and *ỉ*, as found in certain German dialects (cf. *buob*, *liab*), these are also false diphthongs. They give no auditory impression of unity, as with *ỏủ*, *ảỉ*, etc. We cannot pronounce *ủỏ* as an adductive sequence without interruption, except by imposing in some contrived way a unity on the combination which it does not have naturally.

This definition of the diphthong, which relates it to general principles governing adductive sequences, shows that the diphthong is not, as might be thought, an irregularity which resists attempts at phonetic classification. It is pointless to set diphthongs apart in a group of their own. Diphthongs as such are neither of particular interest nor of particular importance. What matters is not determining where the sonant ends, but where it begins.

Sievers and many other linguists distinguish in writing between *i*, *u*, *ü*, *r̥*, *n̥*, etc. and *i̯*, *u̯*, *ü̯*, *r*, *n*, etc. (The *i̯* is said to stand for 'unsilbisches' *i*, 'non-syllabic' *i*; and the *i* to stand for 'silbisches' *i*, 'syllabic' *i*.) Thus they write *mirta*, *mai̯rta*, *mi̯arta* where we prefer *mirta*, *mairta*, [93] *myarta*. Having grasped the fact that *i* and *y* are the same type of sound, they wanted to use the same generic letter for both (in accordance with the same old idea that a sound sequence consists of a succession of juxtaposed types!). But although this transcriptional practice is based on auditory evidence, it is contrary to common sense and obliterates the very distinction it is important to note. The results are: (i) opening *i* and *u* (= *y*, *w*) are confused with closing *i* and *u*, so that no distinction can be made between e.g. *newo* and *neuo*, and (ii) closing *i* and *u*, on the other hand, are each split in two (cf. *mirta* and *mairta*). A few examples of the drawbacks are as follows. Take ancient Greek *dwís* and *dusí*, and *rhéwō* and *rheûma*. These two contrasts appear under exactly the same phonetic conditions and are normally reflected in writing in the same way: depending on whether the *u* is followed by a more open or a less open sound, it has either an opening articulation (*w*) or a closing articulation (*u*). But if one writes *du̯is*, *dusi*, *rheu̯ō*, *rheu̯ma*, all this is lost. Likewise, in Proto-Indo-European the two series *māter*, *mātrai*, *māteres*, *mātrsu* and *sūneu*, *sūnewai*, *sūnewes*, *sūnusu* are strictly parallel both in their treatment of *r* and in their treatment of *u*. In the second series at least, the distinction between adduction and abduction is very obvious in the written forms, but is obscured as soon as we adopt the spellings criticised here (*sūneu̯*, *sūneu̯ai*, *sūneu̯es*, *sūnusu*). Not only should the customary distinctions in spelling be observed, but it would be advantageous to extend them systematically, and write e.g.: *māter*, *mātρai*, *māteρes*, *mātrsu*. In that way, the syllabification would be evident, and the vocalic peaks and syllable boundaries could be inferred automatically.

Editorial note. These theories throw light on various problems, some
[94] of which Saussure dealt with in his lectures. A few examples are appended.

1. Sievers cites *beritn̥nn̥n* (German *berittenen*) as a typical example of the fact that the same sound may function alternately, twice as a sonant and twice as an adsonant. (In fact, *n* functions here only once as an adsonant: the form should be *beritnnn*. But this is irrelevant.) It would be difficult to find a more striking example to show that sounds and sound types are not the same thing. For if in fact the *n* remained the same sound throughout, with adduction followed by sustainment, that would give just one long syllable. In order to alternate between a sonant *n* and an adsonant *n*, it is necessary to follow the adduction of the first *n* with abduction on the second *n*, and then revert to adduction with the third *n*. As the two adductions are not preceded by adductions, they emerge as sonants.

2. In French words like *meurtrier*, *ouvrier*, etc. the endings *-trier*, *-vrier* were formerly monosyllabic (whatever their exact pronunciation may have been: cf. p. [85] footnote). Subsequently, they began to be pronounced as two syllables (*meurtri-er*, with or without hiatus, i.e. *-trie* or *-triye*). The change was brought about not by placing a 'syllabic stress' on the *i*, but by changing its articulation from abduction to adduction.

In popular pronunciation we hear *ouvérier* for *ouvrier*. This is a similar phenomenon. Here the second sound has altered instead of the third, becoming a sonant: *uvrye*→*uvrye*. Later, an *e* developed in front of the sonant *r*.

3. Another example is the well-known case of prothetic vowels before an initial group consisting of *s* followed by a consonant in French: e.g. Latin *scūtum*→*iscūtum*→French *escu*, *écu*. As we have seen (p. [85]), the group *sk* is a broken sequence: *sk* is more natural. But this adductive *s* should constitute a vocalic peak at the beginning of a
[95] phrase, or when the preceding word in the phrase ends in a consonant of small aperture. The prothetic *i* or *e* merely emphasises this sonant quality. All weak phonetic features are strengthened whenever the tendency is to preserve them. The same phenomenon is to be observed in the case of French *esclandre*, and in the popular pronunciations *esquelette*, *estatue* (instead of *squelette*, *statue*). Or again in the popular pronunciation of the preposition *de*, which changes *un œil de tanche* into *un œil ed tanche*. What happens in this case is that syncope alters *de tanche* to *d'tanche*, and to be heard in this position the *d* has to be adductive: *d tanche*. Consequently a vowel develops in front of it, as in the previous example.

4. It is hardly necessary to revert to the question of Indo-European sonants, and ask why for instance Old High German *hagl* became *hagal*, while *balg* remained unchanged. The *l* of the latter word, being the second member of an adductive sequence (*bàlg̀*), acted as an adsonant and had no reason to change its function. Whereas the *l* of *hagl*, likewise adductive, was a vocalic peak. Being a sonant, it developed a more open vowel in front of it (an *a*, according to the evidence of spelling). This vowel weakened in the course of time, *Hagel* being today once again pronounced *hàǵl*. That is what distinguishes the pronunciation of this word from French *aigle*: the *l* is a closing articulation in the German word, but an opening articulation in the French word, where it is followed by a final mute *e* (*èǵlə*).

PART ONE [97]

General Principles

CHAPTER I

Nature of the Linguistic Sign

§1. Sign, signification, signal

For some people a language, reduced to its essentials, is a nomenclature: a list of terms corresponding to a list of things. For example, Latin would be represented as:

: ARBOR

: EQUOS

etc. etc.

This conception is open to a number of objections. It assumes that ideas already exist independently of words (see below, p. [155]). It does not clarify whether the name is a vocal or a psychological entity, for

ARBOR might stand for either. Furthermore, it leads one to assume that the link between a name and a thing is something quite unproblematic, which is far from being the case. None the less, this naive
[98] view contains one element of truth, which is that linguistic units are dual in nature, comprising two elements.

As has already been noted (p. [28]) in connexion with the speech circuit, the two elements involved in the linguistic sign are both psychological and are connected in the brain by an associative link.[1] This is a point of major importance.

A linguistic sign is not a link between a thing and a name, but between a concept and a sound pattern.[2] The sound pattern is not actually a sound; for a sound is something physical. A sound pattern is the hearer's psychological impression of a sound, as given to him by the evidence of his senses. This sound pattern may be called a 'material' element only in that it is the representation of our sensory impressions. The sound pattern may thus be distinguished from the other element associated with it in a linguistic sign. This other element is generally of a more abstract kind: the concept.

The psychological nature of our sound patterns becomes clear when we consider our own linguistic activity. Without moving either lips or tongue, we can talk to ourselves or recite silently a piece of verse. We grasp the words of a language as sound patterns. That is why it is best to avoid referring to them as composed of 'speech sounds'. Such a term, implying the activity of the vocal apparatus, is appropriate to the spoken word, to the actualisation of the sound pattern in discourse. Speaking of the *sounds* and *syllables* of a word need not give rise to any misunderstanding,[3] provided one always bears in mind that this refers to the sound pattern.

[99] The linguistic sign is, then, a two-sided psychological entity, which may be represented by the following diagram (top of p. 67).

These two elements are intimately linked and each triggers the other. Whether we are seeking the meaning of the Latin word *arbor* or the word by which Latin designates the concept 'tree', it is clear

[1] This associative link is to be distinguished from the associative relations which link one sign with another: cf. p. [170] ff. (Translator's note)

[2] Saussure's term 'sound pattern' may appear too narrow. For in addition to the representation of what a word sounds like, the speaker must also have a representation of how it is articulated, the muscular pattern of the act of phonation. But for Saussure a language is essentially something acquired by the individual from the outside world (cf. p. [30]). Saussure's 'sound pattern' is above all the natural representation of the word form as an abstract linguistic item, independently of any actualisation in speech. Hence the articulatory aspect of the word may be taken for granted, or relegated to a position of secondary importance in relation to its sound pattern. (Editorial note)

[3] None the less, as various passages in the *Cours* bear witness, it would have been in the interests of clarity to introduce a terminological distinction and keep to it. (Translator's note)

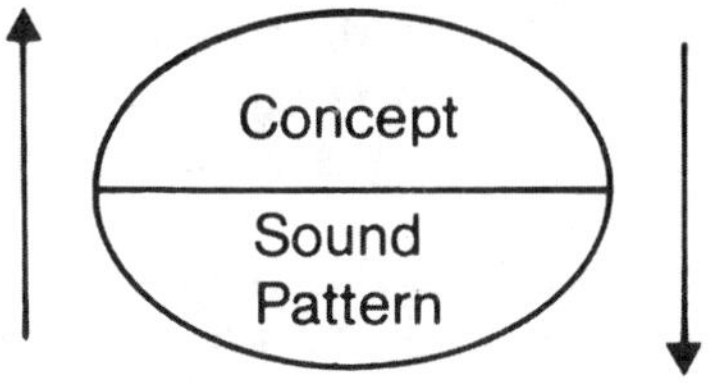

that only the connexions institutionalised in the language appear to us as relevant. Any other connexions there may be we set on one side.

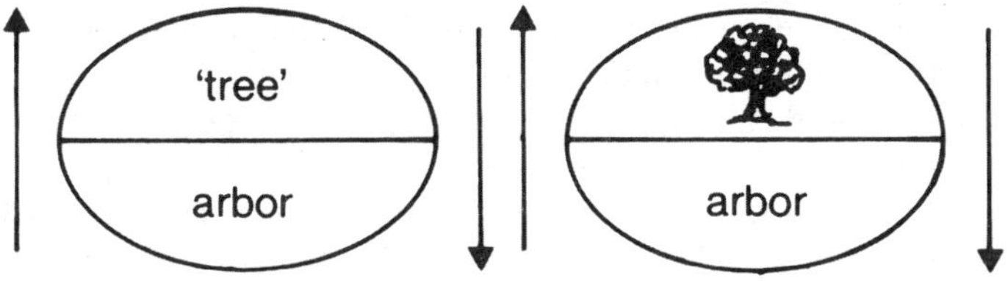

This definition raises an important question of terminology. In our terminology a *sign* is the combination of a concept and a sound pattern. But in current usage the term *sign* generally refers to the sound pattern alone, e.g. the word form *arbor*. It is forgotten that if *arbor* is called a sign, it is only because it carries with it the concept 'tree', so that the sensory part of the term implies reference to the whole.

The ambiguity would be removed if the three notions in question were designated by terms which are related but contrast. We propose to keep the term *sign* to designate the whole, but to replace *concept* and *sound pattern* respectively by *signification* and *signal*. The latter terms have the advantage of indicating the distinction which separates each from the other and both from the whole of which they are part.
We retain the term *sign*, because current usage suggests no alterna- [100]
tive by which it might be replaced.

The linguistic sign thus defined has two fundamental characteristics. In specifying them, we shall lay down the principles governing all studies in this domain.

§2. *First principle: the sign is arbitrary*

The link between signal and signification is arbitrary. Since we are treating a sign as the combination in which a signal is associated with a signification, we can express this more simply as: *the linguistic sign is arbitrary*.

There is no internal connexion, for example, between the idea 'sister' and the French sequence of sounds *s-ö-r* which acts as its signal. The same idea might as well be represented by any other sequence of sounds. This is demonstrated by differences between languages, and even by the existence of different languages. The signification 'ox' has as its signal *b-ö-f* on one side of the frontier,[1] but *o-k-s* (*Ochs*) on the other side.

No one disputes the fact that linguistic signs are arbitrary. But it is often easier to discover a truth than to assign it to its correct place. The principle stated above is the organising principle for the whole of linguistics, considered as a science of language structure. The consequences which flow from this principle are innumerable. It is true that they do not all appear at first sight equally evident. One discovers them after many circuitous deviations, and so realises the fundamental importance of the principle.

It may be noted in passing that when semiology is established one of the questions that must be asked is whether modes of expression which rely upon signs that are entirely natural (mime, for example) fall within the province of semiology. If they do, the main object of study in semiology will none the less be the class of systems based upon the arbitrary nature of the sign. For any means of expression accepted in a society rests in principle upon a collective habit, or on
[101] convention, which comes to the same thing. Signs of politeness, for instance, although often endowed with a certain natural expressiveness are none the less fixed by rule. It is this rule which renders them obligatory, not their intrinsic value. We may therefore say that signs which are entirely arbitrary convey better than others the ideal semiological process. That is why the most complex and the most widespread of all systems of expression, which is the one we find in human languages, is also the most characteristic of all. In this sense, linguistics serves as a model for the whole of semiology, even though languages represent only one type of semiological system.

The word *symbol* is sometimes used to designate the linguistic sign, or more exactly that part of the linguistic sign which we are calling the signal. This use of the word *symbol* is awkward, for reasons connected with our first principle. For it is characteristic of symbols that they are never entirely arbitrary. They are not empty configurations. They show at least a vestige of natural connexion between the signal and its signification. For instance, our symbol of justice, the scales, could hardly be replaced by a chariot.

The word *arbitrary* also calls for comment. It must not be taken to imply that a signal depends on the free choice of the speaker. (We shall see later than the individual has no power to alter a sign in any respect once it has become established in a linguistic community.) The

[1] The frontier between France and Germany. (Translator's note)

term implies simply that the signal is *unmotivated*: that is to say arbitrary in relation to its signification, with which it has no natural connexion in reality.

In conclusion, two objections may be mentioned which might be brought against the principle that linguistic signs are arbitrary.

1. *Onomatopoeic* words might be held to show that a choice of signal is not always arbitrary. But such words are never organic elements of a linguistic system. Moreover, they are far fewer than is generally [102] believed. French words like *fouet* ('whip') or *glas* ('knell') may strike the ear as having a certain suggestive sonority. But to see that this is in no way intrinsic to the words themselves, it suffices to look at their Latin origins. *Fouet* comes from Latin *fāgus* ('beech tree') and *glas* from Latin *classicum* ('trumpet call'). The suggestive quality of the modern pronunciation of these words is a fortuitous result of phonetic evolution.

As for genuine onomatopoeia (e.g. French *glou-glou* ('gurgle'), *tic-tac* 'ticking (of a clock)'), not only is it rare but its use is already to a certain extent arbitrary. For onomatopoeia is only the approximate imitation, already partly conventionalised, of certain sounds. This is evident if we compare a French dog's *ouaoua* and a German dog's *wauwau*. In any case, once introduced into the language, onomatopoeic words are subjected to the same phonetic and morphological evolution as other words. The French word *pigeon* ('pigeon') comes from Vulgar Latin *pīpiō*, itself of onomatopoeic origin, which clearly proves that onomatopoeic words themselves may lose their original character and take on that of the linguistic sign in general, which is unmotivated.

2. Similar considerations apply to *exclamations*. These are not unlike onomatopoeic words, and they do not undermine the validity of our thesis. People are tempted to regard exclamations as spontaneous expressions called forth, as it were, by nature. But in most cases it is difficult to accept that there is a necessary link between the exclamatory signal and its signification. Again, it suffices to compare two languages in this respect to see how much exclamations vary. For example, the French exclamation *aïe!* corresponds to the German *au!* Moreover, it is known that many exclamations were originally meaningful words (e.g. *diable!* 'devil', *mordieu!* 'God's death').

In short, onomatopoeic and exclamatory words are rather marginal phenomena, and their symbolic origin is to some extent disputable.

§3. Second principle: linear character of the signal [103]

The linguistic signal, being auditory in nature, has a temporal aspect, and hence certain temporal characteristics: (a) *it occupies a certain temporal space*, and (b) *this space is measured in just one dimension:* it is a line.

This principle is obvious, but it seems never to be stated, doubtless because it is considered too elementary. However, it is a fundamental principle and its consequences are incalculable. Its importance equals that of the first law. The whole mechanism of linguistic structure depends upon it (cf. p. [170]). Unlike visual signals (e.g. ships' flags) which can exploit more than one dimension simultaneously, auditory signals have available to them only the linearity of time. The elements of such signals are presented one after another: they form a chain. This feature appears immediately when they are represented in writing, and a spatial line of graphic signs is substituted for a succession of sounds in time.

In certain cases, this may not be easy to appreciate. For example, if I stress a certain syllable, it may seem that I am presenting a number of significant features simultaneously. But that is an illusion. The syllable and its accentuation constitute a single act of phonation. There is no duality within this act, although there are various contrasts with what precedes and follows (cf. p. [180]).

CHAPTER II [104]

Invariability and Variability of the Sign

§1. Invariability

The signal, in relation to the idea it represents, may seem to be freely chosen. However, from the point of view of the linguistic community, the signal is imposed rather than freely chosen. Speakers are not consulted about its choice. Once the language has selected a signal, it cannot be freely replaced by any other. There appears to be something rather contradictory about this. It is a kind of linguistic Hobson's choice. What can be chosen is already determined in advance. No individual is able, even if he wished, to modify in any way a choice already established in the language. Nor can the linguistic community exercise its authority to change even a single word.[1] The community, as much as the individual, is bound to its language.

A language cannot therefore be treated simply as a form of contract, and the linguistic sign is a particularly interesting phenomenon to study for this reason. For if we wish to demonstrate that the rules a community accepts are imposed upon it, and not freely agreed to, it is a language which offers the most striking proof.

Let us now examine how the linguistic sign eludes the control of our will. We shall then be able to see the important consequences which follow from this fact.

At any given period, however far back in time we go, a language is [105]
always an inheritance from the past. The initial assignment of names

[1] This is not a denial of the possibility of linguistic legislation, nor even of its potential effectiveness. What Saussure denies is that the collective ratification required is a matter for collective decision. It may be illegal for trade purposes to call Spanish sparkling wine 'champagne': but that will be merely one external factor bearing on speech (*parole*), which may or may not ultimately affect the word *champagne* as a linguistic sign. (Translator's note)

to things, establishing a contract between concepts and sound patterns, is an act we can conceive in the imagination, but no one has ever observed it taking place. The idea that it might have happened is suggested to us by our keen awareness of the arbitrary nature of the linguistic sign.

In fact, no society has ever known its language to be anything other than something inherited from previous generations, which it has no choice but to accept. That is why the question of the origins of language does not have the importance generally attributed to it. It is not even a relevant question as far as linguistics is concerned. The sole object of study in linguistics is the normal, regular existence of a language already established. Any given linguistic state is always the product of historical factors, and these are the factors which explain why the linguistic sign is invariable, that is to say why it is immune from arbitrary alteration.[1]

But to say that a language is an inheritance from the past explains nothing unless we take the question further. Is it not possible from time to time to change established laws which have been handed down from the past?

This question leads us to consider a language in its social context and to pursue our enquiry in the same terms as for any other social institution. How are social institutions handed down from generation to generation? This is the more general question which subsumes the question of invariability. It is first necessary to realise the different degrees of freedom enjoyed by other institutions. Each of them, it will be seen, achieves a different balance between the tradition handed down and society's freedom of action. The next question will be to discover why, in any given case, factors of one kind are more powerful or less powerful than factors of the other kind. Finally, reverting to linguistic matters in particular, it may then be asked why historical
[106] transmission is the overriding factor, to the point of excluding the possibility of any general or sudden linguistic change.

The answer to this question must take many considerations into account. It is relevant to point out, for example, that linguistic changes do not correspond to generations of speakers. There is no vertical structure of layers one above the other like drawers in a piece of furniture; people of all ages intermingle and communicate with one another. The continuous efforts required in order to learn one's native language point to the impossibility of any radical change. In addition, people use their language without conscious reflexion, being largely

[1] For Saussure's generation, questions of language planning had not acquired the importance they have today. Although criticism of commonly accepted linguistic forms of expression has a long history in the Western tradition, only small minorities of thinkers, teachers and writers had ever concerned themselves with such matters. (Translator's note)

unaware of the laws which govern it. If they are not aware of these laws, how can they act to change them? In any case, linguistic facts are rarely the object of criticism, every society being usually content with the language it has inherited.

These considerations are important, but they are not directly to the point. Priority must be given to the following, which are more essential, more immediately relevant, and underlie all the rest.

1. *The arbitrary nature of the linguistic sign.* The arbitrary nature of the linguistic sign was adduced above as a reason for conceding the theoretical possibility of linguistic change. But more detailed consideration reveals that this very same factor tends to protect a language against any attempt to change it. It means that there is no issue for the community of language users to discuss, even were they sufficiently aware to do so. For in order to discuss an issue, there must be some reasonable basis for discussion. One can, for example, argue about whether monogamy is better than polygamy, and adduce reasons for and against. One could likewise discuss the pros and cons of a system of symbols, because a symbol has a rational connexion with what it symbolizes (cf. p. [101]). But for a language, as a system of arbitrary signs, any such basis is lacking, and consequently there is no firm ground for discussion. No reason can be given for preferring [107]
sœur to *sister*, *Ochs* to *bœuf*, etc.[1]

2. *The great number of signs necessary to constitute a language.* The implications of this fact are considerable. A system of writing, comprising between 20 and 40 letters, might conceivably be replaced in its entirety by an alternative system. The same would be true of a language if it comprised only a limited number of elements. But the inventory of signs in any language is countless.

3. *The complex character of the system.* A language constitutes a system. In this respect, it is not entirely arbitrary, for the system has a certain rationality. But precisely for this reason, the community is unable to change it at will. For the linguistic system is a complex mechanism. Its workings cannot be grasped without reflexion. Even speakers who use it daily may be quite ignorant in this regard. Any such change would require the intervention of specialists, grammarians, logicians, and others. But history shows that interference by experts is of no avail in linguistic matters.

4. *Collective inertia resists all linguistic innovations.* We come now to a consideration which takes precedence over all others. At any

[1] Saussure's general point here is confirmed by the fact that current debates about, for instance, whether 'sexist' terms (such as *chairman*) should be replaced by unbiassed terms (e.g. *chairperson*) arise only when a reason *can* be given for preferring one to the other. But in such cases the reason given is usually social or political, rather than linguistic. (Translator's note)

time a language belongs to all its users. It is a facility unrestrictedly available throughout a whole community. It is something all make use of every day. In this respect it is quite unlike other social institutions. Legal procedures, religious rites, ships' flags, etc. are systems used only by a certain number of individuals acting together and for a limited time. A language, on the contrary, is something in which everyone participates all the time, and that is why it is constantly open to the influence of all. This key fact is by itself sufficient to explain why a linguistic revolution is impossible. Of all social insti-
[108] tutions, a language affords the least scope for such enterprise. It is part and parcel of the life of the whole community, and the community's natural inertia exercises a conservative influence upon it.

None the less, to say that a language is a product of social forces does not automatically explain why it comes to be constrained in the way it is. Bearing in mind that a language is always an inheritance from the past, one must add that the social forces in question act over a period of time. If stability is a characteristic of languages, it is not only because languages are anchored in the community. They are also anchored in time. The two facts are inseparable. Continuity with the past constantly restricts freedom of choice. If the Frenchman of today uses words like *homme* ('man') and *chien* ('dog'), it is because these words were used by his forefathers. Ultimately there is a connexion between these two opposing factors: the arbitrary convention which allows free choice, and the passage of time, which fixes that choice. It is because the linguistic sign is arbitrary that it knows no other law than that of tradition, and because it is founded upon tradition that it can be arbitrary.[1]

§2. *Variability*

The passage of time, which ensures the continuity of a language, also has another effect, which appears to work in the opposite direction. It allows linguistic signs to be changed with some rapidity. Hence variability and invariability are both, in a certain sense, characteristic of the linguistic sign.[2]

[1] The epigrammatic concision of this summary of the connexion between the nature of the linguistic sign and its socio-historical role epitomises Saussure's brilliance as a linguistic theorist. It was not until half a century after his death that detailed sociolinguistic investigations began to provide in abundance the kind of evidence which would corroborate the connexion Saussure here postulates. What is ironical is that the evidence in question was often interpreted as throwing doubt upon the validity or adequacy of a Saussurean approach to the study of language. What is perhaps even more ironical is that the Saussurean implications of a reciprocal limitation between choice and tradition remained largely unexplored as a result. (Translator's note)

[2] It would be a mistake to criticise Saussure for being illogical or paradoxical in assigning two contradictory characteristics to the linguistic sign. The striking contrast

In the final analysis, these two characteristics are intimately connected. The sign is subject to change because it continues through [109] time. But what predominates in any change is the survival of earlier material. Infidelity to the past is only relative. That is how it comes about that the principle of change is based upon the principle of continuity.

Change through time takes various forms, each of which would supply the subject matter for an important chapter of linguistics. Without going into detail here, it is important to bring out the following points.

First of all, let there be no misunderstanding about the sense in which we are speaking of change. It must not be thought that we are referring particularly to phonetic changes affecting the signal, or to changes of meaning affecting the concept signified. Either view would be inadequate. Whatever the factors involved in change, whether they act in isolation or in combination, they always result in *a shift in the relationship between signal and signification.*

As examples, one might cite the following. The Latin word *necāre* meaning 'to kill' became in French *noyer* meaning 'to drown'. Here the sound pattern and the concept have both changed. It is pointless to separate one aspect of the change from the other. It suffices to note as a single fact that the connexion between sound and idea has changed. The original relationship no longer holds. If instead of comparing Latin *necāre* with French *noyer*, one contrasts it with Vulgar Latin *necare* of the fourth or fifth century, meaning 'to drown', the case is somewhat different. But even here, although the signal has undergone no appreciable change, there is a shift in the relationship between the idea and the sign.[1]

The Old German word *dritteil* meaning 'a third' became in modern German *Drittel*. In this case, although the concept has remained the same, the relationship has changed in two ways. The signal has altered not only phonetically but also grammatically. We no longer recognise it as a combination including the unit *Teil* meaning 'part': instead, it has become a single unanalysable word. That counts too as a change [110] in relationship.

In Anglo-Saxon, the preliterary form *fōt* meaning 'foot' remained as *fōt* (modern English *foot*), while its plural **fōti*, meaning 'feet', became *fēt* (modern English *feet*). Whatever changes may have been involved here, one thing is certain: a shift in the relationship occurred. New correlations between phonic substance and idea emerged.

---

between these terms is intended simply to emphasise the fact that a language changes even though its speakers are incapable of changing it. One might also say that it is impervious to interference although open to development. (Editorial note)

[1] In the interests of terminological consistency, the term *sign* should here be replaced by *signal*. (Translator's note)

A language is a system which is intrinsically defenceless against the factors which constantly tend to shift relationships between signal and signification. This is one of the consequences of the arbitrary nature of the linguistic sign.

Other human institutions – customs, laws, etc. – are all based in varying degrees on natural connexions between things. They exhibit a necessary conformity between ends and means. Even the fashion which determines the way we dress is not entirely arbitrary. It cannot depart beyond a certain point from requirements dictated by the human body. A language, on the contrary, is in no way limited in its choice of means. For there is nothing at all to prevent the association of any idea whatsoever with any sequence of sounds whatsoever.

In order to emphasise that a language is nothing other than a social institution, Whitney quite rightly insisted upon the arbitrary character of linguistic signs. In so doing, he pointed linguistics in the right direction. But he did not go far enough. For he failed to see that this arbitrary character fundamentally distinguishes languages from all other institutions. This can be seen in the way in which a language evolves. The process is highly complex. A language is situated socially and chronologically by reference to a certain community and a certain period of time. No one can alter it in any particular. On the other hand, the fact that its signs are arbitrary implies theoretically a freedom to establish any connexion whatsoever between sounds and ideas. The result is that each of the two elements joined together in the linguistic sign retains its own independence to an unparalleled
[111] extent. Consequently a language alters, or rather evolves, under the influence of all factors which may affect either sounds or meanings. Evolution is inevitable: there is no known example of a language immune from it. After a certain time, changes can always be seen to have taken place.

This principle must even apply to artificial languages. Anyone who invents an artificial language retains control of it only as long as it is not in use. But as soon as it fulfils its purpose and becomes the property of the community, it is no longer under control. Esperanto is a case in point. If it succeeds as a language, can it possibly escape the same fate? Once launched, the language will in all probability begin to lead a semiological life of its own. Its transmission will follow laws which have nothing in common with those of deliberate creation, and it will then be impossible to turn the clock back. Anyone who thinks he can construct a language not subject to change, which posterity must accept as it is, would be like a hen hatching a duck's egg. The language he created would be subject to the same forces of change as any other language, regardless of its creator's wishes.

The continuity of signs through time, involving as it does their alteration in time, is a principle of general semiology. This principle is confirmed by systems of writing, by deaf-and-dumb languages, and so on.

But on what is the necessity for change based? We may perhaps be criticised for not being as explicit upon this point as upon the principle of invariability. The reason is that we have not gone into the different factors involved in change. A great variety of such factors must be taken into account in order to determine to what extent change is a necessity.

The causes of linguistic continuity are in principle available to observation. The same is not true of the causes of change through time. That is why in the first instance it would be misleading to attempt to identify them precisely. It is more prudent to speak in general terms of shifts in relations. For time changes everything. [112]
There is no reason why languages should be exempt from this universal law.

The argument advanced so far, based on the principles established in the introduction, may be summarised as follows.

1. Avoiding the sterility of merely verbal definitions, we began by distinguishing, within the global phenomenon of *language*, between *linguistic structure* and *speech*. Linguistic structure we take to be language minus speech. It is the whole set of linguistic habits which enables the speaker to understand and to make himself understood.

2. But this definition fails to relate linguistic structure to social reality. It is a definition which misrepresents what a language is, because it takes into account only how the individual is affected. But in order to have a language, there must be a *community of speakers*. Contrary to what might appear to be the case, a language never exists even for a moment except as a social fact, for it is a semiological phenomenon. Its social nature is one of its internal characteristics. A full definition must recognise two inseparable things, as shown in the following diagram:

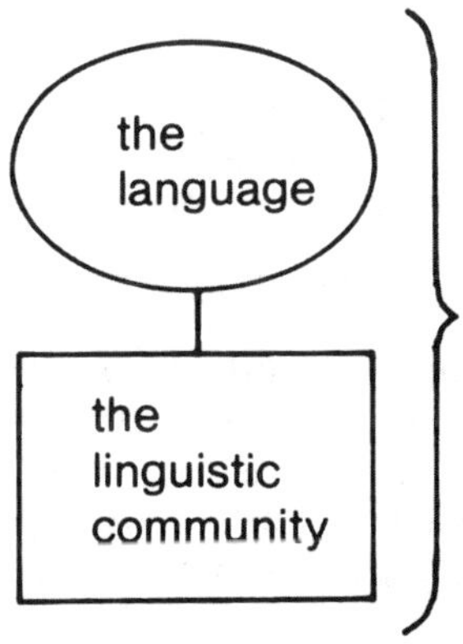

But even then there is something missing. The language thus represented is a viable system, but not a living one. It is a social reality, but not a historical fact.

3. Since the linguistic sign is arbitrary, a language as so far defined would appear to be an adaptable system, which can be organised in any way one likes, and is based solely upon a principle of rationality. Its social nature, as such, is not incompatible with this view. Social psychology, doubtless, must operate on more than a purely logical basis: account must be taken of everything which might affect the
[113] operation of reason in practical relations between one individual and another. But that is not the objection to regarding a language as a mere convention, which can be modified to suit the interests of those involved. There is something else. We must consider what is brought about by the passage of time, as well as what is brought about by the forces of social integration. Without taking into account the contribution of time, our grasp of linguistic reality remains incomplete.

If a language were considered in a chronological perspective, but ignoring the social dimension (as in the case of a hypothetical individual living in isolation for hundreds of years), there might perhaps be no change to observe. Time would leave no mark upon the language. On the other hand, if one looked at the community of speakers without taking the passage of time into account, one would not see the effect of social forces acting upon the language. In order to come to terms with reality, therefore, one must supplement our first diagram by some indication of the passage of time:

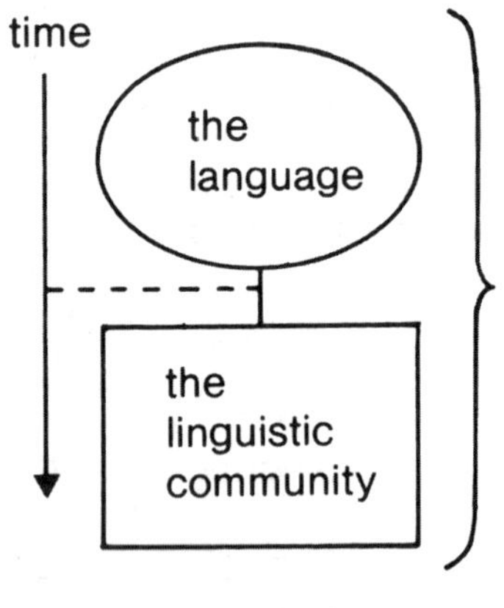

When this is taken into account, the language is no longer free from constraints, because the passage of time allows social forces to be brought to bear upon it. One is left with a principle of continuity which precludes freedom of choice. At the same time, continuity necessarily implies change. Relations will alter in some respect or other.

CHAPTER III [114]

Static Linguistics and Evolutionary Linguistics

§1. Internal duality of all sciences concerned with values

Very few linguists realise that the need to take account of the passage of time gives rise to special problems in linguistics and forces us to choose between two radically different approaches.

Most other sciences are not faced with this crucial choice. For them, what happens with the passage of time is of no particular significance. In astronomy, it is observed that in the course of time heavenly bodies undergo considerable changes. But astronomy has not on that account been obliged to split into two separate disciplines. Geology is constantly concerned with the reconstruction of chronological sequences. But when it concentrates on examining fixed states of the earth's crust, that is not considered to be a quite separate object of study. There is a descriptive science of law and a history of law: but no one contrasts the one with the other. The political history of nations is intrinsically concerned with successions of events in time. None the less, when a historian describes the society of a particular period, one does not feel that this ceases to be history. The science of political institutions, on the other hand, is essentially descriptive: but occasionally it may deal with historical questions, and that in no way compromises its unity as a science.

Economics, by contrast, is a science which is forced to recognise this duality. Unlike the preceding cases, the study of political economy [115]
and of economic history constitute two clearly distinguishable disciplines belonging to one and the same science. Recent work in this field emphasises this distinction. Although it may not be fully realised, the distinction is required by an inner necessity of the subject. It is a necessity entirely analogous to that which obliges us to divide linguistics into two parts, each based upon a principle of its own. The

reason is that, as in the study of political economy, one is dealing with the notion of *value*. In both cases, we have a *system of equivalence between things belonging to different orders*. In one case, work and wages; in the other case, signification and signal.

It is certain that all sciences would benefit from identifying more carefully the axes along which the things they are concerned with may be situated. In all cases, distinctions should be drawn on the following basis.

1. *Axis of simultaneity* (AB). This axis concerns relations between things which coexist, relations from which the passage of time is entirely excluded.

2. *Axis of succession* (CD). Along this axis one may consider only one thing at a time. But here we find all the things situated along the first axis, together with the changes they undergo.

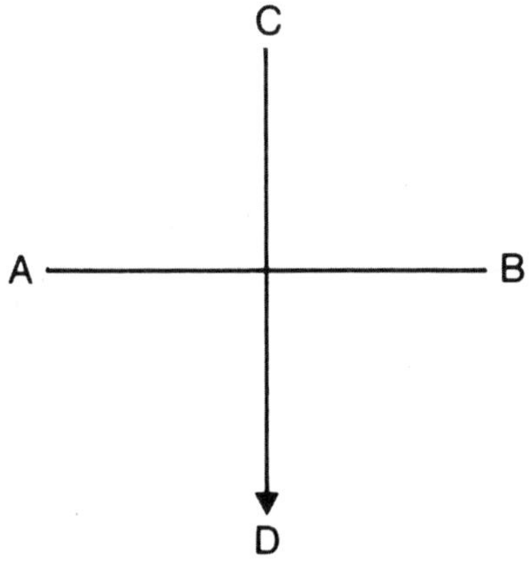

For sciences which involve the study of values, this distinction becomes a practical necessity, and in certain cases is an absolute necessity. In this domain, it is impossible for scholars to organise their
[116] research in any rigorous fashion without taking account of these two axes. They are obliged to distinguish between the system of values considered in itself, and these same values considered over a period of time.

It is in linguistics that this distinction is least dispensable. For a language is a system of pure values, determined by nothing else apart from the temporary state of its constituent elements. Insofar as a value, in one of its aspects, is founded upon natural connexions between things (as, for example, in economics the value of a piece of land depends on the income derivable from it), it is possible up to a point to trace this value through time, bearing in mind that it depends at any one time upon the relevant system of contemporary values. However, its connexion with things inevitably supplies it with a natural basis, and hence any assessment of it is never entirely arbitrary. There are limits upon the range of variability. But, as we have already seen, in linguistics these natural connexions have no place.

It should be added that the more complex and rigorously organised a system of values is, the more essential it becomes, on account of this very complexity, to study it separately in terms of the two axes. Of no system is this as true as it is of a language. Nowhere else do we find comparable precision of values, or such a large number and diversity of terms involved, or such a strict mutual dependence between them. The multiplicity of signs, which we have already invoked to explain linguistic continuity, precludes absolutely any attempt to study simultaneously relations in time and relations within the system.

That is why we must distinguish two branches of linguistics. What should they be called? The terms available are not all equally appropriate to indicate the distinction in question. 'History' and 'historical linguistics' cannot be used, for the ideas associated with them are too vague. Just as political history includes the description of periods as well as the narration of events, it might be supposed that by describing a [117]
sequence of states of a language one was studying the language along the temporal axis. But in order to do that, it would be necessary to consider separately the factors of transition involved in passing from one linguistic state to the next. The terms *evolution* and *evolutionary linguistics* are more exact, and we shall make frequent use of these terms. By contrast, one may speak of the science of linguistic *states*, or *static linguistics*.

But in order to mark this contrast more effectively, and the intersection of two orders of phenomena relating to the same object of study, we shall speak for preference of *synchronic* linguistics and *diachronic* linguistics. Everything is synchronic which relates to the static aspect of our science, and diachronic everything which concerns evolution. Likewise *synchrony* and *diachrony* will designate respectively a linguistic state and a phase of evolution.

§2. Internal duality and the history of linguistics

The first thing which strikes one on studying linguistic facts is that the language user is unaware of their succession in time: he is dealing with a state. Hence the linguist who wishes to understand this state must rule out of consideration everything which brought that state about, and pay no attention to diachrony. Only by suppressing the past can he enter into the state of mind of the language user. The intervention of history can only distort his judgment. It would be absurd to try to draw a panorama of the Alps as seen from a number of peaks in the Jura simultaneously. A panorama must be taken from just one point. The same is true of a language. One cannot describe it or establish its norms of usage except by taking up a position in relation to a given state. When the linguist follows the evolution of the language, he is like the observer moving from one end of the Jura to the other in order to record changes in perspective.

[118] Since its beginnings, it would be true to say that modern linguistics has been entirely taken up with diachronic study. The comparative grammar of the Indo-European languages uses the facts it has available in order to reconstruct hypothetically an earlier type of language. Comparison is only a means for resurrecting the past. The method is the same in the study of particular linguistic sub-groups (the Romance languages, Germanic languages, etc.). Linguistic states are considered only in fragments and very imperfectly. This was the approach inaugurated by Bopp, and the conception of a language it offers is hybrid and uncertain.

But what was the method followed by those who studied languages before the foundation of linguistics? How did the traditional 'grammarians' proceed? It is a curious fact that on this particular point their approach was quite flawless. Their writings show us clearly that they were concerned with the description of linguistic states. Their programme was a strictly synchronic one. The grammar of Port Royal, for instance, attempts to describe the state of the French language under Louis XIV and to set out the relevant system of values. For this purpose, it has no need to make reference to the French of the Middle Ages; it keeps strictly to the horizontal axis (cf. p. [115]) and never departs from it. Its method is thus perfectly correct. That is not to say, however, that the application of the method is perfect. Traditional grammar pays no attention to whole areas of linguistic structure, such as word formation. It is normative grammar, concerned with laying down rules instead of observing facts. It makes no attempt at syntheses. Often, it even fails to distinguish between the written word and the spoken word. And so on.

Traditional grammar has been criticised for not being scientific. None the less, its basis is less objectionable and its object of study better defined than is the case for the kind of linguistics inaugurated by Bopp. The latter attempts to cover an inadequately defined area,
[119] never knowing exactly where it is going. It has a foot in each camp, having failed to distinguish clearly between states and sequences.

Having paid too much attention to history, linguistics will go back now to the static viewpoint of traditional grammar, but in a new spirit and with different methods. The historical approach will have contributed to this rejuvenation. It will have been instrumental in facilitating a better grasp of linguistic states. The old grammar saw no further than synchronic facts. Linguistics has made us aware of a different order of phenomena. But that is not enough. The opposition between these two orders must be grasped in order to draw out all the consequences which it implies.

§3. Examples of internal duality

The contrast between the two points of view – synchronic and diachronic – is absolute and admits no compromise. A few examples will illustrate what this difference consists in, and why it is irreducible.

The Latin word *crispus* ('wavy, curly') supplied French with a stem *crép-*, on which are based the verbs *crépir* ('to rough-render') and *décrépir* ('to strip the plaster from'). Then French at a certain stage borrowed from Latin the word *dēcrepitus* ('worn by age'). This became in French *décrépit*, and its etymology was forgotten. Nowadays, it is certain that most speakers connect *un mur décrépi* ('a dilapidated wall') and *un homme décrépit* ('a decrepit man'), although historically the two words have nothing to do with each other. People often speak of the *façade décrépite* ('dilapidated façade') of a house. That is a static fact, because it involves a relationship between two terms coexisting in the language. But in order to bring it about, certain evolutionary changes had to coincide. The original *crisp-* had to come to be pronounced *crép-*, and at the right moment a new word had to be borrowed from Latin. These diachronic facts, it is clear, have no con- [120]
nexion with the static fact which they brought about. They are of quite a different order.

Another example with quite general implications is the following. In Old High German, the plural of *gast* ('guest') was originally *gasti*, the plural of *hant* ('hand') was *hanti*, and so on. Subsequently, this *-i* produced an umlaut; that is to say, it had an effect upon the vowel of the preceding syllable, changing *a* into *e*. So *gasti* became *gesti*, and *hanti* became *henti*. Then this *-i* weakened, giving *geste*, etc. Today as a result we have *Gast* with a plural *Gäste*, *Hand* with a plural *Hände*, and so on for a whole class of words. Something similar happened in Anglo-Saxon, where originally *fōt* ('foot') had a plural **fōti*, *toþ* ('tooth') had a plural **toþi*, *gōs* ('goose') had a plural *gōsi*, etc. A first phonetic change gave rise to an umlaut, so that **fōti* became **fēti*; and then as the result of a second phonetic change, the fall of the final *i*, **fēti* became *fēt*. Thus *fōt* then had a plural *fēt*, *tōþ* a plural *tēþ*, *gōs* a plural *gēs* (Modern English *foot* : *feet*, *tooth* : *teeth*, *goose* : *geese*).

Previously, at the stage *gast* : *gasti*, *fōt* : *fōti*, the plural had been marked simply by adding an *-i*. But *Gast* : *Gäste* and *fōt* : *fēt* show a new way of marking the plural. The mechanism is not the same in the two cases, since in Old English there is simply a contrast of vowels, whereas in German there is in addition the presence or absence of a final *-e*. But this difference does not affect the example.

The relation between singular and plural at any given time, irrespective of the actual forms, can be represented along a horizontal axis:

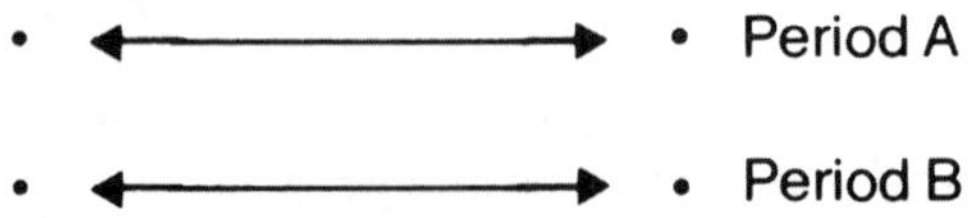

The developments, whatever they may have been, which gave rise
[121] to changes in the forms, can be represented along a vertical axis. So
we have a complete figure as follows:

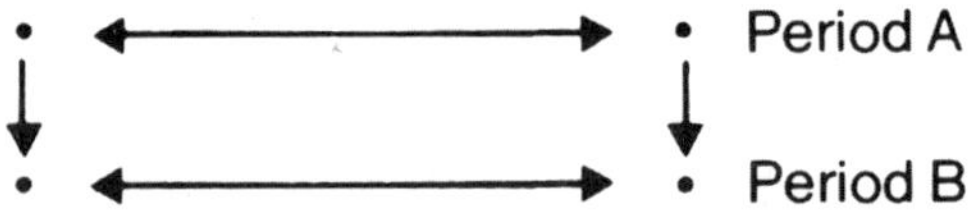

This type of case suggests a number of observations which are very relevant to the present discussion.

1. The diachronic developments are in no way directed towards providing a new sign to mark a given value. The fact that *gasti* changed to *gesti* and then to *geste* (*Gäste*) has nothing to do with the plurals of nouns. In *tragit→trägt* we see the same umlaut affecting the flexion of a verb. So the reason for a diachronic development lies in the development itself. The particular synchronic consequences which may ensue have nothing to do with it.

2. These diachronic events do not even tend to change the system. There was no intention to replace one system of relations by another. The change affected not the organisation as such, but merely the particular items involved.

This illustrates a principle already stated earlier: the language system as such is never directly altered. It is in itself unchangeable. Only certain elements change, but without regard to the connexions which integrate them as part of the whole. It is as if one of the planets circling the sun underwent a change of dimensions and weight: this isolated event would have general consequences for the whole solar system, and disturb its equilibrium. In order to mark pluralisation, a contrast between two terms is required: *fōt* vs. **fōti* or *fōt* vs. *fēt* are equally viable for this purpose. Substituting one for the other leaves the distinction itself untouched. It is not the system as a whole which has been changed, nor one system which has engendered a second. All that happened was the one element in the original system changed, and that sufficed to bring a new system into being.

3. Once we see this, we can better appreciate the fact that a linguistic state always has a *fortuitous* character. Languages are not [122] mechanisms created and organised with a view to the concepts to be expressed, although people are mistakenly inclined to think so. On the contrary, our example shows that the state which resulted from the change was in no way destined to express the meanings it took on. A fortuitous state is given (*fōt* : *fēt*), and this is pressed into service to mark the distinction between singular and plural: but *fōt* vs. *fēt* is no better designed for that purpose than *fōt* vs. **fōti*. At each stage, spirit is breathed into the matter given, and brings it to life. This view, inspired by historical linguistics, is unknown to traditional grammar, which would never have come to it by the traditional methods. It is a view equally foreign to most philosophers of language: and yet it is of the greatest philosophical significance.

4. Are the facts belonging to the diachronic series at least of the same order as those of the synchronic series? In no way. For the changes brought about, as we have already observed, are entirely unintentional. Whereas a synchronic fact is always significant, being based always upon two coexisting terms. It is not *Gäste* which expresses the plural, but the opposition *Gast* vs. *Gäste*. With a diachronic fact, just the opposite is true. It involves one term only. If a new term (*Gäste*) is to appear, the old term (*gasti*) must make way for it.

Any notion of bringing together under the same discipline facts of such disparate nature would be mere fantasy. In the diachronic perspective one is dealing with phenomena which have no connexion with linguistic systems, even though the systems are affected by them.

Other examples which may be adduced to corroborate and amplify the conclusions drawn from those already cited include the following.

In French, the stress falls always on the final syllable, unless it contains a mute *e* (ə). This is a synchronic fact, a relationship between the whole French vocabulary and stress. Where does it come from? [123] From an antecedent linguistic state. Latin had a different and more complex system of stress, in which stress fell upon the penultimate syllable if that syllable were long, but otherwise upon the antipenultimate (e.g. *amī́cus*, *ánĭma*). This rule involves factors which have no parallel at all in the case of French. None the less, it is the same stress we are dealing with, in the sense that it still falls in the same place. In a French word, the stress falls always on the same syllable which bore the stress in Latin. Thus *amī́cum* becomes French *amí*, and *ánimam* becomes *âme*. However, the Latin and French stress patterns are different because the forms of the words have changed. In French words, vowels following the stressed syllable have either disappeared or been reduced to a mute *e*. As a consequence of these changes, the position of stress in the word was no longer the same. From that point on French speakers, aware of the new situation, instinctively placed stress on the final syllable, even in the case of foreign words originally borrowed in written form (*facile*, *consul*, *ticket*, *burgrave*, etc.). It is evident that there was no intention to change the system or apply a new rule, since in a case like *amícum*→*amí* the stress remains throughout on the same syllable. But a diachronic fact intervened. The place of the stress changed without anyone moving it. A stress law, like everything else in a linguistic system, is an arrangement of elements, the fortuitous and involuntary outcome of evolution.

An even more striking example is this. In early Slavonic, *slovo* ('word') had an instrumental case *slovemъ* in the singular, a nominative plural *slova*, and a genitive plural *slovъ*. It was a declension in which each case had its own ending. But today the 'weak' vowels ь and ъ, which were the Slavic representatives of Proto-Indo-European *ĭ* and *ŭ*, have disappeared. So in Czech, for example, we have *slovo*, *slovem*, *slova*, *slov*. Likewise *žena* ('woman') has an accusative singular *ženu*, a nominative plural *ženy*, and a genitive plural *žen*. Here we see that the genitive ending (*slov*, *žen*) is zero. So it is not [124] even necessary to have any material sign in order to give expression to an idea: the language may be content simply to contrast something with nothing. In this particular example, we can recognize the genitive plural *žen* simply by the fact that it is neither *žena*, nor *ženu*, nor any of the other forms of the declension. At first sight it seems strange that such a specific notion as that of genitive plural should have acquired the sign zero. But that is precisely what demonstrates that it is purely a matter of chance. Languages are mechanisms which go on functioning, in spite of the damage caused to them.

All this confirms the principles already formulated above, which may be summed up as follows.

A language is a system of which all the parts can and must be considered as synchronically interdependent.

Since changes are never made to the system as a whole, but only to its individual elements, they must be studied independently of the system. It is true that every change has a repercussion on the system. But initially only one point is affected. The change is unrelated to the internal consequences which may follow for the system as a whole. This difference in nature between chronological succession and simultaneous coexistence, between facts affecting parts and facts affecting the whole, makes it impossible to include both as subject matter of one and the same science.

§4. Difference between the two orders illustrated by comparisons

In order to clarify at the same time the autonomy and interdependence of the synchronic and diachronic approaches, it is useful to compare synchrony to the projection of a three-dimensional object on a two-dimensional plan. Any projection depends directly upon the object projected, but none the less differs from it. The projection is something apart. Otherwise there would be no need for a whole science of projection: it would be enough to consider the objects themselves. In linguistics, we find the same relation between historical reality and a [125]
linguistic state. The latter is a projection of the former at one given moment. Studying objects, that is to say diachronic events, will give us no insight into synchronic states, any more than we can hope to understand geometrical projections simply by studying, however thoroughly, different kinds of object.

If we cut crosswise through the stem of a plant, we can observe a rather complex pattern on the surface revealed by the cut. What we are looking at is a section of the plant's longitudinal fibres. These fibres will be revealed if we now make a second cut perpendicular to the first. Again in this example, one perspective depends on the other. The longitudinal section shows us the fibres themselves which make up the plant, while the transversal section shows us their arrangement on one particular level. But the transversal section is distinct from the longitudinal section, for it shows us certain relations between the fibres which are not apparent at all from any longitudinal section.

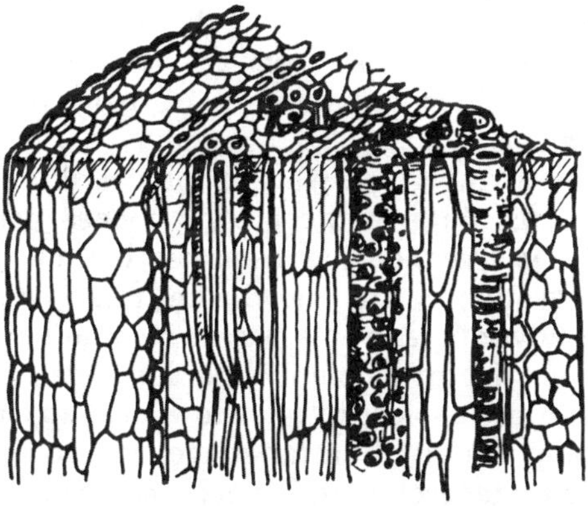

But of all the comparisons one might think of, the most revealing is the likeness between what happens in a language and what happens in a game of chess. In both cases, we are dealing with a system of values and with modifications of the system. A game of chess is like an artificial form of what languages present in a natural form.

Let us examine the case more closely.

In the first place, a state of the board in chess corresponds exactly to a state of the language. The value of the chess pieces depends on
[126] their position upon the chess board, just as in the language each term has its value through its contrast with all the other terms.

Secondly, the system is only ever a temporary one. It varies from one position to the next. It is true that the values also depend ultimately upon one invariable set of conventions, the rules of the game, which exist before the beginning of the game and remain in force after each move. These rules, fixed once and for all, also exist in the linguistic case: they are the unchanging principles of semiology.

Finally, in order to pass from one stable position to another or, in our terminology, from one synchronic state to another, moving one piece is all that is needed. There is no general upheaval. That is the counterpart of the diachronic fact and all its characteristic features. For in the case of chess:

(*a*) One piece only is moved at a time. Similarly, linguistic changes affect isolated elements only.

(*b*) In spite of that, the move has a repercussion upon the whole system. It is impossible for the player to foresee exactly where its consequences will end. The changes in values which result may be, in any particular circumstance, negligible, or very serious, or of moderate importance. One move may be a turning point in the whole game, and have consequences even for the pieces which are not for the moment involved. As we have just seen, it is exactly the same where a language is concerned.

(*c*) Moving a piece is something entirely different from the preceding state of the board and also from the state of the board which results. The change which has taken place belongs to neither. The states alone are important.

In a game of chess, any given state of the board is totally independent of any previous state of the board. It does not matter at all whether the state in question has been reached by one sequence of
[127] moves or another sequence. Anyone who has followed the whole game has not the least advantage over a passer-by who happens to look at the game at that particular moment. In order to describe the position on the board, it is quite useless to refer to what happened ten seconds ago. All this applies equally to a language, and confirms the radical distinction between diachronic and synchronic. Speech operates only upon a given linguistic state, and the changes which supervene between one state and another have no place in either.

There is only one respect in which the comparison is defective. In chess, the player *intends* to make his moves and to have some effect upon the system. In a language, on the contrary, there is no premeditation. Its pieces are moved, or rather modified, spontaneously and fortuitously. The umlaut of *Hände* for *hanti*, of *Gäste* for *gasti* (cf. p. [120]) produced a new plural formation, but also produced at the same time a verb form like *trägt* for *tragit*, etc. If the game of chess were to be like the operations of a language in every respect, we would have to imagine a player who was either unaware of what he was doing or unintelligent. This sole difference, moreover, makes the comparison even more instructive, by showing the absolute necessity for distinguishing in linguistics between the two orders of phenomena. For if diachronic facts cannot be reduced to the synchronic system they affect, even when a change of this kind is made deliberately, this will be the case even less when blind forces of change disturb the organisation of a system of signs.

§5. Synchronic and diachronic linguistics: their methods and principles contrasted

Diachronic and synchronic studies contrast in every way.

For example, to begin with the most obvious fact, they are not of [128]
equal importance. It is clear that the synchronic point of view takes precedence over the diachronic, since for the community of language users that is the one and only reality (cf. p. [117]). The same is true for the linguist. If he takes a diachronic point of view, he is no longer examining the language, but a series of events which modify it. It is often claimed that there is nothing more important than knowing how a given state originated. In a certain sense, that is true. The conditions which gave rise to the state throw light upon its true nature and prevent us from entertaining certain misconceptions (cf. p. [121] ff.). But what that proves is that diachrony has no end in itself. One might say, as has been said of journalism as a career, that it leads nowhere until you leave it behind.

Their methods are also different in two respects:

(*a*) Synchrony has only one perspective, that of the language users; and its whole method consists of collecting evidence from them. In order to determine to what extent something is a reality, it is necessary and also sufficient to find out to what extent it exists as far as the language users are concerned. Diachronic linguistics, however, needs to distinguish two perspectives. One will be *prospective*, following the course of time, and the other *retrospective*, going in the opposite direction. It follows that two diachronic methods are required, and these will be discussed later in Part V.

(*b*) A second difference derives from the different areas covered by the two disciplines. The object of synchronic study does not comprise everything which is simultaneous, but only the set of facts correspond-

ing to any particular language. In this, it will take into account where necessary a division into dialects and sub-dialects. The term *synchronic*, in fact, is not sufficiently precise. *Idiosynchronic* would be a better term, even though it is somewhat cumbersome. Diachronic
[129] linguistics, on the contrary, needs no such particularisation, and indeed rejects it. The items diachronic linguistics deals with do not necessarily belong to a single language. (Compare Proto-Indo-European **esti*, Greek *ésti*, German *ist*, French *est*.) It is precisely the succession of diachronic facts and their proliferation in space which gives rise to the diversity of languages. In order to justify comparing two forms, it is sufficient that there should be some historical connexion between them, however indirect.

These are not the most striking contrasts, nor the most profound. The consequences of the radical difference between facts of evolution and static facts is that all notions pertinent to the former and all notions pertinent to the latter are mutually irreducible. Any of the notions in question may be used to demonstrate this truth. No synchronic phenomenon has anything in common with any diachronic phenomenon (cf. p. [122]). One is a relationship between simultaneous elements, and the other a substitution of one element for another in time, that is to say an event. We shall also see (p. [150]) that diachronic identities and synchronic identities are two very different things. Historically, the French negative particle *pas* is the same as the noun *pas* ('pace'), whereas in modern French these two units are entirely separate. Realising these facts should be sufficient to bring home the necessity of not confusing the two points of view. But nowhere is this necessity more evident than in the distinction we are about to draw.

§6. *Synchronic laws and diachronic laws*

There is a great deal of talk nowadays about laws in linguistics. But are linguistic facts really governed by laws? And if so, of what kind can these laws be? A language being a social institution, one might *a*
[130] *priori* think it is governed by prescriptions of the kind which regulate communities. Now any social law has two fundamental characteristics: it is *imperative* and it is *general*. It demands compliance, and it covers all cases, within certain limits of time and place, of course.

Do the laws which govern a language answer to this definition? Once again, to find out we must first distinguish between synchrony and diachrony. For the two cases are not to be conflated. To speak of a 'linguistic law' in general is like trying to lay hands on a ghost.

The following are examples from Greek, in which 'laws' of a synchronic and diachronic nature have been deliberately intermingled.

1. Proto-Indo-European voiced aspirates became voiceless aspirates, e.g. **dhūmos* → *thūmós* ('breath of life'), **bherō* → *phérō* ('I carry').

2. Stress never falls on a syllable preceding the antipenultimate syllable of a word.

3. All words end either in a vowel or in *-s*, *-n*, *-r*; but no other consonant.

4. Initial *s* before a vowel became *h* (denoted by the 'rough breathing' mark), e.g. **septm* (Latin *septem*) → *heptá*.

5. Final *-m* became *-n*, e.g. **jugom* → *zugón* (cf. Latin *jugum*).[1]

6. Final stops fall, e.g. **gunaik* → *gúnai*, **epheret* → *éphere*, **epheront* → *épheron*.

In the above examples, Law 1 is diachronic: it states that what had been *dh* becomes *th*, etc. Law 2 states a relationship between word-unit and stress: it is a kind of contract between two coexisting terms: [131] it is thus a synchronic law. Law 3 is the same, since it concerns the word-unit and its final sound. Laws 4, 5 and 6 are diachronic: they state, respectively, that what had been *s* became *h*, that *-n* replaced *-m*, and that *-t*, *-k*, etc. disappeared without trace.

It should also be noted that Law 3 is the result of Laws 5 and 6. Two diachronic facts created a synchronic fact.

Once the two categories of laws are distinguished, one sees that Laws 2 and 3 are not of the same nature as Laws 1, 4, 5 and 6.

Synchronic laws are general, but not imperative. It is true that a synchronic law is imposed upon speakers by the constraints of communal usage (cf. p. [107]). But we are not envisaging here an obligation relative to the language users. What we mean is that *in the language* there is nothing which guarantees the maintenance of regularity on any given point. A synchronic law simply expresses an existing order. It registers a state of affairs. What it states is of the same order as a statement to the effect that in a certain orchard the trees are planted in the form of a quincunx. The order a synchronic law defines is precarious, precisely because it is not imperative. Nothing could be more regular than the synchronic law governing stress in Latin (a law exactly comparable to Law 2 above). This system of stress, none the less, offered no resistance to factors of change, and eventually gave place to a new law, which we find in French (cf. p. [122] ff.). In short, when one speaks of a synchronic law, one is speaking of an arrangement, or a principle of regularity.

Diachrony, on the other hand, presupposes a dynamic factor through

[1] According to Meillet (*Mem. de la Société de Linguistique, IX*, p. 365 ff.) and Gauthiot (*La fin de mot en indo-européen*, p. 158 ff.) Proto-Indo-European had only final *-n* and not *-m*. If this is accepted, law 5 becomes: 'Final *-n* is maintained'. Its value as an example is unchanged, since the phonetic conservation of an earlier state of affairs is not different in nature from the phonetic alteration of an earlier state of affairs. Cf. p. [200]. (Editorial note)

which an effect is produced, a development carried out. But this imperative character does not justify applying the notion of law to facts of evolution. One speaks of a law only when a set of facts is governed by the same rule. In spite of appearances to the contrary, diachronic events are always accidental and particular in nature.

[132] This is quite obvious in the case of semantic facts. For example, the French word *poutre*, meaning 'mare', took on the meaning of 'beam, rafter'. The change can be explained by reference to particular circumstances, and has no connexion with other changes that may have occurred at the same time. It is merely one accident among many recorded in the history of a language.

As regards syntactic and morphological changes, at first sight this is not so clear. At a certain period, for instance, nearly all the forms of the Old French nominative case disappeared. Is this not an example of a whole set of facts governed by the same law? No. For all these are merely multiple examples of a single isolated fact. It was the notion of a nominative case itself which was affected, and the disappearance of that case naturally involved the disappearance of a whole set of forms.[1] For anyone who looks only at the language from the outside, the single phenomenon is obscured by the multiplicity of its manifestations. But the phenomenon itself is one in its underlying nature, and it constitutes a historical event as isolated of its kind as the semantic change of the word *poutre*. It only appears to be a law because it is actualised in a system. It is the rigorous organisation of the system which creates the illusion that the diachronic fact is subject to the same conditions as the synchronic.

Exactly the same applies to phonetic changes, even though people nowadays speak of 'phonetic laws'. It is indeed observable that at a given time in a given region, all the words which have a certain phonetic feature are subject to the same change. For example, Law 1 on p. [130] (**dhūmos → Greek thūmós*) applies to all Greek words with a voiced aspirate (cf. **nebhos → néphos*, **medhu → méthu*, **anghō → ánkhō*, etc.). Law 4 (**septm → heptá*) applies to **serpō → hérpo*, **sūs → hûs*, and all words beginning with *s*. This regularity, which has sometimes been disputed, is in our view very well estab-
[133] lished: the apparent exceptions do not diminish the ineluctability of changes of this kind, for they are to be explained either by more specialised phonetic laws (e.g. *tríkhes* : *thriksí*, cf. p. [138]), or else by the intervention of facts of a different order (analogy, etc.). So it would appear that nothing could better fit the definition of the term *law* given above. And yet, however many cases confirm a phonetic

[1] It is not altogether clear how this explanation is to be reconciled with the claims that a language system itself is never changed as such (p. [124]) and that case distinctions belong among the abstract entities of grammar (p. [189] ff.). (Translator's note)

law, all the facts it covers are simply manifestations of a single particular fact.

The real question is whether phonetic changes affect words or only sounds. The answer is not in doubt. In *néphos*, *méthu*, *ánkhō*, etc. it is a particular sound; a Proto-Indo-European voiced aspirate which becomes a voiceless aspirate, the initial *s* of early Greek which changes to *h*, and so on. Each of these facts is an isolated fact. It is independent of other events of the same order, and also independent of the words in which it occurs.[1] All the words in question, naturally, are modified phonetically; but that must not mislead us as to the real nature of what is taking place.

On what do we base the claim that words themselves are not directly subject to phonetic change? On the simple observation that sound changes do not affect words as such, and cannot alter them essentially. The word as a unit is not made up simply of a set of sounds:[2] it depends on other characteristics than its material nature. Imagine that one [134]
note on a piano is out of tune. Every time this note is played in the performance of a piece, there will be a false note. But where? In the melody? Surely not. Nothing has happened to the melody, only to the piano. It is exactly the same in the case of sound change. The sound system is the instrument we play in order to articulate the words of the language. If one element in the sound system changes, this may have various results; but in itself, the fact does not affect the words, for they are, so to speak, the melodies in our repertoire.

Thus diachronic facts are individual facts. The alteration of a system takes place through events which not only lie outside it (cf. p. [121]), but are isolated events and form no system among themselves.[3]

To summarise, synchronic facts of whatever kind present a certain regularity, but they have no imperative character. Diachronic facts, on the contrary, are forced upon the language, but there is nothing general about them.

[1] It need hardly be said that the examples cited are merely an indication. Currently, linguistics attempts – rightly – to relate as many series of changes as possible to the operation of the same initial principle. Meillet, for example, explains all changes in Greek stops as due to a gradual weakening of articulation (*Mem. de la Société de Linguistique, IX*, p. 163 ff.). Where such general facts are to be found it is to them, in the final analysis, that the conclusions concerning the nature of phonetic change apply. (Editorial note)

[2] But elsewhere (p. [98]) it is denied that a word consists of sounds at all. If that is the case, there is no need to justify the claim that words are not subject to sound change, since it is true by definition. If, on the other hand, the signal is treated as a fixed set of sound units, corresponding to the sequence of letters in a written form (p. [32]), it is less obvious that sound change does not affect the sound pattern of a word directly. There is some inconsistency here, which Saussure's editors cannot be said to have resolved satisfactorily. (Translator's note)

[3] The thesis that a system as such does not evolve, but is merely affected by unrelated external developments, subsequently became one of the major subjects of controversy among structuralists. (Translator's note)

In short, we conclude that neither synchronic nor diachronic facts are governed by laws in the sense defined above. If, none the less, one insists on speaking of linguistic laws, the term will mean something entirely different as applied to synchronic facts and to diachronic facts.

§7. *Is there a panchronic point of view?*

Hitherto, we have taken the term *law* in its legal sense. But might there perhaps be in languages laws as understood in the physical and natural sciences? In other words, relations which hold in all cases and for ever? In short, is it not possible to study languages from a panchronic point of view?

It is possible, no doubt. Since phonetic changes occur, and will
[135] always occur, one may consider that general phenomenon in itself as one of the constant features of language: hence it is a linguistic law. In linguistics as in chess (cf. p. [125] ff.) there are rules which outlast all events. But they are general principles existing independently of concrete facts. As soon as one comes down to particular, tangible facts, there is no panchronic point of view. Every phonetic change, whatever its extension may be, is limited to a certain period and a certain geographical area. There is no such change which occurs all the time and everywhere. Its existence is merely diachronic. That very fact is a criterion for judging what belongs to linguistic structure and what does not. Any concrete fact amenable to panchronic explanation could not be part of linguistic structure. Take the French word *chose* ('thing'). From a diachronic point of view, it is to be distinguished from Latin *causa*, from which it is derived. From a synchronic point of view, it is to be distinguished from all the words it might be associated with in modern French. Only the sounds of the word considered in themselves (*šọz*) may be considered panchronically: but they are devoid of linguistic value. Even from a panchronic point of view, *šọz* as part of a sequence like *ün šọz admirablə* (*une chose admirable* 'an admirable thing') is not a unit. It is just a formless mass, which lacks definition. Why pick out *šọz*, rather than *ọza* or *nšọ*? There is no value, because there is no meaning. The panchronic point of view never gets to grips with specific facts of language structure.

§8. *Consequences of the confusion of synchrony with diachrony*

There are two cases to consider.

(a) The synchronic facts appear to conflict with the diachronic facts. Looking at the case superficially, it appears that we have to choose between the two. In fact, this is not necessary. One does not exclude the other. For instance, the word *dépit* in French used to mean 'scorn'; [136] but that does not prevent it nowadays having a quite different meaning. Etymology and synchronic value are two separate things. Similarly, in modern French, according to traditional grammar, the present participle is sometimes variable and behaves like an adjective, agreeing with its noun (*une eau courante*, 'running water'), but is in other cases invariable (*une personne courant dans la rue*, 'a person running in the street'). But historical grammar shows us that we are not dealing with one and the same form. In one case there is the continuation of the Latin participle (*currentem*), which is variable; but in the other case we are dealing with a survival of the Latin ablative gerund (*currendō*), which is invariable.[1] Do the synchronic facts contradict the diachronic facts in this case? Is traditional grammar to be condemned in the name of historical grammar? No. That would be to see only one side of the reality. One must not suppose that historical facts are the only important ones, or that they suffice to constitute a language. It is undoubtedly true that, as far as its origins are concerned, the modern French participle *courant* subsumes two originally separate forms. But as language users we no longer distinguish two forms: we recognise only one.[2] Both facts are equally absolute and incontestable.

(b) The synchronic facts agree so closely with the diachronic facts that they are confused, or it is considered superfluous to distinguish them. For instance, the present meaning of the French word *père* ('father') is explained by appeal to the fact that its Latin etymon *pater* meant 'father'. To take another example, Latin short *a* in a non-initial open syllable became *i*: so beside *faciō* one has *conficiō*, beside *amīcus* one has *inimīcus*, etc. The law is often stated as being that the *a* of *faciō* ('I make') changes to *i* in *conficiō* ('I make ready, complete') because it is no longer in the initial syllable. This is incorrect. The *a* of *faciō* never 'became' the *i* of *conficiō*. In order to establish the truth of the matter, one must distinguish between two periods and four different forms. Originally, the forms were *faciō* and *confaciō*. Then [137] *confaciō* became *conficiō*, while *faciō* stayed as it was: so the forms in use were *faciō* – *conficiō*.

[1] This theory, although generally accepted, was challenged by E. Lerch (*Das invariable Participium praesentis*, Erlangen, 1913), but unsuccessfully in our view. The example has therefore been allowed to stand. In any case, its didactic value would be unimpaired. (Editorial note)

[2] The example is not entirely convincing. For semantically, and on the basis of both syntagmatic and associative relations, there seem to be adequate grounds for distinguishing the variable *courant* from its invariable counterpart in modern French, without any appeal to diachronic considerations. (Translator's note)

faciō $\longleftrightarrow$ confaciō		Period A
$\downarrow$ $\qquad\qquad$ $\downarrow$		
faciō $\longleftrightarrow$ conficiō		Period B

If a 'change' occurred, it was that *confaciō* changed to *conficiō*. But the rule, badly formulated as it is, does not even mention *confaciō*. Furthermore, in addition to this change, which is a diachronic fact, there is a second fact which is quite different. It concerns the purely synchronic contrast between *faciō* and *conficiō*. One may be tempted to regard this not as a separate fact, but as a consequence of the first. None the less, it is a fact in its own right; and indeed all synchronic facts are of this kind. What prevents our recognising the proper value of the contrast *faciō* – *conficiō* is that its role is not particularly important. But when we consider pairs like German *Gast* – *Gäste*, *gebe* – *gibt*, we realise that these contrasts too are fortuitous results of phonetic evolution: they none the less embody, synchronically, quite essential grammatical distinctions. Since synchronic and diachronic facts are closely connected in other respects, each presupposing the other, in the end distinguishing between them is felt to be pointless. For years, linguistics has muddled them up without even noticing the muddle.

This mistake becomes very apparent, however, in certain cases. In order to explain Greek *phuktós*, it might be supposed that it is sufficient to point out that in Greek *g* and *kh* become *k* before a voiceless consonant, and to state this fact in terms of synchronic correspondences such as *phugeîn* : *phuktós*, *lékhos* : *léktron*, etc. But then we come up against cases like *tríkhes* : *thriksí*, where a complication
[138] appears in the form of a 'change' from *t* to *th*. The forms of this word can be explained only in historical terms, by appeal to relative chronology. The primitive stem **thrikh*, followed by the ending *-si*, gave *thriksí*. This was a very early development, like that which produced *léktron* from the root *lekh-*. At a later stage, any aspirate followed by another in the same word lost its aspiration, and so **thríkhes* became *tríkhes*, while *thriksí* naturally remained unaffected by this development.

§9. Conclusions

Linguistics is thus faced with a second parting of the ways. In the first place, we found it necessary to choose between studying languages and studying speech (cf. p. [36]). Now we find ourselves at the junction where one road leads to diachrony and the other to synchrony.

Once this dual principle of classification is grasped, one may add that *everything which is diachronic in languages is only so through speech.* Speech contains the seeds of every change, each one being pioneered in the first instance by a certain number of individuals before entering into general usage. Modern German has *ich war, wir waren,* whereas at an earlier period, up to the sixteenth century, the conjugation was *ich was, wir waren* (English still has *I was, we were*). How did this substitution of *war* for *was* come about? A few people, on the basis of *waren,* created the analogical form *war.* This form, constantly repeated and accepted by the community, became part of the language. But not all innovations in speech meet with the same success. As long as they are confined to certain individuals, there is no need to take them into account, since our concern is solely with the language. They enter our field of observation only when they have become accepted by the community.

An evolutionary development is always preceded by a similar de- [139]
velopment, or rather many similar developments, in the sphere of speech. That in no way invalidates the distinction established previously: rather, it offers a confirmation. For in the history of any innovation one always finds two distinct phases: (1) its appearance in individual cases, and (2) its incorporation into the language in exactly the same form, but now adopted by the community.

The following table indicates a rational structure for the pursuit of linguistic studies:

- Language
  - Languages
    - Synchrony
    - Diachrony
  - Speech

It must be conceded that the theoretically ideal form a science should take is not always the form imposed upon it by practical necessities. In linguistics, practical necessities are more demanding than in any other subject. To some extent, the confusion which at present reigns in linguistic research is due to them. Even if the distinctions drawn here were accepted once and for all, it might not be possible in practice to translate this ideal schema into a systematic programme of studies.

In the synchronic study of Old French, the linguist uses facts and principles which have nothing in common with those which would be revealed by the history of the same language from the thirteenth to the twentieth century, but are comparable to those which would emerge from the description of a modern Bantu language, or Attic

Greek in 400 B.C., or French at the present day. These different synchronic investigations are concerned with similar relations: for although each language constitutes a closed system, all presuppose certain constant principles. These do not vary from one case to the next, because the facts studied belong to the same order of phenomena. In the case of historical studies, it is no different. Whether one is
[140] studying the development of French over a certain period (from the thirteenth to the twentieth century, for example), or a period in the history of Javanese, or of any other language, one is dealing with similar facts. Comparing these facts is sufficient to enable one to establish valid diachronic generalisations. The ideal programme would be for each scholar to concentrate either on synchronic or on diachronic research, and include as much as possible of the material falling within his chosen field. But it is difficult to achieve a scientific understanding of widely differing languages. Furthermore, each language in practice constitutes a single unit for purposes of study, and one is led inevitably to study it from both a static and a historical viewpoint in turn. Such units, we must none the less remember, are merely superficial in theoretical terms. On the contrary, the disparity between different languages conceals an underlying unity. In studying a language from either point of view, it is of the utmost importance to assign each fact to its appropriate sphere, and not to confuse the two methods.

The two branches of linguistics thus defined will now be considered in turn.

Synchronic linguistics will be concerned with logical and psychological connexions between coexisting items constituting a system, as perceived by the same collective consciousness.

Diachronic linguistics on the other hand will be concerned with connexions between sequences of items not perceived by the same collective consciousness, which replace one another without themselves constituting a system.

PART TWO [141]

Synchronic Linguistics

CHAPTER I

General Observations

The aim of general synchronic linguistics is to establish the fundamental principles of any idiosynchronic system, the facts which constitute any linguistic state. Many matters already discussed in the preceding section properly belong to synchrony. The general properties of the linguistic sign may be considered an integral part of synchronic studies, although we previously examined these properties in order to demonstrate the necessity for distinguishing synchronic from diachronic linguistics.

To synchrony belongs everything called 'general grammar'; for only through linguistic states are the various relations involved in grammar established. In what follows we shall simply be concerned with certain essential principles, without which it would be impossible to tackle more specific problems connected with states, or to give any detailed explanation of a linguistic state.

Generally speaking, static linguistics is much more difficult than historical linguistics. Facts of evolution are more concrete, and stir
the imagination more readily: the connexions link sequences of terms [142]
which are easily grasped. It is simple, and often entertaining even, to follow through a series of linguistic changes. But a linguistics concerned with values and coexisting terms is much harder going.

In practice, a linguistic state occupies not a point in time, but a period of time of varying length, during which the sum total of changes occurring is minimal. It may be ten years, a generation, a century, or even longer. A language may hardly change at all for a long period, only to undergo considerable changes in the next few years. Of two contemporary languages, one may evolve considerably and the other hardly at all over the same period. In the latter case, any study will necessarily be synchronic, but in the former case diachronic. An absolute state is defined by lack of change. But since languages are always changing, however minimally, studying a linguistic state amounts in practice to ignoring unimportant changes. Mathematicians do likewise when they ignore very small fractions for certain purposes, such as logarithmic calculation.

Historians distinguish between *epochs* and *periods*. The former are points in time, and the latter lengths of time. None the less, a historian speaks of the 'Antonine epoch' or the 'Crusading epoch' when he is taking into consideration a set of features which remained constant over the period in question. One could likewise say that static linguistics is also in this sense concerned with epochs; but the term *state* is preferable. The beginning and end of an epoch are usually marked by some more or less sudden upheaval which tends to alter the established order. The term *state* avoids the suggestion that anything like that occurs in a language. In addition, the term *epoch*, precisely because it is borrowed from history, directs attention less to the language
[143] itself than to the circumstances and conditions in which it occurs. In short, *epoch* suggests more the idea of what we have called 'external linguistics' (cf. p. [40]).

Demarcation in time is not the only problem encountered in defining a linguistic state. Exactly the same question arises over demarcation in space. So the notion of a linguistic state can only be an approximation. In static linguistics, as in most sciences, no demonstration is possible without a conventional simplification of the data.

CHAPTER II [144]

Concrete Entities of a Language

§1. Entities and units. Definitions

The signs comprising a language are not abstractions, but real objects (cf. p. [32]). Linguistics studies these objects and the relations between them. They may be termed the *concrete entities* of that science.

Let us remind ourselves first of all of two principles which bear on the whole question.

1. Any linguistic entity exists only in virtue of the association between signal and signification (cf. p. [99]). It disappears the moment we concentrate exclusively on just one or the other. We are then left with a pure abstraction in place of a concrete object. There is a constant risk of taking one part or other of the entity and believing that we are dealing with the totality. That is what would happen, for instance, if one were to begin by dividing the spoken sequence into syllables. A syllable is defined solely in phonetic terms. But a sequence of sounds is a linguistic sequence only if it is the bearer of an idea:[1] in itself, it is merely an item for physiological investigation.

The same is true of the signification as soon as we separate it from its signal.[2] Concepts like 'house', 'white', 'see', etc. considered in themselves belong to psychology. They become linguistic entities only by association with sound patterns. In linguistic structure, a concept

[1] An unfortunate way of putting the point, since it seems to imply that certain sound sequences are linguistic phenomena, while others are merely speech phenomena. Whereas only signals, i.e. sound patterns, belong to the language in Saussure's sense. (Translator's note)

[2] The parallel is by no means convincing. While it is reasonably clear how one might study sounds separately from studying the words they express, it is far from clear in what sense concepts like 'house' can be separated at all for purposes of investigation from their association with particular English word forms. Cf. the remarks on the amorphousness of thought on p. [155]. (Translator's note)

[145] becomes an identifying characteristic of a certain sound, just as a given sound is an identifying characteristic of the corresponding concept.

This unified duality has often been compared with that of the human being, comprising body and soul. But the parallel is unsatisfactory. A better one would be with chemical compounds, such as water. Water is a combination of hydrogen and oxygen: but taken separately neither element has any of the properties of water.

2. A linguistic entity is not ultimately defined until it is *delimited,* i.e. separated from whatever there may be on either side of it in a sequence of sounds. It is these delimited entities or *units* which contrast with one another in the mechanism of the language.

At first, one may be tempted to assimilate linguistic signs to visual signs, which are observed to coexist in space without confusion. One perhaps imagines that the separation of significant elements can be carried out in the same kind of way, without requiring any mental analysis. The word *form*, which is often used to designate these entities (as in *verb form, noun form,* etc.), tends to confirm us in this error. But, as we have already noted, a primary characteristic of the spoken sequence is its linearity (cf. p. [103]). In itself, it is merely a line, a continuous ribbon of sound, along which the ear picks out no adequate or clearly marked divisions. In order to do so, recourse must be had to meanings. When we listen to an unknown language, we are not in a position to say how the sequence of sounds should be analysed: for the analysis is impossible if one takes into account nothing more than the phonic side of the linguistic event. But when we know what meaning and what role to attribute to each segment in the sequence, then we see those segments separated one from another, and the shapeless ribbon is cut up into pieces. But the analysis involved is in no way a material analysis.

[146] To summarise, a language does not present itself to us as a set of signs already delimited, requiring us merely to study their meanings and organisation. It is an indistinct mass, in which attention and habit alone enable us to distinguish particular elements. The unit has no special phonic character, and the only definition it can be given is the following: *a segment of sound which is, as distinct from what precedes and follows in the spoken sequence, the signal of a certain concept.*

§2. *Method of delimitation*

Anyone familiar with a language can determine the units by a very simple method – at least in theory. The method takes speech as its linguistic evidence and envisages it as representing two parallel sequences, one of concepts (*a*) and one of sound patterns (*b*).

Correct delimitation of signs requires that the divisions established in the sound sequence (α′, β′, γ′ . . .) match the divisions in the sequence of concepts (α, β, γ . . .).

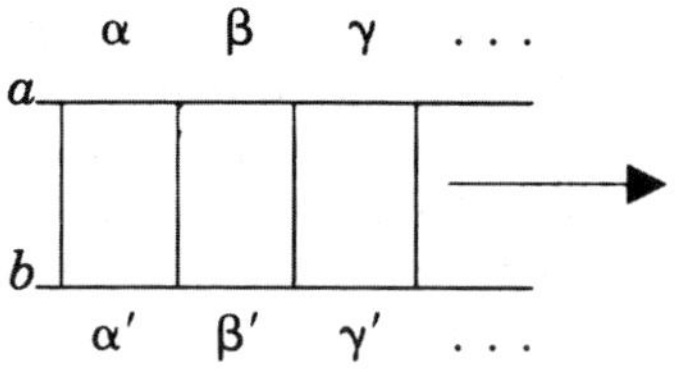

Take the French sequence *sižlaprã*. Can I introduce a division after *l* and take *sižl* as a unit? No. One has only to consider the concepts to see that this division is a mistake. The division into syllables (*siž-la-prã*) is not *a priori* a linguistic division either. The only divisions admissible are: (1) *si-ž-la-prã* (*si je la prends*, 'if I take it/her'), and (2) *si-ž-l-aprã* (*si je l'apprends*, 'if I learn it'). These divisions are determined by the sense one attaches to the words.

To check the results of this analysis and make sure that one has picked out the units, it is necessary to compare series of phrases in [147]
which the same unit occurs, and be able in each case to separate the unit in question from its context in a way corroborated by the sense. In the two phrases *lafǫrsdüvã* (*la force du vent*, 'the strength of the wind') and *abudfǫrs* (*à bout de force*, 'exhausted'),[1] the same concept coincides with the same sound-segment *fǫrs* in both cases: thus it is clearly a linguistic unit. But in *ilməfǫrsaparlę* (*il me force à parler*, 'he forces me to speak'), *fǫrs* has quite a different meaning: so it is a different unit.

§3. *Practical difficulties of delimitation*

Can this method, in theory so straightforward, be easily applied in practice? It is tempting to think so, if one supposes that the units to be delimited will turn out to be words; for what is a phrase but a combination of words? What could be easier to grasp? To go back to the example discussed above, it can be said that the sequence *sižlaprã* divides into four units by our method of analysis, and these are four words: *si-je-l'-apprends*. But a note of caution must be sounded here. For there has been a great deal of controversy about what a word is. On further reflection, it becomes clear that what a word is usually taken to be does not correspond to our notion of a concrete unit.

To convince oneself of this, it suffices to consider the singular form

[1] i.e. 'at the end of one's strength'. (Translator's note)

cheval ('horse') and its plural *chevaux* ('horses'). It is commonly said that these are two forms of the same word. But, taking each as a whole, it is clear that we are dealing with two quite distinct items, as regards both meaning and sound. Or compare *mwa* in *le mois de décembre* ('the month of December') and *mwaz* in *un mois après* ('a month later').[1] The same word appears in two phonetic guises, so there is no question of its being a single concrete unit: for although the meaning is the same, the sound-segments are different. So as soon as
[148] we try to equate concrete units with words, we find ourselves in a dilemma. Either ignore the connexion, even though it is an obvious one, between *cheval* and *chevaux*, *mwa* and *mwaz*, etc., and say that these are different words: or else dispense with concrete units and be content with the abstraction which groups together various forms of the same word. It is useless, evidently, to look upon the word as a concrete unit. In any case, many words are complex units, in which one can clearly distinguish smaller units (suffixes, prefixes, stems). Derived forms like *désir-eux* ('desir-ous'), *malheur-eux* ('un-fortun-ate') divide into distinct parts, each with its own clear meaning and function. On the other hand, there are units larger than single words. These include compounds (*porte-plume*, 'pen holder'), phrases (*s'il vous plaît*, 'if you please'), flexional forms (*il a été*, 'he has been'), etc. These units raise the same problems of delimitation as words proper, and it is extremely difficult to unravel in a sequence of sounds the arrangement of units present, and to say which are the concrete elements the language is using.

Doubtless these difficulties do not arise for the language-users themselves. Anything which is significant in any way strikes them as being a concrete unit, and they do not fail to notice it in discourse. However, it is one thing to sense this rapid and subtle interplay of units, but quite another thing to give an account of it by means of a systematic analysis.

A widely held view claims that the only concrete linguistic units are sentences. We speak in sentences, it is said: analysing sentences into words is a secondary operation. But first of all it must be asked to what extent sentences belong to the language itself (cf. p. [172]). If the sentence as such belongs to speech, it can hardly be counted a linguistic unit. However, let us leave that difficulty on one side. If we think of all the sentences which could be uttered, what strikes us most forcibly is the lack of resemblance between them. We might at first be tempted to compare the immense diversity of sentences to the anal-
[149] ogous diversity of individuals included in a zoological species. But that is an illusion. In animals of the same species the common character-

[1] Here the alternation of the two pronunciations of the word for 'month', *mwa* and *mwaz*, depends on whether the following word begins with a vowel. (Translator's note)

istics are much more important than the individual differences. With sentences, on the contrary, it is diversity which is predominant. As soon as one looks for something to link them together in spite of this diversity, one finds that one has unintentionally come back to the word and its grammatical features, with all the attendant difficulties already familiar.

§4. Conclusion

In most scientific domains, the question of units does not even arise: they are given in advance. In zoology, the animal is the obvious unit. In astronomy, likewise, there are items already separated out in space: the stars, planets, etc. In chemistry, one can study the nature and composition of bichromate of potash without worrying for a moment about whether it is a well defined object.

When a science offers no immediately recognizable concrete units, that means they are not essential. In history, for example, is the unit the individual, the epoch, or the nation? No one knows. But does it matter? To study history it is not at all necessary to decide.

But just as chess is based entirely on the combinations afforded by the various pieces, so too a language has the character of a system based entirely on the contrasts between its concrete units. One cannot dispense with identifying them, nor move a step without having recourse to them. And yet delimiting them is such a tricky problem that one is led to ask whether they are really there.

A language thus has this curious and striking feature. It has no immediately perceptible entities. And yet one cannot doubt that they exist, or that the interplay of these units is what constitutes linguistic structure. That is undoubtedly a characteristic which distinguishes languages from all other semiological institutions.

[150]

CHAPTER III

Identities, Realities, Values

The foregoing considerations raise a crucial problem. It is all the more important in that the fundamental concepts of static linguistics are directly based upon, or even merge with, the concept of a linguistic unit. This we now propose to show, by examining the notions of synchronic identity, synchronic reality, and synchronic value.

A. What is a synchronic *identity*? What is at issue here is not the kind of identity which links the French negative particle *pas* ('not') to the Latin noun *passum* ('pace'): that is a diachronic identity (cf. p. [249]). It is the no less interesting kind of identity which permits us to say that two sentences like *je ne sais pas* ('I don't know') and *ne dites pas cela* ('Don't say that') include the same element (*pas*, 'not'). An idle question, it may be thought. For clearly the identity resides in the fact that these two sentences include the same sequence of sound (*pas*) bearing the same meaning in both cases. But this explanation will not do. Although correlations of phonic segments and concepts establish identities (as in the example previously given: *la force du vent* and *à bout de force*, p. [147]), the converse does not hold. It is possible to have an identity without any such correlation. For example, we may hear in the course of a lecture several repetitions of the word *Messieurs!* ('Gentlemen!'). We feel that in each case it is the same expression: and yet there are variations of delivery and intonation
[151] which give rise in the several instances to very noticeable phonic differences – differences as marked as those which in other cases serve to differentiate one word from another (e.g. *pomme* from *paume*, *goutte* from *goûte*, *fuir* from *fouir*, etc.).[1] Furthermore, this feeling of identity persists in spite of the fact that from a semantic point of view too

[1] Comparable English pairs would be *come – comb*, *look – luck*, *fear – fir*. (Translator's note)

there is no absolute reduplication from one *Messieurs!* to the next. A word can express quite different ideas without seriously compromising its own identity (cf. *adopter une mode*, 'to adopt a fashion', *adopter un enfant*, 'to adopt a child'; *la fleur du pommier* 'the flower of the apple-tree', *la fleur de la noblesse*, 'the flower of the nobility').

The mechanism of a language turns entirely on identities and differences. The latter are merely counterparts of the former. The problem of identities crops up everywhere. It merges in part with the problem of entities and units, to which it adds complications. But the complications are valuable complications. Let us examine the problem of identity in linguistics in the light of some non-linguistic examples. We assign identity, for instance, to two trains ('the 8.45 from Geneva to Paris'), one of which leaves twenty-four hours after the other. We treat it as the 'same' train, even though probably the locomotive, the carriages, the staff etc. are not the same. Or if a street is demolished and then rebuilt, we say it is the same street, although there may be physically little or nothing left of the old one. How is it that a street can be reconstructed entirely and still be the same? Because it is not a purely material structure. It has other characteristics which are independent of its bricks and mortar; for example, its situation in relation to other streets. Similarly, the train is identified by its departure time, its route, and any other features which distinguish it from other trains. Whenever the same conditions are fulfilled, the same entities reappear. But they are not abstractions. The street and the train are real enough. Their physical existence is essential to our [152]
understanding of what they are.

A quite different kind of case would be, say, a suit of mine which is stolen, but which I find subsequently on a second-hand stall. That suit is indeed a material object, made up simply of various inert substances – cloth, lining, facings, etc. Any other suit, however similar, would not be my suit. Now linguistic identity is not the kind of identity the suit has, but the kind of identity the train and the street have. Every time I utter the word *Messieurs* ('Gentlemen'), I renew its material being: it is a new act of phonation and a new psychological act. The link between two uses of the same word is not based upon material identity, nor upon exact similarity of meaning, but upon factors the linguist must discover, if he is to come anywhere near to revealing the true nature of linguistic units.

B. What is a synchronic *reality*? What concrete or abstract elements of linguistic structure can be thus designated?

Take the distinctions between the various parts of speech. On what is the classification of words into nouns, adjectives, etc. based? Is it on some purely logical principle of an extra-linguistic nature, applied to grammar from outside like lines of longitude and latitude on the

earth's globe? Or does it correspond to something which belongs within, and is determined by the language system? In other words, is it a synchronic reality? The second answer seems likely to be correct, but there may be something to be said in favour of the first. In the French sentence *ces gants sont bon marché* ('these gloves are good value'), is *bon marché* ('good value') an adjective? Logically, it has the right meaning. But grammatically it is less clear. For *bon marché* does not behave like a normal French adjective: it is invariable, never precedes its noun, and so on. Furthermore, it consists of two words. What the parts of speech provide is a classification of individual words:
[153] so how can a group of two words belong to one or other of the parts of speech? Yet if we split it up into two words, and say *bon* ('good') is an adjective, whereas *marché* ('value') is a noun, we have not accounted for the single expression *bon marché* ('good value'). The conclusion is that our 'parts of speech' classification must be defective or incomplete: its division of words into nouns, verbs, adjectives, etc. does not correspond to any undeniable linguistic reality.

Linguistics is always working with concepts originally introduced by the grammarians. It is unclear whether or not these concepts really reflect constituent features of linguistic structure. But how can we find out? And if they are illusory, what realities can we put in their place?

To avoid being misled, it is first of all important to realise that concrete linguistic entities do not just present themselves for inspection of their own accord. It is in seeking them out that one makes contact with linguistic reality. Taking this as our point of departure, we have to proceed to work out all the classifications linguistics needs to accommodate the facts it has to deal with. But to base these classifications on anything other than concrete entities – to say, for instance, that the parts of speech do reflect linguistic structure, simply because they are logically viable categories – is to forget that linguistic facts do not exist independently of sound-sequences divided into meaningful segments.

C. Finally, the notions discussed above do not differ in essentials from what we have elsewhere referred to as *values*. The point can be brought out once again by comparison with chess (cf. p. [125] ff.). Consider a knight in chess. Is the piece by itself an element of the game? Certainly not. For as a material object, separated from its square on the board and the other conditions of play, it is of no significance for the player. It becomes a real, concrete element only when it takes on or becomes identified with its value in the game. Suppose that during a game this piece gets destroyed or lost. Can it
[154] be replaced? Of course it can. Not only by some other knight, but even by an object of quite a different shape, which can be counted as a

knight, provided it is assigned the same value as the missing piece. Thus it can be seen that in semiological systems, such as languages, where the elements keep one another in a state of equilibrium in accordance with fixed rules, the notions of identity and value merge.

That is why in the final analysis the notion of value covers units, concrete entities and realities. There is no fundamental difference between these notions, but they allow the same problem to be formulated in a variety of different ways. Whether we are trying to determine units, realities, concrete entities, or values, it will always come down to the same central question, which runs throughout the whole of static linguistics.

From a practical point of view, it would be of interest to begin with units; to determine units, and recognize the various kinds of units by providing a classification. It would be necessary to examine what the basis is for division into words. For the word, in spite of being so difficult to define, is a unit which compels recognition by the mind. It has a central role in the linguistic mechanism. (But a discussion of that topic alone would fill a book.) Then one would proceed to classify smaller units, larger units, and so on. By determining in this way the elements to be dealt with, a science of linguistics would fully achieve its goals, having related all relevant phenomena in its domain to one first principle. It cannot be said that this central problem has ever been tackled, or that the scope and difficulty of it have been realised. Where languages are concerned, people have always been satisfied to work with poorly defined units.

However, in spite of the capital importance of units, it is preferable to approach the problem by considering values. For that, in our view, is the heart of the matter.

[155]

CHAPTER IV

Linguistic Value

§1. The language as thought organised in sound

In order to realise that the language itself can be nothing other than a system of pure values, one need only consider the two elements which are involved in the way it functions: ideas and sounds.

Psychologically, setting aside its expression in words, our thought is simply a vague, shapeless mass. Philosophers and linguists have always agreed that were it not for signs, we should be incapable of differentiating any two ideas in a clear and constant way. In itself, thought is like a swirling cloud, where no shape is intrinsically determinate. No ideas are established in advance, and nothing is distinct, before the introduction of linguistic structure.

But do sounds, which lie outside this nebulous world of thought, in themselves constitute entities established in advance? No more than ideas do. The substance of sound is no more fixed or rigid than that of thought. It does not offer a ready-made mould, with shapes that thought must inevitably conform to. It is a malleable material which can be fashioned into separate parts in order to supply the signals which thought has need of. So we can envisage the linguistic phenomenon in its entirety – the language, that is – as a series of adjoining
[156] subdivisions simultaneously imprinted both on the plane of vague, amorphous thought (*A*), and on the equally featureless plane of sound (*B*). This can be represented very approximately as in the following sketch (top of p. 111).

The characteristic role of a language in relation to thought is not to supply the material phonetic means by which ideas may be expressed. It is to act as intermediary between thought and sound, in such a way that the combination of both necessarily produces a mutually complementary delimitation of units. Thought, chaotic by nature, is made precise by this process of segmentation. But what happens is neither

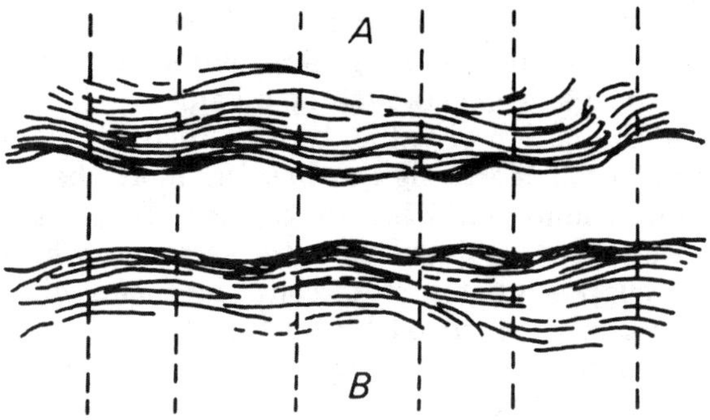

a transformation of thoughts into matter, nor a transformation of sounds into ideas. What takes place, is a somewhat mysterious process by which 'thought-sound' evolves divisions, and a language takes shape with its linguistic units in between those two amorphous masses. One might think of it as being like air in contact with water: changes in atmospheric pressure break up the surface of the water into series of divisions, i.e. waves. The correlation between thought and sound, and the union of the two, is like that.

Linguistic structure might be described as the domain of articulations, taking this term in the sense defined earlier (p. [26]). Every linguistic sign is a part or member, an *articulus*, where an idea is fixed in a sound, and a sound becomes the sign of an idea.

A language might also be compared to a sheet of paper. Thought is [157]
one side of the sheet and sound the reverse side. Just as it is impossible to take a pair of scissors and cut one side of paper without at the same time cutting the other, so it is impossible in a language to isolate sound from thought, or thought from sound. To separate the two for theoretical purposes takes us into either pure psychology or pure phonetics, not linguistics.

Linguistics, then, operates along this margin, where sound and thought meet. *The contact between them gives rise to a form, not a substance.*

These observations clarify our earlier remarks about the arbitrary nature of the linguistic sign (p. [100]). Not only are the two areas which are linguistically linked vague and amorphous in themselves, but the process which selects one particular sound-sequence to correspond to one particular idea is entirely arbitrary. If this were not so, the notion of value would lose something. For it would involve a certain element of imposition from the outside world. But in fact values remain entirely a matter of internal relations, and that is why the link between idea and sound is intrinsically arbitrary.

In turn, the arbitrary nature of the sign enables us to understand more easily why it needs social activity to create a linguistic system.

A community is necessary in order to establish values. Values have no other rationale than usage and general agreement. An individual, acting alone, is incapable of establishing a value.

Furthermore, the notion of value, thus defined, shows us that it is a great mistake to consider a sign as nothing more than the combination of a certain sound and a certain concept. To think of a sign as nothing more would be to isolate it from the system to which it belongs. It would be to suppose that a start could be made with individual signs, and a system constructed by putting them together. On the contrary, the system as a united whole is the starting point, from which it becomes possible, by a process of analysis, to identify its constituent elements.

[158] To develop this idea, we shall look at it first from the point of view of the signification or concept (§2), then from that of the signal (§3), and finally from that of the sign as a whole (§4).

Since we cannot have direct access to concrete entities and linguistic units, we shall take words as examples. Although, as previously noted (p. [147]), words do not answer exactly to our definition of linguistic units, they will be adequate to give a rough idea, and will obviate the necessity for talking in abstract terms. So we will treat them for present purposes as specimens supposedly equivalent to the actual signs of a synchronic system. The principles which will emerge may be taken as valid for linguistic entities in general.

§2. Linguistic value: conceptual aspects

The value of a word is mainly or primarily thought of in terms of its capacity for representing a certain idea. That is indeed an aspect of linguistic value. But in that case, does its linguistic value differ from what is called its *meaning*? Are *value* and *meaning* synonymous terms? Not in our view, although it is easy to confuse them. For the subtlety of the distinction, rather than any analogy between the two terms, invites confusion.

Value, in its conceptual aspect, is doubtless part of meaning. It is by no means easy, indeed, to draw the distinction in view of this interconnexion. Yet it must be drawn, if a language is not to be reduced to a mere nomenclature (cf. p. [97]).

Let us first consider meaning, as usually understood, in the light of our previous analysis (p. [99]). As the arrows in the diagram indicate, a meaning is simply the counterpart of a sound pattern. The relevant
[159] relation is one between a sound pattern and a concept, within the limits of the word, which is for this purpose treated as a self-contained unit, existing independently.

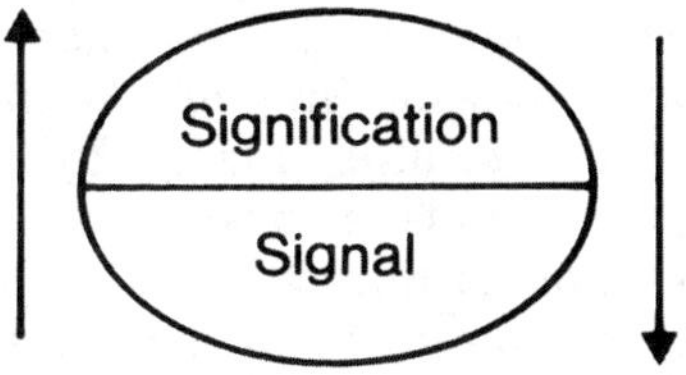

The paradoxical part of it is this. On the one hand, the concept appears to be just the counterpart of a sound pattern, as one constituent part of a linguistic sign. On the other hand, this linguistic sign itself, as the link uniting the two constituent elements, likewise has counterparts. These are the other signs in the language.

A language is a system in which all the elements fit together, and in which the value of any one element depends on the simultaneous coexistence of all the others. It may be represented as follows.

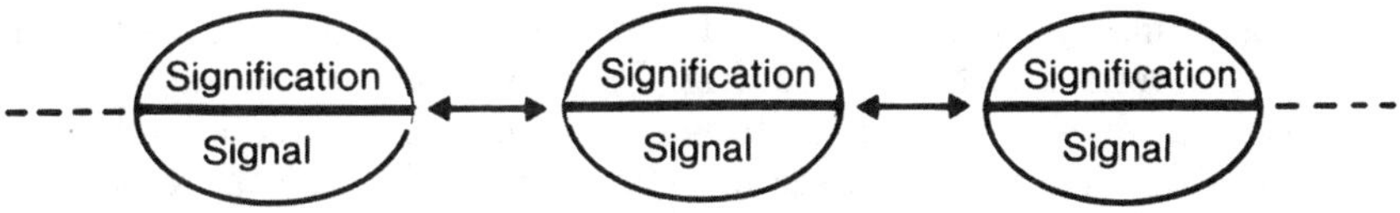

So how does it come about that value, as defined, can be equated with meaning, i.e. with the counterpart of the sound pattern? For it looks impossible to assimilate the relations represented here by horizontal arrows to those other relations represented in the previous diagram by vertical arrows. In other words, to go back to our comparison with the sheet of paper (p. [157]), it is difficult to see how the relation between different shapes cut out (call them A, B, C, D, etc.) can fail to be different from the relation between one side of any given shape and its reverse side (A/A′, B/B′, etc.).

In answering this question, it is relevant to point out that even in non-linguistic cases values of any kind seem to be governed by a paradoxical principle. Values always involve:

(1) something *dissimilar* which can be exchanged for the item whose value is under consideration, and
(2) *similar* things which can be *compared* with the item whose value is under consideration.

These two features are necessary for the existence of any value. To determine the value of a five-franc coin, for instance, what must be [160]
known is: (1) that the coin can be exchanged for a certain quantity of something different, e.g. bread, and (2) that its value can be compared with another value in the same system, e.g. that of a one-franc coin, or of a coin belonging to another system (e.g. a dollar). Similarly, a

word can be substituted for something dissimilar: an idea. At the same time, it can be compared to something of like nature: another word. Its value is therefore not determined merely by that concept or meaning for which it is a token. It must also be assessed against comparable values, by contrast with other words. The content of a word is determined in the final analysis not by what it contains but by what exists outside it. As an element in a system, the word has not only a meaning but also – above all – a value. And that is something quite different.

A few examples will show that this is indeed the case. The French word *mouton* may have the same meaning as the English word *sheep*; but it does not have the same value. There are various reasons for this, but in particular the fact that the English word for the meat of this animal, as prepared and served for a meal, is not *sheep* but *mutton*. The difference in value between *sheep* and *mouton* hinges on the fact that in English there is also another word *mutton* for the meat, whereas *mouton* in French covers both.

In a given language, all the words which express neighbouring ideas help define one another's meaning. Each of a set of synonyms like *redouter* ('to dread'), *craindre* ('to fear'), *avoir peur* ('to be afraid') has its particular value only because they stand in contrast with one another. If *redouter* ('to dread') did not exist, its content would be shared out among its competitors. On the other hand, words are also enriched by contact with other words. For instance, the new element introduced into *décrépit* (as in *un vieillard décrépit*, cf. p. [119]) is a result of the coexistence of *décrépi* (as in *un mur décrépi*). So the value of any given word is determined by what other words there are in that particular area of the vocabulary. That is true even of a word
[161] like *soleil* ('sun'). No word has a value that can be identified independently of what else there is in its vicinity. There are languages, for example, in which it is impossible to say the equivalent of *s'asseoir au soleil* ('to sit in the sun').

The above remarks apply not only to words but to all linguistic elements, including grammatical entities. The value of a French plural, for instance, does not match that of a Sanskrit plural, even though they often mean the same. This is because in Sanskrit, in addition to singular and plural, there is a third category of grammatical number. In Sanskrit the equivalents of expressions like *mes yeux* ('my eyes'), *mes oreilles* ('my ears'), *mes bras* ('my arms'), *mes jambes* ('my legs') would be neither in the singular nor in the plural but in the dual. It would thus be inaccurate to attribute the same value to the Sanskrit plural as to the French plural, because Sanskrit cannot use the plural in all the cases where it has to be used in French. Its value thus does indeed depend on what else there is in its vicinity.

If words had the job of representing concepts fixed in advance, one would be able to find exact equivalents for them as between one language and another. But this is not the case. French uses the same verb *louer* ('hire, rent') both for granting and for taking a lease, whereas German has two separate verbs, *mieten* and *vermieten*: so there is no exact correspondence between the values in question. The German verbs *schätzen* ('to value') and *urteilen* ('to judge') have meanings which answer roughly to those of the French verbs *estimer* and *juger*: but in various respects there is no one-to-one correspondence.

Flexion offers some particularly striking examples. The distinctions of tense which are so familiar to us are unknown in certain languages. The Hebrew verb does not even mark the fundamental difference between past, present and future. Proto-Germanic has no separate verb form for the future: it is sometimes said that it uses the present tense for this purpose, but that is misleading because the value of a present tense is not the same in Germanic as in those languages which have future tense forms in addition to present tense forms. The Slavic languages regularly distinguish two verbal aspects: the perfective [162] aspect represents an action as a whole, as a single point, taking no development into account, whereas the imperfective aspect represents the same action in the process of development, taking place in time. These categories are difficult for a Frenchman, because his language does not recognise them. If they were predetermined categories, there would be no such difficulty. In all these cases what we find, instead of *ideas* given in advance, are *values* emanating from a linguistic system. If we say that these values correspond to certain concepts, it must be understood that the concepts in question are purely differential. That is to say they are concepts defined not positively, in terms of their content, but negatively by contrast with other items in the same system. What characterises each most exactly is being whatever the others are not.

The full significance of our diagram representing the linguistic sign should now be apparent.

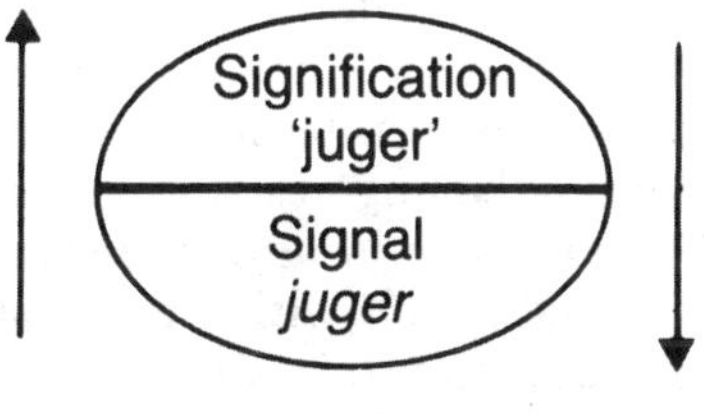

This means that in French, the concept 'juger' ('to judge') is linked to the sound pattern *juger*. So the diagram represents what the word means. But it must not be supposed that the concept in question has any kind of priority. On the contrary, that particular concept is simply a value which emerges from relations with other values of a similar kind. If those other values disappeared, this meaning too would vanish. If I say, simply, that a certain word means this or that – going no further than identifying the concept associated with that particular sound pattern – then what I am saying may in some respects be accurate, and succeed in giving a correct picture. But I fail inevitably to capture the real linguistic fact, either in its basic essentials or in its full scope.

[163] ### *§3. Linguistic value: material aspects*

Just as the conceptual part of linguistic value is determined solely by relations and differences with other signs in the language, so the same is true of its material part. The sound of a word is not in itself important, but the phonetic contrasts which allow us to distinguish that word from any other. That is what carries the meaning.

This may seem surprising. But how could it possibly be otherwise? No particular configuration of sound is more aptly suited to express a given message than any other such configuration. So it is clearly the case – indeed, it must be the case – that no linguistic item can ever be based, ultimately, upon anything other than its non-coincidence with the rest. Here the terms *arbitrary* and *differential* designate two correlative properties.

The processes of linguistic change amply demonstrate this correlation. It is precisely because two signs *a* and *b* are never grasped as such by our linguistic consciousness, but only the difference between *a* and *b*, that each sign remains free to change in accordance with laws quite unconnected with their signifying function. The Czech genitive plural *žen* (cf. p. [123]) has no positive case maker. Yet the contrast *žena* vs. *žen* works just as well as *žena* vs. *zenъ*, which preceded it. The reason is that all that matters is the difference between the signs: *žena* functions effectively simply because it is different.

Another example which brings out even more clearly the systematic nature of such contrasts is the following. In Greek *éphēn* is an imperfect and *éstēn* an aorist, even though their morphological format-
[164] ion is identical. The former belongs to the present indicative system of *phēmi* ('I say'), whereas there is no present form **stēmi*. It is the relation between *phēmi* and *éphēn* which corresponds to the relation between present and imperfect (cf. *deíknūmi* – *edeíknūn*). These signs thus function not according to their intrinsic value but in virtue of their relative position.

In any case, it is impossible that sound, as a material element, should in itself be part of the language. Sound is merely something ancillary, a material the language uses. All conventional values have the characteristic of being distinct from the tangible element which serves as their vehicle. It is not the metal in a coin which determines its value. A crown piece nominally worth five francs contains only half that sum in silver. Its value varies somewhat according to the effigy it bears. It is worth rather more or rather less on different sides of a political frontier. Considerations of the same order are even more pertinent to linguistic signals. Linguistic signals are not in essence phonetic. They are not physical in any way. They are constituted solely by differences which distinguish one such sound pattern from another.

This fundamental principle applies to every material element used by a language, even the basic speech sounds. Each language constructs its words out of some fixed number of phonetic units, each one clearly distinct from the others. What characterises those units is not, as might be thought, the specific positive properties of each; but simply the fact that they cannot be mistaken for one another. Speech sounds are first and foremost entities which are contrastive, relative and negative.[1]

What proves this is the latitude speakers are allowed in pronunciation, provided they distinguish one sound from another. In French, for instance, the fact that *r* is usually pronounced as a uvular consonant does not prevent many speakers from pronouncing it as an apical trill. It makes no difference to the French language, which requires [165] only that *r* should be distinct from other consonants. There is no necessity that it be pronounced always in exactly the same way. I can even pronounce a French *r* like the German *ch* in *Bach*, *doch*, etc.; whereas I could not in German substitute *r* for *ch* because German, unlike French, distinguishes between *r* and *ch*. Likewise in Russian, there is no latitude of pronounciation for *t* in the direction of *t'* (i.e. palatalised *t*), because the result would be to confuse two sounds distinguished by the language (cf. *govorit'*, 'to speak' vs. *govorit* 'he speaks'). But a Russian is more at liberty to aspirate a *t*, because *th* is not a separate sound in the Russian system.

An identical state of affairs is to be found in that other system of signs, writing. Writing offers a useful comparison, which throws light upon the whole question. We find that:

1. The signs used in writing are arbitrary. The letter *t*, for instance, has no connexion with the sound it denotes.

[1] When this passage is compared with the detailed account of speech sounds given earlier (p. [63] ff.), it is evident that the published text of the *Cours* lacks any careful and consistently drawn distinction between phonetic and phonological units. The speech sounds discussed on p. [63] ff. are clearly language-neutral elements, characterised in physiological terms; whereas the speech sounds discussed here are defined contrastively in the context of particular languages. Cf. p. [180] fn. (Translator's note)

2. The values of the letters are purely negative and differential. So the same individual may write *t* in such variant forms as:

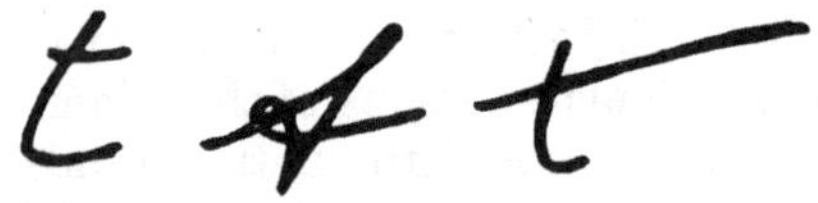

The one essential thing is that his *t* should be distinct from his *l*, his *d*, etc.

3. Values in writing are solely based on contrasts within a fixed system, having a determinate number of letters. This feature, although not the same as 2 above, is closely connected with it; for both 2 and 3 follow from 1. Since the written sign is arbitrary, its form is of little importance; or rather, is of importance only within certain limits imposed by the system.

[166] 4. The actual mode of inscription is irrelevant, because it does not affect the system. (This also follows from 1.) Whether I write in black or white, in incised characters or in relief, with a pen or a chisel – none of that is of any importance for the meaning.

§4. *The sign as a whole*

Everything we have said so far comes down to this. *In the language itself, there are only differences.* Even more important than that is the fact that, although in general a difference presupposes positive terms between which the difference holds, in a language there are only differences, *and no positive terms.* Whether we take the signification or the signal, the language includes neither ideas nor sounds existing prior to the linguistic system, but only conceptual and phonetic differences arising out of that system. In a sign, what matters more than any idea or sound associated with it is what other signs surround it. The proof of this lies in the fact that the value of a sign may change without affecting either meaning or sound, simply because some neighbouring sign has undergone a change (cf. p. [160]).

But to say that in a language everything is negative holds only for signification and signal considered separately. The moment we consider the sign as a whole, we encounter something which is positive in its own domain. A linguistic system is a series of phonetic differences matched with a series of conceptual differences. But this matching of a certain number of auditory signals and a similar number of items carved out from the mass of thought gives rise to a system of values. It is this system which provides the operative bond between phonic and mental elements within each sign. Although signification and signal are each, in isolation, purely differential and negative,

their combination is a fact of a positive nature. It is, indeed, the only order of facts linguistic structure comprises. For the essential function [167]
of a language as an institution is precisely to maintain these series of differences in parallel.

Certain diachronic developments are most revealing in this respect. We find countless cases where a change in the signal brings with it a change in the idea expressed. Time and again we observe that in principle the number of ideas distinguished matches the number of distinct signals available. When two words merge through phonetic change (e.g. *décrépit* from Latin *decrepitus*, and *décrépi* from Latin *crispus*, cf. p. [119]), the ideas tend to merge as well, however dissimilar they may be. What happens when one word gives birth to two alternative pronunciations (e.g. French *chaise* and *chaire*, both from Latin *cathedra*)? Inevitably the phonetic difference which has emerged will tend to acquire significance, although perhaps not always immediately or always successfully. Conversely, any difference in ideas distinguished by the mind will seek expression in different linguistic signals; whereas two ideas the mind no longer differentiates will tend to find expression in the same signal.

The moment we compare one sign with another as positive combinations, the term *difference* should be dropped. It is no longer appropriate. It is a term which is suitable only for comparisons between sound patterns (e.g. *père* vs. *mère*), or between ideas (e.g. 'father' vs. 'mother'). Two signs, each comprising a signification and a signal, are not different from each other, but only distinct. They are simply in *opposition* to each other. The entire mechanism of language[1], which we shall consider below, is based on oppositions of this kind and upon the phonetic and conceptual differences they involve.

What is true of values is also true of units (cf. p. [154]). A unit is a segment of a spoken sequence which corresponds to a certain concept. Both are purely differential in nature.

Applied to units, the principle of differentiation may be formulated [168]
as follows. *The characteristics of the unit merge with the unit itself.* In a language, as in every other semiological system, what distinguishes a sign is what constitutes it, nothing more. Difference is what makes characteristics, just as it makes values and units.

Another consequence, and a rather surprising one, of the same principle is this. What is usually called a 'grammatical fact' corresponds in the final analysis to our definition of a unit. For there is always an opposition of terms involved. What is special is that the opposition happens to be particularly important, e.g. German plural formations of the type *Nacht* vs. *Nächte* (cf. p. [120] ff.). Each of the

[1] The term used in the text here is *langage*, but the chapter referred to is entitled 'Mécanisme de la langue'. (Translator's note)

items which contrast grammatically (the singular form without the umlaut and without the final *-e*, contrasting with a plural form having both) is itself the product of the operation of oppositions within the system. In isolation, *Nacht* and *Nächte* are nothing: the opposition between them is everything. In other words, one might express the relation *Nacht* vs. *Nächte* by an algebraic formula *a/b*, where *a* and *b* are not simple terms, but each represents a complex of relations. The language is, so to speak, an algebra which has only complex terms. Some of the oppositions it includes are more important than others. But 'units' and 'grammatical facts' are only different names for different aspects of the same general fact: the operation of linguistic oppositions. So much so that it would be perfectly possible to tackle the problem of units by beginning with grammatical facts. Starting from an opposition like *Nacht* vs. *Nächte*, one would inquire what are the units involved. Are they just two words? Or are they whole series of similar words? Or are they just *a* and *ä*? Or are they all singulars and all plurals?

Units and grammatical facts would not merge in this way if a linguistic sign was constituted by anything apart from differences.
[169] But linguistic structure being what it is, however one approaches it, nothing is simple. Always and everywhere one finds this same complex equilibrium of terms holding one another in mutual juxtaposition. In other words, *the language itself is a form, not a substance* (cf. p. [157]). The importance of this truth cannot be overemphasised. For all our mistakes of terminology, all our incorrect ways of designating things belonging to the language originate in our unwittingly supposing that we are dealing with a substance when we deal with linguistic phenomena.

CHAPTER V [170]

Syntagmatic Relations and Associative Relations

§1. *Definitions*

In a linguistic state, then, everything depends on relations. How do they work?

The relations and differences between linguistic items fall into two quite distinct kinds, each giving rise to a separate order of values. The opposition between these two orders brings out the specific character of each. They correspond to two different forms of mental activity, both indispensable to the workings of a language.

Words as used in discourse, strung together one after another, enter into relations based on the linear character of languages (cf. p. [103]). Linearity precludes the possibility of uttering two words simultaneously. They must be arranged consecutively in spoken sequence. Combinations based on sequentiality may be called *syntagmas*.[1] The syntagma invariably comprises two or more consecutive units: for example, *re-lire* ('re-read'), *contre tous* ('against all'), *la vie humaine* ('the life of man'), *Dieu est bon* ('God is good'), *s'il fait beau temps, nous sortirons* ('if it's fine, we'll go out'). In its place in a syntagma, any [171]
unit acquires its value simply in opposition to what precedes, or to what follows, or to both.

Outside the context of discourse, words having something in common are associated together in the memory. In this way they form groups, the members of which may be related in various ways. For instance, the word *enseignement* ('teaching') will automatically evoke a host of other words: *enseigner* ('to teach'), *renseigner* ('to inform'), etc., or *armement* ('armament'), *changement* ('change'), etc., or *édu-*

[1] Needless to say, the study of *syntagmas* is not to be equated with *syntax*. The latter is only part of the former, as will be seen (cf. p. [185]ff.). (Editorial note)

cation ('education'), *apprentissage* ('apprenticeship'). All these words have something or other linking them.

This kind of connexion between words is of quite a different order. It is not based on linear sequence. It is a connexion in the brain. Such connexions are part of that accumulated store which is the form the language takes in an individual's brain. We shall call these *associative relations*.

Syntagmatic relations hold *in praesentia*. They hold between two or more terms co-present in a sequence. Associative relations, on the contrary, hold *in absentia*. They hold between terms constituting a mnemonic group.

Considered from these two points of view, a linguistic unit may be compared to a single part of a building, e.g. a column. A column is related in a certain way to the architrave it supports. This disposition, involving two units co-present in space, is comparable to a syntagmatic relation. On the other hand, if the column is Doric, it will evoke mental comparison with the other architectural orders (Ionic, Corinthian, etc.), which are not in this instance spatially co-present. This relation is associative.

Each of these two orders of relationship calls for certain special comments.

[172] *§2. Syntagmatic relations*

The examples given above (p. [170]) already make it clear that the notion of a syntagma applies not only to words, but to groups of words, and to complex units of every size and kind (compound words, derivative forms, phrases, sentences).

It is not sufficient to consider merely the relation between the parts of a syntagma, e.g. between *contre* ('against') and *tous* ('all') in *contre tous* ('against all'), or between *contre* ('over') and *maître* ('master') in *contremaître* ('overseer'). Account must also be taken of the relation between the whole and the parts, e.g. between *contre tous* and *contre*, *contre tous* and *tous*, *contremaître* and *contre*, *contremaître* and *maître*.

An objection might be raised at this point. The most typical kind of syntagma is the sentence. But the sentence belongs to speech, not to the language (cf. p. [30]). So does it not follow that the syntagma is a phenomenon of speech too? Not in our view. The characteristic of speech is freedom of combination: so the first question to ask is whether all syntagmas are equally free.

There are, in the first place, a large number of expressions belonging to the language: these are ready-made phrases, absolutely invariable in usage, in which it may even require reflection to distinguish the constituent parts: e.g. *à quoi bon?* ('what's the use?'), *allons donc!* ('come along!'). The same is true, although not to the same extent, for expressions like *prendre la mouche* ('to take offence'), *forcer la main à quelqu'un* ('to force someone's hand'), *rompre une lance* ('to break a lance'), *avoir mal à la tête* ('to have a headache'), *à force de* ('by dint of'), *que vous en semble?* ('what do you think of it?') *pas n'est besoin de* . . . ('no need to . . .'), etc. These are idiomatic expressions involving oddities of meaning or syntax. These oddities are not improvised, but handed down by tradition. In this connexion one might also cite morphological oddities which, although perfectly analysable, represent irregularities maintained solely by prevalence of usage: e.g. *difficulté* [173] ('difficulty') as compared with *facilité* ('ease') and *facile* ('easy'); *mourrai* ('I will die'), *mourir* ('to die'), as compared with *dormirai* ('I will sleep'), *dormir* ('to sleep'), and *finirai* ('I will finish'), *finir* ('to finish').[1]

But that is not all. To the language, and not to speech, must be attributed all types of syntagmas constructed on regular patterns. Since there is nothing abstract in linguistic structure, such types will not exist unless sufficiently numerous examples do indeed occur. When a new word such as *indécorable* ('undecoratable') crops up in speech (cf. p. [228] ff.), it presupposes an already existing type, and the type in question would not exist were it not for our recollection of a sufficient number of similar words already in the language, e.g. *impardonnable* ('unpardonable'), *intolérable* ('intolerable'), *infatigable* ('indefatigable'), etc. Exactly the same holds for sentences and groups of words based upon regular models. Combinations like *la terre tourne* ('the earth rotates'), *que vous dit-il?* ('what does he say to you?'), etc. correspond to general combinatory types, which in turn are based in the language on specific examples heard and remembered.

Where syntagmas are concerned, however, one must recognise the fact that there is no clear boundary separating the language, as confirmed by communal usage, from speech, marked by freedom of the individual. In many cases it is difficult to assign a combination of units to one or the other. Many combinations are the product of both, in proportions which cannot be accurately measured.

§3. *Associative relations*

Groups formed by mental association do not include only items sharing something in common. For the mind also grasps the nature of the relations involved in each case, and thus creates as many associative

[1] The 'regular' forms ought presumably to be **difficilité* and **mourirai*. (Translator's note)

series as there are different relations. In *enseignement* ('teaching'), *enseigner* ('to teach'), *enseignons* ('(we) teach'), etc., there is a common
[174] element in all the terms, i.e. the stem *enseign-* ('teach-'). But the word *enseignement* also belongs to another series based upon a different common element, the suffix *-ment*: e.g. *enseignement* ('teaching'), *armement*, ('armament'), *changement* ('change'), etc. The association may also be based just on similarity of significations, as in *enseignement* ('teaching'), *instruction* ('instruction'), *apprentissage* ('apprenticeship'), *éducation* ('education'), etc. Similarly, it may be based just on similarity of sound patterns, e.g. the final syllables of *enseignement* ('teaching') and *justement* ('precisely').[1] So sometimes there is a double associative link based on form and meaning, but in other cases just one associative link based on form or meaning alone. Any word can evoke in the mind whatever is capable of being associated with it in some way or other.

While a syntagma brings in straight away the idea of a fixed sequence, with a specific number of elements, an associative group has no particular number of items in it; nor do they occur in any particular order. In a series like *désir-eux* ('desirous'), *chaleur-eux* ('warm'), *peur-eux* ('fearful'), etc. it is impossible to say in advance how many words the memory will suggest, or in what order. Any given term acts as the centre of a constellation, from which connected terms radiate *ad infinitum*.

Of these two characteristics found in associative series – indeterminate order and indefinite number – only the former is constant. The
[175] latter may not be found in certain cases. This is so with a very common type of associative group, flexional paradigms. In a Latin series like *dominus*, *dominī*, *dominō*, etc. we have an associative group based on a common element: the noun stem *domin-*. But the series is not open-ended, like *enseignement*, *changement*, etc., since the number of case forms is limited. Their sequence, however, is not fixed. It is purely arbitrary that grammarians list them in one order rather than another. As far as language-users are concerned, the nominative is not

[1] This case is rare and may be treated as abnormal. For the mind naturally discards all associations likely to impede understanding and discourse. Nonetheless, the existence of such associative groups is proved by the category of feeble puns based upon the ridiculous confusions which may result from homonymy pure and simple. E.g. *Les musiciens produisent les sons et les grainetiers les vendent* ('Musicians produce [sounds/bran], which seedsmen sell' – *son* meaning both 'sound' and also 'bran'). Such cases must be distinguished from those in which word assoication, although fortuitous, is backed by a certain connexion of ideas: e.g. French *ergot* ('spur, spike') and *ergoter* ('to quibble'), or German *blau* ('blue') and *durchbläuen* ('to beat, thrash'). What is involved here is a new interpretation of one or other of the terms. These are cases of popular etymology (cf. p. [238]). Although of interest in the study of semantic change, from a synchronic viewpoint they merely fall into the category of *enseigner*, *enseignement*, etc. mentioned above. (Editorial note)

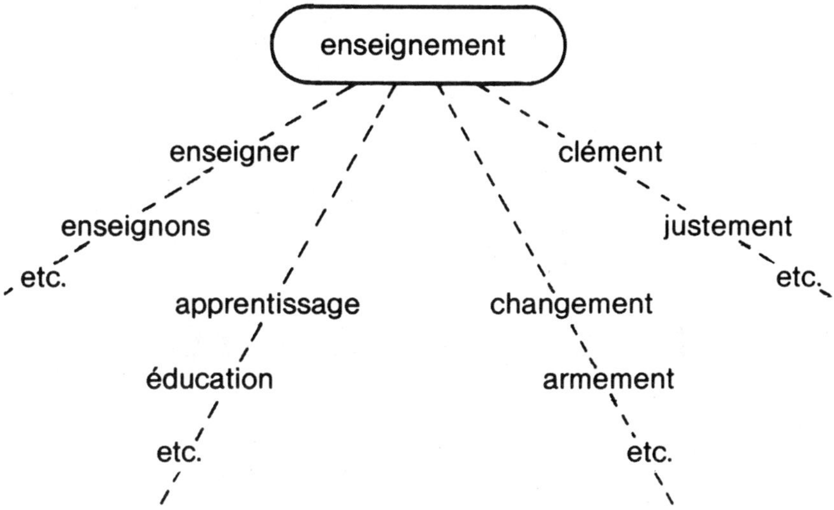

in any sense the 'first' case in the declension: the forms may be thought of in any variety of orders, depending on circumstances.

[176]

CHAPTER VI

The Language Mechanism

§1. Syntagmatic interdependences

The whole set of phonetic and conceptual differences which constitute a language are thus the product of two kinds of comparison, associative and syntagmatic. Groups of both kinds are in large measure established by the language. This set of habitual relations is what constitutes linguistic structure and determines how the language functions.

The first thing that strikes us in this organisation are the *syntagmatic interdependences*. Almost all linguistic units depend either on what precedes or follows in the spoken sequence, or else on the successive parts of which they are themselves composed.

This is amply demonstrated by word formation. A unit like *désireux* ('desirous') divides into two smaller units: *désir-eux* ('desir-ous'). But these two are not independent units merely added together: *désir+eux*. They form a product, a combination of interdependent elements, their value deriving solely from their mutual contributions within a higher unit, which we may represent as: *désir×eux*. For the suffix *-eux*, in isolation, never occurs. Its place in the language depends on the existence of a series of terms in use, such as *chaleur-eux*, *chanc-eux*, etc. Nor is the stem *désir-* autonomous. It exists only when [177] combined with a suffix. In *roulis* ('rolling') the element *roul-* ('roll-') is nothing without the suffix added to it. The whole depends on the parts, and the parts depend on the whole. That is why the syntagmatic relation between part and whole is just as important as the syntagmatic relation between one part and another.

This is a general principle, which can be seen to operate in all the types of syntagma previously listed (p. [172]). There are always larger units, composed of smaller units, with a relation of interdependence holding between both.

It is true that there are independent linguistic units. These have no syntagmatic relations, either between their parts or with other units. Words like *oui* ('yes'), *non* ('no'), *merci* ('thank you'), which are equivalent to whole sentences, provide good examples. But this phenomenon, which is in any case rare, does not undermine the general principle. Normally we do not express ourselves by using single linguistic signs, but groups of signs, organised in complexes which themselves are signs. In linguistic structure everything in the end comes down to differences, and also to groups. This mechanism, which involves interrelations of successive terms, is like the functioning of a machine in which the components all act upon one other, even though they are arranged in one dimension only.

§2. *Simultaneous functioning of both types of group*

Syntagmatic groups formed in this way are linked by interdependence, each contributing to all. Linear ordering in space helps to create associative connexions, and these in turn play an essential part in syntagmatic analysis.

Take the compound *dé-faire* ('un-do'). We can represent it along a [178]
horizontal strip corresponding to the spoken sequence:

But at the same time, along another axis, there are subconsciously present one or more associative series, each based on a common element. For example:

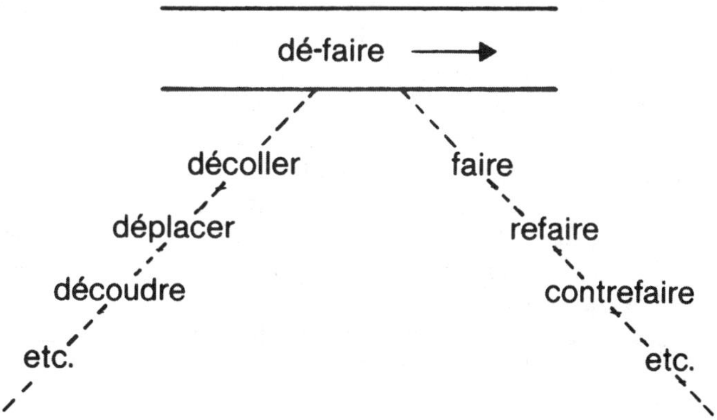

Similarly, as a syntagma the Latin word *quadruplex* ('four-fold') is supported by two associative series:

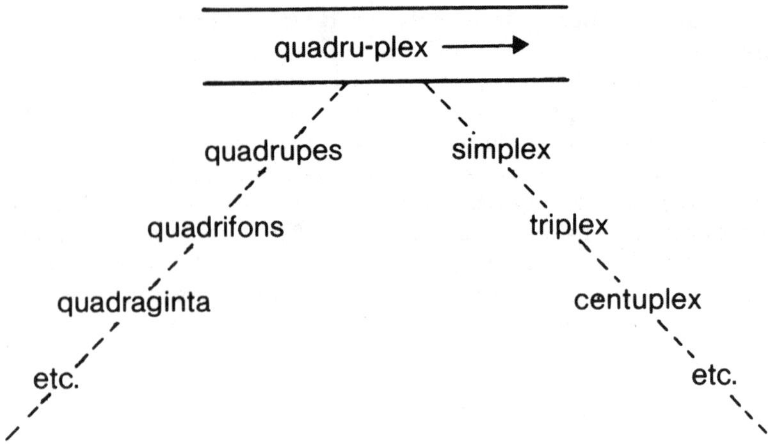

It is insofar as *défaire* and *quadruplex* are surrounded by these other forms that they are themselves analysable into smaller units – that they are syntagmas, in other words. *Défaire* would become unanalysable if the other words containing *dé-* or *faire* disappeared from the
[179] language. *Défaire* would then be one simple unit, with no parts to contrast internally.

We can now see how this dual system works in discourse.

Our memory holds in store all the various complex types of syntagma, of every kind and length. When a syntagma is brought into use, we call upon associative groups in order to make our choice. So when someone says *marchons!* ('let's march!'), he thinks unconsciously of various associative groups, at whose common intersection appears the syntagma *marchons!* This syntagma belongs to one series which includes the singular imperative *marche!* ('march!') and the 2nd person plural imperative *marchez!* ('march!'), and *marchons!* stands in opposition to both as a form selected from this group. At the same time, it belongs to another series which includes *montons!* ('let's go up!'), *mangeons!* ('let's eat!') etc., and represents a selection from this group as well. In each series, it is known which factor to vary in order to obtain the differentiation appropriate to the unit sought. If the idea to be expressed is a different one, other oppositions will be brought into play to produce a different value, thus yielding some other form, such as *marchez!* or *montons!*

It is thus an oversimplification to say, looking at the matter positively, that *marchons!* is selected because it means what the speaker intends to express. In reality, the idea evokes not just one form but a whole latent system, through which the oppositions involved in the constitution of that sign are made available. The sign by itself would have no meaning of its own. If the forms *marche!* and *marchez!* were to disappear from the language, leaving *marchons!* in isolation, certain oppositions would automatically collapse and *ipso facto* the value of *marchons!* would be different.

This principle applies to syntagmas and sentences of all types, even the most complex. In uttering the words *que vous dit-il?* ('what does he say to you?'), we vary one element in a latent syntagmatic type of which other examples would be *que te dit-il?*, *que nous dit-il?* etc. ('what does he say to you/us/them . . .?' etc.). This is the process in- [180]
volved in our selection of the pronoun *vous* in *que vous dit-il?*. In this process, which involves eliminating mentally everything which does not lead to the desired differentiation at the point required, associative groupings and syntagmatic types are both involved.

On the other hand, this process of determination and choice governs even the smallest units, right down to phonetic elements, when they have a value. We are thinking here not only of cases like the feminine adjective *pətit* (*petite* 'little') contrasting with the masculine *pəti* (written *petit*), or the Latin genitive singular *dominī* ('of a master') contrasting with the dative singular *dominō* ('to a master'), where it happens to be the case that the difference depends on just one sound, but also of the more typical and subtle way in which speech sounds themselves play their part in the system comprising a given linguistic state. If, for example, in Greek *m,p,t,* etc. never occur at the end of a word, that means that their presence or absence in a certain position counts as a factor in word structure and sentence structure. In all cases of this kind, the individual sound in question, as with all other units, will be selected on the basis of a dual contrast in the mind. If we take a hypothetical sequence like *anma*, the sound *m* is in syntagmatic opposition with the preceding and following sounds, and also in associative opposition with all the sounds that the mind can suggest[1], as shown:

a n m a
v
d

[1] Cf. p. [164] fn. This formulation fails to make it clear exactly what status is to be assigned to the 'sounds' discussed here. The phrase 'all the sounds the mind can suggest' seems to allow, for example, the possibility of imagining an English word *srim*, even though the initial group *sr-* never in fact occurs in English. On the other hand, if the possibilities of contrast are limited to combinations actually occurring in the language, the conclusion would seem to be that the *s* in English *slip* cannot be the same 'sound' as the *s* in *lisp*, since the syntagmatic and associative relations in the two cases are different. (Translator's note)

§3. Absolute arbitrariness and relative arbitrariness

The mechanism of a language can be looked at in another way which is of particular significance.

The fundamental principle of the arbitrary nature of the linguistic sign does not prevent us from distinguishing in any language between what is intrinsically arbitrary – that is, unmotivated – and what is [181] only relatively arbitrary. Not all signs are absolutely arbitrary. In some cases, there are factors which allow us to recognise different degrees of arbitrariness, although never to discard the notion entirely. *The sign may be motivated to a certain extent.*

The French word *vingt* ('twenty') is unmotivated, whereas *dix-neuf* ('nineteen') is not unmotivated to the same extent. For *dix-neuf* evokes the words of which it is composed, *dix* ('ten') and *neuf* ('nine'), and those of the same numerical series: *dix* ('ten'), *neuf* ('nine'), *vingt-neuf* ('twenty-nine'), *dix-huit* ('eighteen'), *soixante-dix* ('seventy'), etc. Taken individually, *dix* and *neuf* are on the same footing as *vingt*, but *dix-neuf* is an example of relative motivation. The same is true of *poirier* ('pear-tree'), which evokes the simple form *poire* ('pear'), and has a suffix *-ier* which recalls that of *cerisier* ('cherry-tree'), *pommier* ('apple-tree'), etc. (But words like *frêne* ('ash-tree') and *chêne* ('oak') offer no parallel.) Again, a word like *berger* ('shepherd') is completely unmotivated, whereas *vacher* ('cowman') is relatively motivated.[1] Similar pairs are: *geôle* ('jail') and *cachot* ('lock-up'), *hache* ('axe') and *couperet* ('chopper'), *concierge* ('porter') and *portier* ('doorman'), *jadis* ('of yore') and *autrefois* ('formerly'), *souvent* ('often') and *fréquemment* ('frequently'), *aveugle* ('blind') and *boiteux* ('limping'), *sourd* ('deaf') and *bossu* ('hunch-backed'), *second* ('second') and *deuxième* ('2nd'), German *Laub* ('foliage') and French *feuillage* ('leafage'), French *métier* ('trade') and German *Handwerk* ('handicraft'). The English plural *ships* adds an *-s*, recalling a whole series like *flags, birds, books*, etc.; whereas the plurals *men* and *sheep* recall no parallel cases. In Greek *dṓsō* ('I will give') expresses the idea of futurity by a sign which links it associatively with other future tense forms like *lū́sō, stḗsō, túpsō*, etc.; whereas the future form *eîmi* ('I will go') is completely isolated.

The factors involved in the motivation of these various cases cannot be examined here. But motivation is always more marked if the syntagmatic analysis is more straightforward and the meaning of the constituent units more obvious. Although some formative elements are transparent enough – e.g. the suffix *-ier* in *poirier* ('pear-tree'), *cerisier* ('cherry-tree'), *pommier* ('apple-tree'), etc. – others are of uncertain meaning, or altogether obscure. What, for instance, is the

[1] Because of *vache* ('cow'). In English, however, the connexions between the forms *shepherd – sheep* and *cowman – cow* make both *shepherd* and *cowman* motivated words. (Translator's note)

meaning, if any, of the suffix *-ot* in *cachot* ('lock-up, nick')? Is there in a series of words like *coutelas* ('cutlas'), *fatras* ('jumble'), *plâtras* ('debris'), *canevas* ('canvas'), an ending *-as* that one can vaguely discern, but [182] without being able to say what it means? Not only are the elements of a motivated sign themselves arbitrary (as are *dix* 'ten', and *neuf* 'nine', in *dix-neuf* 'nineteen'), but the value of the term as a whole is never equal to the sum of the values of its parts. *Poir* × *ier* is not just *poir* + *ier* (cf. p. [176]).

The phenomenon we are considering here finds its explanation in the principles mentioned in the previous section (§2). Relative motivation implies (i) the analysis of the term in question, and hence a syntagmatic relation, and (ii) appeal to one or more other terms, and hence an associative relation. The mechanism is none other than that by which any term whatsoever lends itself to the expression of an idea. So far we have looked upon units as values, as elements of a system, and considered principally the oppositions between them. But now we are taking stock of their interdependences, both associative and syntagmatic, which combine to set a limit to arbitrariness. *Dix-neuf* ('nineteen') is interdependent associatively with *dix-huit* ('eighteen'), *soixante-dix* ('seventy'), etc., and syntagmatically with its constituent elements *dix* ('ten') and *neuf* ('nine') (cf. p. [177]). This dual relationship accounts for part of the value of the sign *dix-neuf*.

Everything having to do with languages as systems needs to be approached, we are convinced, with a view to examining the limitations of arbitrariness. It is an approach which linguists have neglected. But it offers the best possible basis for linguistic studies. For the entire linguistic system is founded upon the irrational principle that the sign is arbitrary. Applied without restriction, this principle would lead to utter chaos. But the mind succeeds in introducing a principle of order and regularity into certain areas of the mass of signs. That is the role of relative motivation. If languages had a mechanism which were entirely rational, that mechanism could be studied in its own right. But it provides only a partial correction to a [183] system which is chaotic by nature. Hence we must adopt the point of view demanded by the nature of linguistic structure itself, and study this mechanism as a way of imposing a limitation upon what is arbitrary.

There exists no language in which nothing at all is motivated. Even to conceive of such a language is an impossibility by definition. Between the two extremes – minimum of organisation and minimum of arbitrariness – all possible varieties are found. Languages always exhibit features of both kinds – intrinsically arbitrary and relatively motivated – but in very varying proportions. This is an important characteristic, which may have to be taken into account in classifying languages.

In one sense – this must not be pressed too far, but it brings out one aspect of the contrast – a distinction could be drawn between *lexicological* languages, in which absence of motivation reaches a maximum, and *grammatical* languages, in which it falls to a minimum. This is not to imply that 'lexical' and 'arbitary' are always synonymous, or 'grammar' and 'relative motivation' either. But they go together in principle. There are, one might say, two opposite poles towards which the whole system is drawn, or two contrary currents sweeping through it. On the one hand there is a tendency to use lexicological means, which favours the unmotivated sign. On the other hand there is a tendency to use grammatical means, which favours regular construction.

English, for example, can be seen to favour lack of motivation more markedly than German. The ultra-lexicological extreme is represented by Chinese, whereas Proto-Indo-European and Sanskrit are examples of the ultra-grammatical. Within the same language, a whole evolutionary trend may be marked by constant movement from motivation to arbitrariness, and vice versa. The result of this to-and-fro is often
[184] a noticeable shift in the proportions of the two categories of sign. French, as compared with Latin, is marked among other things by a huge increase in arbitrariness. Whereas Latin *inimīcus* ('enemy') is motivated by its relations with *in-* ('un-') and *amīcus* ('friend'), the French word *ennemi* ('enemy') lacks motivation entirely. *Ennemi* has relapsed into absolute arbitrariness, and this is the basic condition of the linguistic sign. This shift can be seen in hundreds of French examples: Latin *constāre* 'to cost' (*stāre* 'to stand') vs. French *coûter* ('to cost'), Latin *fabrica* 'workshop' (*faber* 'workman') vs. French *forge* ('forge'), Latin *magister* 'master' (*magis* 'more') vs. French *maître* ('master'), Latin *berbīcārius* 'shepherd' (*berbīx* 'sheep') vs. French *berger* ('shepherd'), etc. These changes have given French a very distinctive character.

CHAPTER VII [185]

Grammar and Its Subdivisions

§1. Definitions. Traditional divisions

Static linguistics, or the description of a linguistic state, may be termed *grammar* in that very precise sense, by no means uncommon, found in expressions like 'the grammar of chess', 'the grammar of the stock market', etc. These are all cases of complex systems, involving coexisting values.

Grammar studies the language as a system of means of expression. 'Grammatical' implies 'synchronic' and 'meaningful'. Since no linguistic system can straddle several eras simultaneously, as far as we are concerned there is no such thing as 'historical grammar'. What is called 'historical grammar' is in reality simply diachronic linguistics.

Our definition is not in accord with the narrower one usually given. Grammar is conventionally restricted to *morphology* and *syntax* combined; and *lexicology* or the science of words is excluded.

But in the first place, do these traditional divisions correspond to linguistic reality? Are they in harmony with the principles we have already indicated?

Morphology deals with the various classes of words (verbs, nouns, adjectives, pronouns, etc.) and with the different forms of flexion (conjugations, declensions). To distinguish this from syntax, it is claimed [186]
that syntax examines the functions associated with linguistic units, while morphology is merely concerned with their forms. Thus morphology simply tells us that the genitive of the Greek word *phúlax* ('guardian') is *phúlakos*. Syntax informs us about the use of these two forms.

But this distinction is illusory. The series of forms of the noun *phúlax* do not constitute a flexional paradigm unless one compares the functions these different forms have. Equally, their functions have nothing to do with morphology unless each answers to a particular phonetic signal. A declension is neither just a list of forms nor just a series of logical abstractions, but a combination of both (cf. p. [144]). Forms and functions are interdependent. It is difficult if not impossible to separate them. Linguistically, morphology has no real, independent object of study: it cannot constitute a discipline distinct from syntax.

On the other hand, is it reasonable to exclude lexicology from grammar? At first sight, words as listed in the dictionary do not seem to lend themselves to grammatical analysis. For grammar is usually limited to studying relations between units. But it soon becomes apparent that many of these relations may be expressed by words just as well as by grammatical devices. In Latin, for example, *fīō* ('I become') and *faciō* ('I make') contrast in the same way as the passive form *dīcor* ('I am said') with its active *dīcō* ('I say'). In Russian the distinction between the perfective and imperfective is expressed grammatically in the case of 'to ask' (*sprosít'* vs. *sprášivat'*), but lexicologically in the case of 'to say' (*skazát'* vs. *govorít'*). Prepositions are usually treated under grammar; nonetheless the prepositional phrase *en considération de* ('in consideration of') is essentially lexicological, since it contains the word *considération* ('consideration') used in its proper sense. If we compare the Greek *peíthō* vs. *peíthomai* with the
[187] French *je persuade* vs. *j'obéis*, we see that the same contrast ('I persuade' vs. 'I obey') is expressed grammatically in the first case and lexicologically in the second. Many relations expressed in certain languages by cases or prepositions are expressed in other languages by compounds, which are closer to words proper, e.g. French *royaume des cieux* ('kingdom of heaven') vs. German *Himmelreich* ('heaven-kingdom'), or by derivational forms, e.g. French *moulin à vent* ('windmill') vs. Polish *wiatr-ak*, or by single words, e.g. French *bois de chauffage* ('firewood', lit. 'wood for heating') vs. Russian *drová*, or French *bois de construction* ('wood for building') vs. Russian *lês*. In the same language, we often find single words and compound expressions as alternatives, e.g. French *considérer* ('consider') and *prendre en considération* ('take into consideration'), *se venger de* ('revenge oneself on') and *tirer vengeance de* ('wreak vengeance upon').

Thus from a functional point of view, lexicological and syntactic devices overlap. Moreover, any word which is not a single, unanalysable unit is essentially no different from a phrase, syntactically speaking. For the arrangement of smaller constituent units obeys the same basic principles as govern the formation of groups of words.

To summarise, the traditional divisions of grammar may have some practical utility, but they do not correspond to natural distinctions and are not unified by any logical principle. Grammar needs a different basis, and a better one.

§2. Rational divisions

The interpenetration of morphology, syntax and lexicology is explained by the fact that all synchronic features are ultimately of the same kind. No boundary between them can be laid down in advance. Only the distinction earlier drawn between syntagmatic relations and associative relations suggests a classification which is indispensable, and which fulfils the requirements for any grammatical systematisation.

Everything in a given linguistic state should be explicable by refer- [188]
ence to a theory of syntagmas and a theory of associations. Certain parts of traditional grammar immediately appear to fall without difficulty under one or the other. Flexion is clearly a typical case of association between forms in speakers' minds. Syntax, on the other hand, as generally understood nowadays – the theory of word sequences – falls under syntagmatics, since word sequences invariably involve at least two units spatially ordered in some way. All syntagmatic facts are not to be classed as syntax, but all syntactic facts belong to syntagmatics.

Any point of grammar will illustrate how important it is to examine each question from both points of view. The concept of a word raises two separate problems, depending on whether one considers the word associatively or syntagmatically. The French adjective *grand* ('big') takes two forms in the syntagma, one before a consonant (*grã garsõ* 'big boy') and another before a vowel (*grãt ãfã* 'big child'). It also takes two forms associatively, a masculine *grã* (written *grand*) and a feminine *grãd* (written *grande*).

The aim should be to assign every fact to its proper domain, either syntagmatic or associative, and thus organize the whole subject-matter of grammar on its two natural axes. Only such a systematisation will show to what extent the traditional framework of synchronic linguistics needs to be altered. This is a task which cannot of course be undertaken here. We are simply concerned to lay down principles of a very general kind.

[189]

CHAPTER VIII

Abstract Entities in Grammar

One important subject has not yet been touched upon. It is one which shows, precisely, how necessary it is to examine every grammatical question from the two points of view distinguished above. It concerns abstract entities in grammar. We shall take first of all the associative aspect.

To associate two forms is not only to feel that they have something in common, but also to distinguish the nature of the relations which govern these connexions. Speakers are aware that the relation between *enseigner* ('to teach') and *enseignement* ('teaching'), or between *juger* ('to judge') and *jugement* ('judgment'), is not the same as that between *enseignement* ('teaching') and *jugement* ('judgment') (cf. p. [173] ff.). This is where the system of associations links up with grammar. One may say that the sum total of deliberate, systematic classifications set up by a grammarian studying a given linguistic state ahistorically must coincide with the sum total of associations, conscious or unconscious, operative in speech. These are the associations which establish in the mind the various word families, flexional paradigms, formative elements (stems, suffixes, endings, etc.) (cf. p. [253] ff.).

But does not association operate only upon material elements? Not at all. As noted previously, association may connect words linked by
[190] meaning only: e.g. *enseignement* ('teaching'), *apprentissage* ('apprenticeship'), *éducation* ('education'), etc. The same must apply in grammar. The three Latin genitives *dominī* ('of a master'), *rēgis* ('of a king') and *rosārum* ('of roses') have three different endings, *-ī*, *-is*, and *-āru*m, which afford no phonetic basis for association. None the less, these endings are linked by one's awareness of their common value, which prescribes identical uses for them. That is sufficient to set up an association, in the absence of any material support. And that is how the notion of 'genitive', as such, takes its place in the

language. A very similar process makes us aware of connexions between the Latin flexional endings *-us, -ī, -ō* etc. in a series like *dominus, dominī, dominō*, etc., and thus emerge our more general notions of case and case flexion. Associations of the same order, but of still wider scope, link all nouns, all adjectives, etc., and thus establish the notion of parts of speech.

All these things exist in the language, but as abstract entities. It is difficult to study them, because one can never be sure whether the awareness of speakers of the language always goes as far as the grammarians' analyses. But the essential point is that *abstract entities are based ultimately upon concrete entities*. No grammatical abstraction is possible unless it has a foundation in the form of some series of material elements, and these are the elements one must always come back to finally.

Let us now look at it from a syntagmatic point of view. The value of a group is often connected with the order of its elements. In analysing a syntagma, the speaker does not stop at distinguishing the various parts: he also recognises their order of occurrence. The meanings of the French word *désir-eux* ('desir-ous') and of Latin *signi-fer* ('standard-bearer') depend on the relative positions of the smaller units. There is no word *eux-désir*, or *fer-signum*. A value may even have no concrete element of its own, unlike *-eux*, *-fer*, etc. It may result simply from the order of elements. In French, for example, *je dois* ('I should') and *dois-je?* ('should I'?) have different meanings, which depend entirely on the word order. A language sometimes uses [191]
the order of elements to express an idea which another language will express by means of one or more concrete terms. English, in types of syntagma like *gooseberry wine* and *gold watch*, uses word order to express relations which French marks by prepositions (*vin de groseilles* 'wine of gooseberries'; *montre en or* 'watch in gold'). French, on the other hand, renders the notion of direct object simply by placing the noun after the transitive verb (*je cueille une fleur* 'I pick a flower'); whereas Latin and other languages do this by using an accusative case form with special endings.

Word order is undeniably an abstract entity. But it is none the less true that it owes its existence to the concrete units involved, which are aligned in a single dimension. It would be a mistake to believe in the existence of an incorporeal syntax apart from these material units distributed in space. In English, *the man I have seen* illustrates a syntactic feature apparently represented by zero, whereas French marks it by *que* ('that'), as in *l'homme que j'ai vu* ('the man that I have seen'). But it is just this comparison with French syntax which produces the illusion that nothing can express something. In reality, the material units in the English example, aligned in a certain order, create this value themselves. Without a set of concrete terms, no discussion of any point of syntax is possible. Furthermore, the very fact that we do understand a complex of forms such as this English example demonstrates its adequacy to express the thought in question.

A material unit exists only in virtue of what it means, what function it has. This principle is particularly important to bear in mind where smaller units are concerned, because there is a temptation to think that they exist simply as material elements. We may be tempted to
[192] think, for instance, that the word *aimer* ('to love') owes its existence entirely to the sounds which go to make it up. On the other hand, as we have just seen, a meaning or function exists only through the support of some material form. This principle was introduced above in connexion with larger syntagmas and syntactic types, simply because in their case the temptation is particularly strong to imagine immaterial abstractions hovering above the actual words in the sentence. The two principles just mentioned are complementary, and conform to our earlier remarks about the delimitation of linguistic units (cf. p. [145]).

PART THREE [193]

Diachronic Linguistics

CHAPTER I

General Observations

Diachronic linguistics studies the relations which hold not between the coexisting terms of a linguistic state, but between successive terms substituted one for another over a period of time.

Absolute stability in a language is never found (cf. p. [110] ff.). All parts of the language are subject to change, and any period of time will see evolution of greater or smaller extent. It may vary in rapidity or intensity. But the principle admits no exceptions. The linguistic river never stops flowing. Whether its course is smooth or uneven is a consideration of secondary importance.

It is true that this uninterrupted evolution is often hidden from us by the attention paid to the corresponding literary language. A literary language (cf. p. [267] ff.) is superimposed upon the vernacular, which is the natural form a language takes, and it is subject to different conditions of existence. Once a literary language is established, it usually remains fairly stable, and tends to perpetuate itself unaltered. Its dependence on writing gives it special guarantees of conservation. Hence this is not the place to look if we wish to see how variable [194]
natural languages are when free from literary regimentation.

Historical phonetics, and historical phonetics in its entirety, is the first object of study in diachronic linguistics. Sound change cannot be reconciled with the notion of a linguistic state. Comparing sounds or groups of sounds with what they were at an earlier period means establishing a diachronic succession. The earlier period may be remote or recent; but as soon as two periods merge, then we are no longer dealing with historical phonetics. We are dealing with the sounds of a single linguistic state, and that is the province of descriptive phonetics.

The diachronic character of historical phonetics is in complete conformity with the principle that nothing in historical phonetics is significant or grammatical, in the broad sense of the term (cf. p. [36]). For establishing the history of the pronunciation of a word, its meaning is irrelevant. One need consider only the material envelope of the word. One can segment it into phonetic parts without inquiring whether these parts have any meaning. One can ask, for example, what happened in Attic Greek to the group *-ewo-*, which has no meaning. If the evolution of a language were nothing more than the evolution of its sounds, the contrast between what belongs to the two branches of linguistics would be immediately conspicuous. One would see clearly that diachronic is to be equated with non-grammatical, and synchronic with grammatical.

But what apart from sounds changes over time? Words change their meanings. Grammatical categories change. Some of the latter disappear along with the forms which served to express them (e.g. the dual in Latin). But if all the various associative and syntagmatic facts have their histories, how can any absolute distinction between diachrony and synchrony be maintained? It becomes very difficult once one goes beyond pure historical phonetics.

[195] Let us note, however, that many changes classed as grammatical changes turn out to be sound changes. In German, the creation of noun plurals of the type *Hand* ('hand') vs. *Hände* ('hands'), and their substitution for plurals of the type *hant* vs. *hanti* (cf. p. [120]), is to be explained entirely by sound change. The same is true of German compounds of the type *Springbrunnen* ('fountain', i.e. 'spring-well'), *Reitschule* ('riding-school'), etc. In Old High German, the first element of these compounds was not a verb but a noun: *beta-hūs* meant 'prayer house'. But when the final vowel fell (*beta*→*bet-*, etc.), it became linked semantically with the verb 'to pray' (*beten*) and *Bethaus* came to mean 'house for praying'.

Something similar happened to the compounds formed in early Germanic with the word *līch* 'external appearance' (e.g. *mannolīch* 'having the appearance of a man', *redolīch* 'having the appearance of reason'). Today, German has a great number of adjectives in which *-lich* has become a suffix (*verziehlich* 'pardonable', *glaublich* 'credible'), rather like the French suffix *-able* (*pardonnable* 'pardonable', *croyable* 'credible'). At the same time, the interpretation of the first element in these German words has changed, being no longer looked upon as a noun but as a verb root. This is because in a number of cases the fall of the final vowel of this first element (e.g. *redo*→*red-*) caused it to be assimilated to a verb root (the *red-* of *reden* 'to speak').

Thus in *glaublich*, *glaub-* is connected with *glauben* ('to believe') rather than *Glaube* ('belief'). Similarly, in spite of the difference in the stems, *sichtlich* ('visibly') is connected with *sehen* ('to see') and no longer with *Sicht* ('sight').

In all these cases and many comparable ones, the distinction between the two orders remains clear. But it is necessary to bear it in mind. Otherwise, one may loosely claim to be doing historical grammar when in fact one is doing two things: first, studying a sound change (which falls in the diachronic domain), and then examining its consequences (which falls in the synchronic domain).

But this does not resolve all the problems one encounters. The [196]
evolution of any grammatical feature, associative group, or syntagmatic type is not comparable to that of a sound. For it is not a single thing. It splits up into a number of separate things, of which only some belong to historical phonetics. In the birth of a new syntagmatic type, such as the French future tense *prendrai* ('I will take') from *prendre* + *ai* ('to take' + 'I have'), at least two factors must be distinguished. One is psychological – the synthesis of two conceptual elements. The other is phonetic and depends on the first – the reduction from two stresses, one on *prendre* and one on *ai*, to a single stress giving *prendrai*.

The flexional system of Germanic strong verbs, represented in modern German by *geben* ('to give'), with past tense *gab* ('gave'), past participle *gegeben* ('given'), etc. (cf. Greek *leípō*, *élipon*, *léloipa*, etc.), is mainly based upon the umlaut affecting stem vowels. The alternations (cf. p. [215] ff.), which were originally fairly straightforward, are clearly the result of a purely phonetic change. For these oppositions to acquire such functional importance, the early flexional system had to undergo simplification by a variety of processes. They included the disappearance of many varieties of present tense forms, together with the different shades of meaning associated with them, the disappearance of the imperfect, the future, the aorist, the reduplicated perfect, and so on. There was nothing essentially phonetic about these changes. But they reduced verb flexion to a very small set of forms. The stem alternations thus acquired a significant value of great importance. We can say that the opposition *e* vs. *a* is more significant for German *geben* vs. *gab* than is the opposition *e* vs. *o* for Greek *leípō* vs. *léloipa*, because of the absence of reduplication in the German perfect.

Although sound change often intervenes in some way or other in linguistic evolution, it does not explain everything. When the phonetic factor has been given its due, there still remains a residue which appears to justify the notion that there is a 'history of grammar'. That
is where the real difficulty lies. The distinction – which must be upheld [197]
– between diachronic and synchronic calls for detailed explanations which cannot be given here.[1]

[1] To this didactic, external reason another must perhaps be added. Saussure never

In what follows, we shall examine in turn sound change, alternation, and analogy. Finally, we shall deal briefly with popular etymology and agglutination.

lectured on the linguistics of speech (cf. p. [36] ff.). It will be recalled that in his view linguistic innovations always begin with various isolated occurrences (cf. p. [138]). One might suppose that Saussure refused to recognise these as grammatical facts, since an isolated occurrence is necessarily divorced from the language and its system, which depends entirely on a whole set of communal habits. As long as facts belong to speech, they are merely special, occasional instances of the use of an established system. Only when an innovation, by frequent repetition, becomes fixed in the memory and thus enters the system does it have the effect of disturbing the equilibrium of values, and the language is *ipso facto* changed immediately. The remarks on p. [36] and p. [121] concerning phonetic evolution could also be applied to grammatical evolution: its development lies outside the system. For one never sees the system itself evolving. It is merely found to be different at different stages. This attempted explanation is no more than a suggestion we should like to put forward. (Editorial note)

CHAPTER II [198]

Sound Changes

§1. *Their absolute regularity*

Sound change, as we have seen (p. [132]) affects not words, but sounds. A given speech sound alters, and this is an isolated occurrence, like all diachronic events. But the consequence is that all the words in which the sound in question occurs alter in an identical way. In this sense, phonetic changes are absolutely regular.

In German, *ī* became *ei*, and then *ai*: thus *wīn*, *trīben*, *līhen*, *zīt*, became *Wein*, *treiben*, *leihen*, *Zeit*. German *ū* became *au*: so *hūs*, *zūn*, *rūch* became *Haus*, *Zaun*, *Rauch*. German *ǖ* became *eu*: so *hǖsir* became *Heusir*, etc. On the other hand, the German diphthong *ie* became *ī*, although it continues to be written *ie*, as in *biegen*, *lieb*, *Tier*. In a parallel way, *uo* became *ū*: so *muot* became *Mut*, etc. German *z* (cf. p. [59]) became *s* (written *ss*): so *wazer* became *Wasser*, *fliezen* became *fliessen*, etc. German *h* between vowels fell: so *līhen* became *leien* (still written *leihen*), and *sehen* became *seen* (still written *sehen*). German *w* became labiodental *v* (still written *w*): so *wazer* became *vasr* (written *Wasser*).

In French, palatal *l'* became a yod (*y*): so *piller*, *bouillir* are now pronounced *piye*, *buyir*, etc.

In Latin, intervocalic *s* became *r*: **genesis* became *generis*, **asēna* became *arēna*, etc.

Any phonetic change, seen in correct perspective, confirms the per- [199]
fect regularity of these developments.

§2. *Conditioning of sound changes*

The foregoing examples show that sound changes, far from being quite general, are usually restricted by specific conditions. In other words, it is not the sound type itself which alters, but the sound as it occurs in certain conditions determined by environment, stress, etc. Thus *s* became *r* in Latin only between vowels and in one or two other positions: otherwise it remained (cf. *est*, *senex*, *equos*).

Unconditioned changes are extremely rare. When they do occur, they often appear to be unconditioned because the conditioning factor is obscure, or else very general. Thus in German *ī* became *ei*, then *ai*, but only in stressed syllables. Proto-Indo-European k_1 becomes *h* in Germanic (cf. Proto-Indo-European *$k_1$olsum*, Latin *collum*, German *Hals*); but the change does not take place after *s* (cf. Greek *skótos*, Gothic *skadus* 'shadow').

The distinction between conditioned and unconditioned changes rests in any case on taking a superficial view of the phenomena involved. It is more rational to speak, as is increasingly done, of *spontaneous* and *combinative* changes. Sound changes are spontaneous when produced by some internal cause, and combinative when the result of the presence of one or more other sounds. The change of Proto-Indo-European *o* to *a* in Germanic (e.g. Gothic *skadus*, German *Hals*) is a spontaneous change. The consonantal mutations, or *Lautverschiebungen*, of Germanic are typical of spontaneous change. Thus Proto-Indo-European k_1 becomes *h* in Proto-Germanic (cf. Latin *collum*, Gothic *hals*). Proto-Germanic *t*, kept in English, becomes *z* (pronounced *ts*) in High German (cf. Gothic *taihun*, English *ten*, German *zehn*). The change of Latin *ct* and *pt* to *tt* in Italian, on the other hand,
[200] (Latin *factum*→Italian *fatto*, Latin *captīvum*→Italian *cattivo*) is a combinative change, since the first consonant was assimilated to the second. The German umlaut is also due to an external cause, the presence of *i* in the following syllable: thus while *gast* remains unchanged, *gasti* becomes *gesti*, then *Gäste*.

In neither type of case, it should be noted, does it make any difference what the result is. Nor is it even important whether a change takes place or not. If we compare Gothic *fisks* with Latin *piscis*, and Gothic *skadus* with Greek *skótos*, it will be observed that in the first case the *i* remains, whereas in the second case there has been a change of *o* to *a*. So in one instance a sound has stayed unchanged, while in the other a sound has altered. But the crucial point is that both developments are spontaneous.

If a sound change is combinative, it is always conditioned. But if it is spontaneous, it is not necessarily unconditioned, because it may be conditioned negatively by the absence of certain factors relevant to change. Proto-Indo-European k_2 spontaneously becomes *qu* in Latin (e.g. *quattuor*, *inquilīna*), but not when followed, for example, by *o* or *u* (cf. *cottīdie*, *colō*, *secundus*, etc.). Likewise, the survival of Proto-Indo-European *i* in Gothic *fisks*, etc. is governed by a condition: it must not be followed by *r* or *h*, in which case it becomes *e* (written *ai*): e.g. *wair* = Latin *vir*, *maihstus* = German *Mist*.

§3. Methodological considerations

The formulations given to statements of diachronic facts may be misleading unless attention is paid to the distinctions drawn above.

Examples of such inaccuracies include the following.

According to the old formulation of Verner's law, 'in Germanic _þ_ in non-initial position became _đ_ if followed by the stress'. So, on the one hand, _*faþer→*fađer_ (German _Vater_) and _*liþumé→*liđumé_ (German _litten_); whereas _þ_ remains in such cases as _*þrīs_ (German _drei_), _*brōþer_ (German _Bruder_), and _*liþo_ (German _leide_). This formulation [201] gives the active role to the stress and introduces a restriction for initial _þ_. In reality, the case is quite different. In Germanic, as in Latin, _þ_ tended to voice in medial position. This was only prevented by stress falling on the preceding vowel. So everything is the other way round. The change was spontaneous, not combinative; and the stress was a conservative factor, not the cause of the change. The correct formulation is thus: 'Medial _þ_ became _đ_, unless prevented by the stress on the preceding vowel'.

In order to distinguish between what is spontaneous and what is combinative, one must analyse the different phases of the change, and not take the eventual outcome for the immediate outcome. Thus, in explaining Latin rhotacisation of _s_, as in _*genesis→generis_, it is inaccurate to say that _s_ became _r_ between vowels, since _s_, being voiceless, cannot become _r_ all at once. In reality, there were two changes. First, _s_ became _z_, a combinative change. Then _z_, not having been retained in the Latin sound system, was replaced by the neighbouring sound _r_: this was a spontaneous change. It was a serious error to misrepresent these two disparate changes as a single phenomenon. The mistake consisted on the one hand of taking the eventual outcome for the immediate outcome (_s→r_ instead of _z→r_); and on the other hand of treating the change as combinative, whereas only its first phase is combinative. It is rather like saying that in French _e_ became _a_ before a nasal. In fact what happened was a combinative change, the nasalisation of _e_ by _n_ (e.g. Latin _ventum_→French _vẽnt_, Latin _fēmina_→ French _femə_, _fẽmə_), followed by the spontaneous change of _ẽ_ to _ã_ (_vãnt_, _fãmə_; now _vã_ and _fam_). It is no objection to say that this happened only before a nasal consonant: the reason why _e_ became nasalised is not to be confused with the question of whether _ẽ_ to _ã_ was spontaneous or combinative.

Although it is not connected with the principles formulated above, [202] the most serious error which must be mentioned here is that of formulating a phonetic law in the present tense, as if what it stated held for all time, instead of being developments confined to a specific period. Chaos results, for in this way all reference to chronological succession of events is eliminated. The point has already been made earlier (p.

[137]) in connexion with the sequences of changes explaining why Greek *tríkhes* appears beside *thriksí*. If we say '*s* becomes *r* in Latin' it sounds as if we are saying that the rhotacisation is inherent in the language, and *causa, rīsus* etc. then appear to be awkward exceptions. Only 'intervocalic *s* became *r* in Latin at a certain period' allows for the possibility that when *s* changed to *r* there was no intervocalic *s* in *causa, rīsus,* etc., so that these words were not affected. This was indeed the case, for the words in question were still at that period *caussa, rīssus*. For an analogous reason, one should say '*ā* became *ē* in the Ionic dialect' (e.g. *mā́tēr→mḗtēr*, etc.); for otherwise there is no way to account for Greek forms like *pâsa, phāsi*, etc., which were still *pansa, phansi*, etc. at the period when the change occurred.

§4. Causes of sound change

Investigating the causes of sound change is one of the most difficult tasks in linguistics. Various explanations have been proposed. None is entirely satisfactory.

I. It is said that racial predispositions determine the direction of sound changes. There is a question of comparative anthropology involved. But does the vocal apparatus vary from one race to another? No. Hardly more than from one individual to another. An African brought to France at birth speaks French as well as any Frenchman. Furthermore, to speak of 'the Italian vocal apparatus' or to say 'the German
[203] mouth does not allow this' is to risk presenting as a permanent characteristic what is merely a historical fact. It is a mistake comparable to formulating a sound change in the present tense. To claim that the Ionian vocal apparatus rejects long *ā* and changes it to *ē* is quite as erroneous as saying that *ā* 'becomes' *ē* in Ionic.

The Ionian vocal apparatus had not the slightest reluctance to pronounce *ā*, for that vowel is indeed found in certain cases. Thus there is no question of any physiological incapacity, but simply of a change of articulatory habits. Similarly Latin, which had not kept intervocalic *s* (**genesis→generis*), reintroduced it a little later (**rīssus→rīsus*). These changes do not point to any permanent disposition of the Latin vocal apparatus.

It is indeed possible to recognise a general tendency in phonetic changes at a given period in a given community. The reduction of diphthongs to monophthongs in modern French manifests the same general tendency. But one could find similar general movements in political history, without being led on that account to question their purely historical nature or to suspect the operation of some underlying racial factor.

II. Phonetic change has often been regarded as an adaptation to geographical and climatic conditions. In Europe, certain languages of the north are full of consonants, while certain languages of the south make a more liberal use of vowels, and thus strike the ear as harmonious. Climate and living conditions may well have some effect upon a language. But the problem becomes complicated as soon as one looks at the details. For example, although Scandinavian languages may be overburdened with consonants, the languages of the Laps and the Finns are more vocalic even than Italian. It must also be noted that the accumulation of consonants in modern German is, in most cases, a quite recent development due to the fall of post-tonic vowels; that some dialects of southern France are less reluctant to accept [204]
consonant groups than northern French; that Serbian has as many as the Russian of Moscow; and so on.

III. Appeal has been made to the law of least effort. This is held to explain the replacement of a double articulation by a single articulation, or a difficult one by an easier one. The idea, whatever may be said of it, is worth considering. It may to some extent throw light on the cause of sound change, or at least indicate where to look for it.

The law of least effort appears to explain a certain number of cases: changes from stop to fricative (e.g. *b*→*v* in Latin *habēre*→French *avoir*); the fall of enormous numbers of final syllables in many languages; assimilation (e.g. *ly*→*ll* in **alyos*→Greek *állos*, *tn*→*nn* in **atnos*→Latin *annus*); monophthongization of diphthongs, which is simply one type of assimilation (e.g. *ai*→ẹ in French *maizōn*→*mẹzō*, 'house'); and others.

The difficulty is that one can cite just as many cases where exactly the opposite happens. With monophthongisation one can contrast for instance the change of German *ī*, *ū* and *ū* to *ei*, *au* and *eu*. If it is held that the Slavic shortening of *ā*, *ē* to *ă*, *ĕ* is due to economy of effort, it must be supposed that the opposite phenomenon in German (*făter*→*Vāter*, *gĕben*→*gēben*) is due to increase of effort. If voiced sounds are held to be easier to pronounce than voiceless sounds (e.g. *p*→*b* in Latin *opera*→Provençal *obra*), the opposite must require greater effort; and yet Spanish changed *ž* to χ (*hiχo* 'son', written *hijo*) and Germanic changed *b*, *d*, *g*, to *p*, *t*, *k*. If loss of aspiration (as in Proto-Indo-European **bherō*→Germanic *beran*) is considered a diminution of effort, what is one to say of German, which puts it in where it used not to be (*Tanne*, *Pute*, etc. pronounced *Thanne*, *Phute*)?

These observations are not intended to provide a refutation of the explanation proposed. The fact is, however, that it is scarcely possible to determine for every language what is easier or more difficult to pronounce. If it is true that shortening demands less effort as regards [205]
duration, it is equally true that careless pronunciation favours length-

ening, and a short sound requires more careful attention. So by assuming different tendencies to be operative it is possible to explain quite opposite facts as being alike. Likewise, if we take *k* changing to *tš*, as in Latin *cēdere*→Italian *cedere*, and consider only the initial and final stages of the process, it looks like a case of increased effort. But it might look different if we were to reconstruct the chain of events. Thus *k* becomes palatal *k'* by assimilation to the following vowel, and then *k'* moves to *ky*. This does not make the pronunciation any more difficult, as two elements run together in *k'* have now been clearly differentiated. Next, from *ky* we move in stages to *ty*, *tχ'* and *tš*: each stage involves progressively less effort.

There is a vast field of study here. In order to be exhaustive, it should take into account at the same time both physiological considerations (questions of articulation) and also psychological considerations (questions of attention).

IV. An explanation favoured for some years now attributes changes in pronunciation to our phonetic education in infancy. The seeds of change lie in the many hesitations, trials and corrections the infant has to make in order to manage to pronounce what he hears around him. Certain inaccuracies which go uncorrected supposedly survive in the pronunciation of the individual and become established in that generation growing up. Children often pronounce *t* instead of *k*, but there is no corresponding sound change in the evolution of languages. That is not the case, however, with other mispronunciations. For example, many Parisian children say *fl'eur*, *bl'anc* with a palatal *l'*; and this is analogous to the process by which in Italian *florem* became *fl'ore* and then *fiore*.

Observations of this nature cannot be ignored: but they leave the
[206] problem unsolved. For it is difficult to see why one generation settles for preserving certain inaccuracies and not others, since all of them are just as natural. The selection of certain mispronunciations appears to be purely arbitrary, and one can see no reason for it. Furthermore, one is led to ask why the mispronunciation survived on one particular occasion but not on another occasion.

A similar question could, moreover, be asked in respect of all the preceding causes, if they are admitted as valid. Climatic influences, racial predispositions, and a tendency to less effort are permanent or long-standing factors. Why should they act intermittently, affecting now one point and now another in the sound system? Any historical event must have a determining factor: but in these cases we are not told what triggered a change for which the general cause had long existed. This is the most difficult point to clear up.

V. Sometimes the causes of sound changes are sought in the general state of a nation at a given period. Languages go through periods of relatively greater upheaval at certain times. It is claimed that these periods correspond to periods of historical upheaval, and so a connexion is established between political instability and linguistic instability. The next step is to apply these conclusions about the language in general to sound changes in particular. It is observed, for example, that the most radical changes in Latin in the course of its development into the Romance languages coincide with the very disturbed period of the barbarian invasions. If we do not wish to be led astray in these matters, two distinctions must be kept clearly in mind.

(*a*) Political stability does not influence the language in the same way as instability. There is no *quid pro quo.* When political stability slows down linguistic evolution, that is the action of a positive factor, albeit an external one. Political instability, with the opposite effect, can act only negatively. Linguistic immobility, the relative stabilisation of a language, may be the result of factors external to it (the influence of a court, of education, of an academy, of writing, etc.) which [207] in turn are actively favoured by social and political stability. On the other hand, if some external upheaval in the life of the nation sets off linguistic evolution, that means that the language simply regains its freedom to follow a normal course of change. The immobility of Latin during the Classical period was due to external factors, and cannot be compared with the changes it later underwent, since these occurred of their own accord in the absence of certain external conditions.

(*b*) Sound changes only are under consideration here, and not linguistic change in general. It is understandable that grammatical change should be affected by these factors, since grammar involves thought in some way, and thus is more sensitive to the repercussions of external upheavals, which have a direct effect upon the mind. But nothing warrants accepting the idea that the turbulent periods in a nation's history correspond to the precipitation of evolution in the sound system.

In any case, it is impossible to find any period, even when the language is superficially stable, which is free from sound change altogether.

VI. Appeal has also been made to the hypothesis of an 'earlier linguistic substratum'. On this hypothesis, certain changes are due to an indigenous population absorbed by newcomers. Thus the difference between Provençal and French is held to be explained by reference to a different proportion of the indigenous Celtic population in the two areas of Gaul. A similar theory has been applied to the different dialects of Italian, which are attributed to Ligurian, Etruscan, etc.

influences, according to the region in question. It must first of all be pointed out that this hypothesis appeals to circumstances which occur only rarely. Furthermore, the hypothesis stands in need of clarifica-
[208] tion. Does it claim that in adopting the new language the earlier population introduced something of their own habits of pronunciation? That is acceptable, and quite natural. But if this is another appeal to imponderable racial factors, it takes us back to the obscurities already mentioned above.

VII. Finally, there is an explanation – which scarcely merits the name – which likens sound changes to changes in fashion. But no one has accounted for changes in fashion: all we know is that they are based on laws of imitation, in which psychologists take a great interest. However, even if this explanation does not solve the problem it has the advantage of making that problem part of a much bigger problem. It treats the principle underlying sound changes as purely psychological. The difficulty is, however, to identify the starting point of the imitative process. That is what is obscure, both in the case of sound change and of changes of fashion.

§5. The scope of sound change is unpredictable

If one attempts to evaluate the effect of these changes, one soon sees that it is unrestricted and incalculable. It is impossible, in other words, to foresee where they will end. It would be naive to suppose that a word can change only up to a certain point, as if there were something in it which could preserve it. This limitless character of sound change derives from the arbitrary nature of linguistic signs. They are in no way tied to their meaning.

It is possible at any given time to ascertain that the sounds of a word have changed, and to what extent. But it is impossible to say in advance to what extent the word has become or will become unrecognisable.

In Germanic, Proto-Indo-European **aiwom* (cf. Latin *aevom*) became **aiwan*, **aiwa*, and then **aiw*, like all words with the same ending. Next, **aiw* became in early German *ew*, like all words including the
[209] sequence *aiw*. Then, since any final *w* changes to *o*, this gave *ēo*. In turn, *ēo* became *eo*, *io* in accordance with other similarly general rules. Then *io* became *ie*, *je*, ending up in modern German as *jē* 'ever' (as in *das schönste, was ich je gesehen habe* 'the most beautiful I have ever seen').

If we consider just the initial and final forms, the word now no longer has any of its original elements. Nonetheless, each stage, taken in isolation, is quite certain and regular. Moreover, each change is limited in its effect. But the whole gives the impression of a limitless sum of modifications. The same might be said of Latin *calidum*, comparing it first with what it became in modern French (*šọ*, written *chaud*), and then reconstructing the intermediate stages: *calidum, calidu, caldu, cald, calt, tšalt, tšaut, šaut, šọt, šọ*. Cf. also Vulgar Latin **waidanju*→French *gẽ* (written *gain*), Latin *minus*→French *mwẽ* (written *moins*), Latin *hoc illī*→*wi* (written *oui*).

Sound change is furthermore unrestricted and incalculable in that it affects any type of sign. It makes no distinction between an adjective or a noun, a stem, a suffix or an ending, etc. Thus must be so *a priori*; for if grammar entered into the question, sound change would merge with synchronic fact, and that is intrinsically impossible. It is in this sense that one may speak of the blind operation of phonetic evolution.

In Greek, for example, *s* fell after *n* not only in **khānses* 'geese', **mēnses* 'months' (giving *khênes, mênes*), where it had no grammatical value, but also in verb forms of the type **etensa*, **ephansa*, etc. (giving *éteina, éphēna*, etc.), where it characterised the aorist. In Middle High German, the post-tonic vowels *ĭ, ĕ, ă, ŏ* all became uniformly *e* (*gibil*→*Giebel*, *meistar*→*Meister*), in spite of the fact that the difference of vowel quality distinguished various endings. So the [210] accusative singular *boton* and the genitive and dative singular *boten* came together as *boten*.

If then, sound changes know no limits, it follows that they must bring about far-reaching disturbances in the grammatical system. This is the point of view from which we are now going to consider them.

[211] CHAPTER III

Grammatical Consequences of Phonetic Evolution

§1. Breaking grammatical links

One consequence of sound change is to break the grammatical link connecting two or more terms. Thus it comes about that one word is no longer felt to be derived from another. For example:

(Latin)	*mansiō*—**mansiōnāticus*	'house – household'
(French)	*maison* ‖ *ménage*	

Formerly, linguistic awareness recognised in **mansiōnāticus* a derivative from *mansiō*. Then phonetic vicissitudes separated them. Similarly:

(Latin)	*vervēx*—*vervēcārius*	
(Vulgar Latin)	*berbīx*—*berbīcārius*	'sheep – shepherd'
(French)	*brebis* ‖ *berger*	

This separation naturally has an effect upon the value of the terms: hence in some local patois French *berger* becomes specialised to mean 'oxherd'.

Similar cases are:

(Latin)	*Grātiānopolis*—*grātiānopolitānus*	'Grenoble – of Grenoble'
(French)	*Grenoble* ‖ *Grésivaudan*	

(Latin)	*decem*—*undecim*	'ten – eleven'
(French)	*dix* ‖ *onze*	

Another is that of Gothic *bītan* ('to bite') — *bitum* ('we have bitten') [212]
— *bitr* ('biting, bitter'), which, as a result of the change *t*→*ts* (*z*) and the conservation of the group *tr*, became in West Germanic *bīʒan*, *biʒum* || *bitr*.

Sound change also breaks the usual links between inflected forms of the same word. Thus Latin *comes — comitem* becomes in Old French *cuens* || *comte*; *barō — barōnem* → *ber* || *baron*; *presbiter — presbiterum* → *prestre* || *provoire*.

In other cases, a flexional ending may split in two. Proto-Indo-European marked all accusative singulars with a final *-m*,[1] e.g. *ek_1wom*, **owim*, **podm*, **māterm*. In Latin, this state of affairs underwent no important change. But in Greek, the very different treatment of nasal sonants and adsonants created two separate series of forms: *híppon*, *ó(w)in* || *póda*, *mấtera*. The Greek accusative plural shows a similar development: *híppous* || *pódas*.

§2. *Obliteration of word-composition*

Another grammatical effect of sound change is that distinct parts of a word, which contributed to fixing its value, may cease to be analysable: the word becomes an indivisible whole. Examples are: French *ennemi* ('enemy') from Latin *in-imīcus* (cf. *amīcus* 'friend'); Latin *perdere* ('to lose') from *per-dare* (cf. *dare* 'to give'); Latin *amiciō* ('I cover') from **ambjaciō* (cf. *jaciō* 'I throw'); German *Drittel* ('third') from *drit-teil* (cf. *teil* 'part').

It is clear that these cases resemble those of the preceding paragraph. If *ennemi* is unanalysable, that means it is no longer possible to connect it with another form in the way that *in-imīcus* is connected with *amīcus*. The formula

(Latin)	*amīcus — inimīcus*
(French)	*ami* || *ennemi*

is entirely comparable to [213]

(Latin)	*mansiō — mansiōnāticus*
(French)	*maison* || *ménage*

The same applies to *decem — undecim* : *dix* || *onze*.

The Classical Latin simple forms of the demonstrative *hunc*, *hanc*, *hāc*, etc. ('this') go back to *hon-ce*, *han-ce*, *hā-ce* etc., as is shown by forms on old inscriptions. These are the result of agglutination of a

[1] Or *–n*? cf. p. [130], footnote. (Editorial note)

pronoun and the particle _-ce_. Originally, _hon-ce_ etc. could be related to _ec-ce_ ('behold'); but with the eventual fall of final _-e_ this became impossible. In other words, the constituent elements of _hunc_, _hanc_, _hăc_, etc. were no longer distinguishable.

Sound change begins by making word analysis difficult, before making it altogether impossible. Noun flexion in Proto-Indo-European provides an example.

The Proto-Indo-European declension once had the following pattern: nominative singular *_pod-s_ ('foot'), accusative *_pod-m_, dative*_pod-ai_, locative *_pod-i_, nominative plural *_pod-es_, accusative *_pod-ns_, etc. The declension of *_ek$_1$wos_ ('horse') was exactly parallel at first: *_ek$_1$wo-s_,*_ek$_1$wo-m_, *_ek$_1$wo-ai_, *_ek$_1$wo-i_, *_ek$_1$wo-es_, *_ek$_1$wo-ns_, etc. At that stage, the stem *_ek$_1$wo-_ could be identified as easily as the stem *_pod-_. But later vocalic contractions altered this: dative *_ek$_1$wōi_, locative *_ek$_1$woi_, nominative plural *_ek$_1$wōs_. From this point on, the identity of the stem *_ek$_1$wo-_ was compromised, and analysis could be misled. Later still, new developments such as the differentiation of accusatives (cf. p. [212]) obliterated the last traces of the original state of affairs. Xenophon's contemporaries probably thought the stem of the word for 'horse' was _hipp-_, and the endings were vocalic: _hipp-os_, etc. Hence the types *_ek$_1$wo-s_ and *_pod-s_ were now entirely separate. In the domain of flexion, as everywhere else, whatever interferes with analysis contributes to a loosening of grammatical connexions.

[214] ### §3. *There are no phonetic doublets*

In both types of case examined in §§ 1 and 2, evolution separates entirely two forms which were once grammatically united. This phenomenon might lead to a serious error of interpretation.

When we realise the relative identity of Late Latin _barō_ : _barōnem_ as compared with the disparity between Old French _ber_ and _baron_, are we not tempted to say that one and the same primitive unit (_bar-_) has developed divergently and produced two forms? No. For the same element cannot simultaneously undergo two different changes in the same place. That would be contradictory to the very definition of sound change. In itself, the evolution of sounds is incapable of creating two forms in place of one.

Certain objections may be raised to this thesis. They can be illustrated by the following examples.

Latin _collocāre_ ('to place'), it may be urged, gave in French both _coucher_ ('to lay down') and _colloquer_ ('to collocate'). No. _Collocare_ gave only _coucher_. _Colloquer_ is only a learned borrowing of the Latin word. Cf. _rançon_ and _rédemption_.[1]

[1] Latin _redemptionem_ 'redemption' gave in French _rançon_, but _rédemption_ was later borrowed from Latin. (Translator's note)

But did not Latin *cathedra* ('chair') give the two forms *chaire* ('throne') and *chaise* ('chair'), both of them authentically French? The fact is that *chaise* in French is a dialect form. In Parisian pronunciation, intervocalic *r* became *z*: *père* ('father') and *mère* ('mother') became *pèse*, *mèse*. But literary French retained only two examples of this local pronunciation: they are *chaise* and *bésicles* ('goggles'), the latter a doublet of *béricles*, derived from *béryl* ('beryl'). The case is exactly comparable to that of the Picard form *rescapé* ('survivor'), which has recently passed into general French usage and thus belatedly finds itself contrasting with the corresponding French form *réchappé* ('survivor'). French also has side by side *cavalier* ('rider') and *chevalier* ('knight'), as well as *cavalcade* ('cavalcade') and *chevauchée* ('ride'); but *cavalier* and *cavalcade* come from Italian. (In the final analysis, these cases are parallel to Latin *calidum* ('hot') giving *chaud* ('hot') in French, but *caldo* ('hot') in Italian.) All these are instances of borrowing.

It may perhaps be claimed that the Latin pronoun *mē* ('me') is [215] represented in French by two forms, *me* and *moi* (cf. *il me voit* 'he sees me' vs. *c'est moi qu'il voit* 'It's me he sees'). The answer is that it was the Latin unstressed *mē* which became French *me*, whereas the stressed form *mē* became *moi*. Now presence or absence of stress depends not on the phonetic laws which changed *mē* into both *me* and *moi*, but upon the role of the word in the phrase. The duality is a grammatical one. In German, similarly, **ur-* remained as *ur-* when stressed, but changed to *er-* in a protonic syllable (cf. *úrlaub* 'leave' vs. *erlaúben* 'allow'). But this variation of stress is itself bound up with the types of word-composition in which *ur-* played a part, and hence with conditions of a grammatical, synchronic nature. Finally, to revert to our first example, the differences of form and accent seen in the pair *bárō* : *barṓnem* are clearly earlier than the sound change in question.

The fact is that one never finds examples of phonetic doublets. Phonetic evolution increases already existing differences, nothing more. Wherever these differences are not due to external causes, as in the case of borrowed words, they are based on grammatical and synchronic dualities which have nothing whatever to do with sound change.

§4. Alternation

In two words like French *maison* ('house') and *ménage* ('household'), one finds little temptation to inquire into the difference between the two forms, either because the contrasting elements *-ezō* and *-en-* do not easily lend themselves to comparison, or because no other pair of French words shows a parallel opposition. But often it happens that two neighbouring terms differ only in respect of one or two elements easily picked out, and that the same difference recurs regularly in a series of parallel pairs of forms. This is a case of the most widespread and common grammatical feature in which sound change plays a part: it is termed *alternation*.

[216] In French every Latin *ŏ* in an open syllable became *eu* when stressed, or *ou* if protonic. Hence French pairs like *pouvons* ('(we) can') vs. *peuvent* ('(they) can'), *œuvre* ('work') vs. *ouvrier* ('workman'), *nouveau* ('new') vs. *neuf* ('new'). In these pairs, one detects without difficulty an element of differentiation and regular variation. In Latin, rhotacisation brings about alternations between *gerō* ('I carry') and *gestus* ('carried'), *oneris* ('of a burden') and *onus* ('burden'), *maeror* ('sorrow') and *maestus* ('sorrowful'), etc. In Germanic the varying treatment of *s* according to where the stress falls produces in Middle High German *ferliesen* ('to lose') vs. *ferloren* ('lost'), *kiesen* ('to choose') vs. *gekoren* ('chosen'), *friesen* ('to freeze') vs. *gefroren* ('frozen'), etc. The fall of Proto-Indo-European *e* is reflected in modern German in such oppositions as *beissen* ('to bite') vs. *biss* ('bit'), *leiden* ('to suffer') vs. *litt* ('suffered'), *reiten* ('to ride') vs. *ritt* ('rode'), etc.

In all these examples, it is the stem of the word which is affected. But it goes without saying that any part of a word may show oppositions of the same kind. Nothing is commoner, for example, than a prefix appearing in different forms depending on the nature of the first sound of the stem: e.g. Greek *apo-dídōmi* ('give back') vs. *ap-érchomai* ('go away'), French *ẽ* in *inconnu* ('unknown') vs. *in-* in *inutile* ('useless'). The Proto-Indo-European alternation *e* : *o*, which must ultimately be phonetic in origin, is found in a great number of suffixal elements in Greek: e.g. nominative *híppos* ('horse') vs. vocative *híppe*, *phér-o-men* ('we carry') vs. *phér-e-te* ('you carry'), nominative *gén-os* ('race') vs. genitive *gén-e-os* (for **gén-es-os*). Old French has a special development of Latin stressed *a* after palatals, which results in the alternation *i:ie* in a number of endings: e.g. *chant-er* ('to sing'), *chant-é* ('sung'), *chant-ez* ('(you) sing') vs. *jug-ier* ('to judge'), *jug-ié* ('judged'), *jug-iez* ('(you) judge').

Alternation may thus be defined as: *a correspondence between two sounds or groups of sounds, changing regularly as between two coexisting series of forms.*

Just as sound change alone does not explain doublets, so it is easily seen that sound change is neither the sole nor the most important cause of alternation. When it is said that the Latin root *nov-* became through sound change both *neuv-* and *nouv-* in French (*neuve* 'new' from Latin *novam*, and *nouveau* 'new' from Latin *novellus*), that amounts to inventing an imaginary unit and overlooking a synchronic
[217] duality already in existence. Latin *nov-* in *nov-am* was already in a different position in the word from *nov-* in *novellus*. That difference

was both grammatical in nature (cf. *barō* : *barōnem*) and also prior to any French phonetic development; and it was that difference which lay at the origin of the French alternation and made it possible. This was not a case of sound change splitting up an original unit, but of sound change making an already established opposition of coexisting terms more obvious by distinguishing the sounds. It is an error many linguists make: to suppose that alternation is a phonetic phenomenon, simply because sounds are the vehicle for it, and changes in sounds lie at its origins. But in fact, whether one looks at the starting point or the conclusion of the process, alternation belongs invariably to grammar and to synchrony.

§5. Laws of alternation

Can alternations be reduced to laws, and if so of what nature are these laws?

Take the alternation *e:i*, which is so common in modern German. If one takes all the cases together, without sorting them out, it seems impossible to formulate any general principle: *geben* ('to give') vs. *gibt* ('gives'), *Feld* ('field') vs. *Gefilde* ('field, region'), *Wetter* ('weather') vs. *wittern* ('to smell'), *helfen* ('to help') vs. *Hilfe* ('aid'), *sehen* ('to see') vs. *Sicht* ('sight'). But if from this jumble we extract the pair *geben* vs. *gibt* and set it beside pairs like *schelten* ('to scold') vs. *schilt* ('scolds'), *helfen* ('to help') vs. *hilft* ('helps'), *nehmen* ('to take') vs. *nimmt* ('takes'), etc. one can see that this alternation corresponds to a difference of tense, person, etc. In *lang* ('long') vs. *Länge* ('length'), *stark* ('strong') vs. *Stärke* ('strength'), *hart* ('hard') vs. *Härte* ('hardness'), etc. a similar contrast *a*: *ä* is connected with the formation of nouns from corresponding adjectives. In *Hand* ('hand') vs. *Hände* ('hands'), *Gast* ('guest') vs. *Gäste* ('guests'), etc. it is connected with the formation of plurals. This is so in all the many different cases that German scholars call *Ablaut* ('vowel gradation'). These include *finden* ('to find') vs. *fand* ('found') vs. *Fund* ('discovery'), *binden* ('to bind') vs. *band* ('bound') vs. *Bund* ('band'), *schiessen* ('to shoot') vs. *schoss* ('shot') vs. *Schuss* ('shot, shooting'), *fliessen* ('to flow') vs. *floss* ('flowed') vs. *Fluss* ('stream'). The *Ablaut*, or root vowel variation coinciding with a grammatical distinction is a prime example of alternation; but it differs in no special [218]
way from the general phenomenon.

It is clear that an alternation is ordinarily distributed among several terms in a regular manner, and coincides with an important contrast of function, of category, or of determination. One may speak of grammatical laws of alternation; but these laws are only a chance result of the sound changes which gave rise to them. Once sound change has created a regular phonetic difference between two series of terms contrasting in value, the mind seizes upon this material difference and endows it with significance, making it a bearer of the conceptual difference (cf. p. [121] ff.). These laws, like all synchronic laws, are merely principles of arrangement, with no imperative force. It is quite incorrect to say, as is commonly said, that the *a* of German *Nacht* ('night') changes to *ä* in the plural *Nächte*. For that gives the false impression that linking one term to the other there is a process governed by some imperative principle. In reality, we are simply dealing with an opposition of forms resulting from phonetic evolution. It is true that analogy, which we shall consider shortly, is able to create new pairs showing the same phonetic difference (e.g. *Kranz* ('wreath') vs. *Kränze* ('wreaths'), based on *Gast* ('guest') vs. *Gäste* ('guests'), etc.). The law then seems to apply in the manner of a rule governing usage to the extent of actually changing it. But it must not be forgotten that in a language these permutations are at the mercy of contrary analogical influences. That alone suffices to indicate that rules of this kind are always precarious, and conform entirely to our definition of a synchronic law.

It may also happen that the phonetic conditions which gave rise to the alternation in the first place are still operative. The pairs cited on p. [217] had in Old High German the forms *geban* vs. *gibit*, *feld* vs. *gafildi*, etc. At that period, when the stem is followed by an *i*, it
[219] appears with an *i* itself in place of *e*, but keeps the *e* in all other cases. The alternations between Latin *faciō* ('I make') : *conficiō* ('I complete'), *amīcus* ('friend') : *inimīcus* ('enemy'), *facilis* ('easy') : *difficilis* ('difficult'), etc. are likewise linked to a phonetic condition, which the language-users would have recognised as being the following: the *a* of a word like *faciō*, *amīcus*, etc. alternates with *i* in members of the same word family where that *a* occurs in a medial syllable.

But these sound contrasts give rise to exactly the same remarks as all grammatical laws: they are synchronic. The moment that is forgotten, there is a risk of committing the error of interpretation already pointed out (p. [136]). In connexion with a pair of forms like Latin *faciō* : *conficiō*, care must be taken not to confuse the relation between these coexisting terms with the relation linking two successive terms in the diachronic process (*confaciō*→*conficiō*). If one is tempted to do so, it is because the cause of the phonetic differentiation is still visible in this pair of forms. But its implementation belongs to the past. For the language-users, there is only a simple synchronic opposition.

All this confirms what has already been said about the strictly grammatical character of alternation. A term used to designate this phenomenon – and quite properly so – is *permutation*. None the less, *permutation* is best avoided, precisely because it has so often been applied to sound change. It evokes a misleading idea of movement, whereas in fact there is only a state.

§6. Alternation and grammatical link

We have seen how phonetic evolution, by changing the forms of words, has the effect of severing the grammatical links uniting them. But that applies only to isolated pairs such as French *maison* ('house') vs. *ménage* ('household'), German *Teil* ('part') vs. *Drittel* ('third'). As soon as alternation appears, this is no longer so.

It is evident in the first place that any more or less regular sound [220] contrast between two elements tends to establish a link between them. In German *Wetter* ('weather') is instinctively connected with *wittern* ('to smell') because there is a familiar alternation of *e* and *i*. Even more so, when speakers feel that a sound contrast is governed by a general law this habitual correlation compels attention and contributes to strengthening the grammatical link rather than loosening it. Thus it is that the German *Ablaut* ('vowel gradation') reinforces a perception of the unity of the stem through its vocalic variations (cf. p. [217]).

The same applies to alternations which are not significant, but are bound up with purely phonetic conditions. The French prefix *re-* (as in *reprendre* 'to retake', *regagner* 'to regain', *retoucher* 'to retouch') is reduced to *r-* before a vowel (e.g. *rouvrir* 'to reopen', *racheter* 'to buy back'). Likewise the French prefix *in-* , very much alive in spite of its learned origin, appears in two different forms under the same conditions as *re-*: as *ẽ-* in *inconnu* ('unknown'), *indigne* ('unworthy'), *invertébré* ('invertebrate') etc., but as *in-* in *inavouable* ('unavowable'), *inutile* ('useless'), *inesthétique* ('unaesthetic'), etc. This difference in no way disrupts the conceptual unity, because meaning and function are conceived as identical, and because the language has decided which form to use in which case.

[221] CHAPTER IV

Analogy

§1. Definition and examples

Sound change, it is clear from the preceding chapter, is a source of linguistic disturbance. Wherever it does not give rise to alternations, it contributes towards loosening the grammatical connexions which link words together. It increases the sum total of linguistic forms to no purpose. The linguistic mechanism becomes obscure and complicated inasmuch as irregularities produced by sound change take precedence over forms grouped under general types; in other words, inasmuch as what is absolutely arbitrary takes precedence over what is only relatively arbitrary (cf. p. [183]).

Fortunately, the effect of these changes is counterbalanced by analogy. Analogy is responsible for all the normal modifications of the external aspect of words which are not due to sound change.

Analogy presupposes a model, and regular imitation of a model. *An analogical form is a form made in the image of one or more other forms according to a fixed rule.*

The Latin nominative singular *honor* ('honour') is analogical. Originally it was *honōs*, with an accusative *honōsem*. Then, following the rhotacisation of *s* (cf. p. [201]), it was *honōs*, with an accusative *honōrem*. Thus the stem then took two different forms. This duality was reduced by creating a new nominative *honor*, on the model of
[222] *ōrātor*: *ōrātōrem*. The process will be examined in detail below. In essence, it involves a computation of the missing fourth term in the proportion:

ōrātōrem : *ōrātor* = *honōrem* : *x*.

Here the solution is: *x* = *honor*.

It can thus be seen that, in order to counterbalance the diversifying effect of sound change (*honōs* : *honōrem*), analogy has once more brought the forms together and re-established regularity (*honor*: *honōrem*).

In French, the forms of the verb *prouver* ('to prove') for a long period included *preuve* ('(he) proves'), *prouvons* ('(we) prove'), and *preuvent* ('(they) prove'). Today *preuve* and *preuvent* have been replaced by *prouve* and *prouvent*, forms which cannot be explained by sound change. Whereas *aime* ('(he) loves') can be traced back phonetically to Latin *amat*, *aimons* ('(we) love') is an analogical replacement of Old French *amons*. Similarly *aimable* ('kind') is an analogical replacement of *amable*. In Greek, intervocalic *s* fell, with the result that *-eso-* became *-eo-* (e.g. *géneos* for **genesos*). However, this intervocalic *s* is found in the future and aorist forms of all verbs with vowel stems, e.g. *lū́sō* ('I shall loose'), *élūsa* ('I loosed'). Here the analogy of other forms like *túpsō* and *étupsa*, where the *s* did not fall, preserved the *s* in the future and aorist. In German, while *Gast* ('guest') : *Gäste* ('guests'), *Balg* ('skin') : *Bälge* ('skins') are phonetically regular plurals, *Kranz* ('wreath') : *Kränze* ('wreaths') is analogical, replacing *kranz* : *kranza*. So too is *Hals* ('neck') : *Hälse* ('necks'), where the plural was formerly *halsa*.

Analogy works in favour of regularity and tends to unify formational and flexional processes. But it is sometimes capricious. In German, beside *Kranz* : *Kränze* etc. one finds also *Tag* ('day') : *Tage* ('days'), *Salz* ('salt') : *Salze* ('salts'), etc. which for one reason or another have resisted analogy. So it is impossible to say in advance how far imitation of a model will extend, or which patterns are destined to provoke it. It is not always the more numerous forms which set analogy working. In Greek, the perfect of *pheúgō* ('flee') has active forms *pépheuga*, *pépheugas*, *pepheúgamen*, etc., but all the middle voice flexions lack the *a*: *péphugmai*, *pephúgmetha*, etc. The language of Homer shows that this *a* was originally missing from the plural and the dual of the active voice (cf. Homeric Greek *ídmen*, *éïkton*, etc.). The analogy began just with the active first person singular and was [223] extended to almost the whole of the perfect indicative paradigm. The case is also remarkable because here analogy attaches to the stem an element (*-a-*) which is flexional in origin (hence *pepheúga-men*); whereas the opposite development – a stem element becoming attached to a suffix – is, as will be seen (cf. p. [233]), much more frequent.

Often two or three isolated words are enough to create a general form – an ending, for instance. In Old High German, weak verbs of the type *habēn*, *lobōn*, etc. have an *-m* in the first person singular of the present: *habēm*, *lobōm*. This *-m* originates with a few verbs, *bim*, *stām*, *gēm*, *tuom*, which are like the Greek verbs in *-mi*. These few alone imposed their *-m* on the whole class of weak verbs. In this case it should be noted that analogy did not regularise any phonetic diversity, but generalised a morphological formation.

§2. *Analogies are not changes*

The early linguists failed to understand the nature of analogical phenomena, which they described as 'false analogy'. They thought that by inventing the nominative form *honor* to replace *honōs* (cf. p. [221]), Latin had made a 'mistake'. In their view, anything which departed from an established order was an irregularity, a violation of an ideal form. Their illusion, very characteristic of the period, was that the original state of the language represented something superior, a state of perfection. They did not even inquire whether that earlier state had not been preceded by a still earlier one. Any liberty taken with it was an anomaly. The Neogrammarians were the first scholars to assign analogy to its rightful place, by showing that it is, along with sound change, the main factor in the evolution of languages, and the process by which they pass from one state of organisation to another.

[224] But what is the nature of analogical phenomena? Are they, as is commonly believed, changes?

Every analogy is a drama involving three characters. They are: (i) the legitimate heir to the succession (e.g. Latin *honōs*), (ii) the rival (*honor*), (iii) a collective character, made up of the forms which sponsored this rival (*honōrem*, *ōrātor*, *ōrātōrem*, etc.). *Honor* is often regarded as a modification or 'metaplasm' of *honōs*, from which it derives most of its substance. But the one form which plays no part at all in the genesis of *honor* is *honōs* itself!

The phenomenon can be represented as follows:

TRANSMITTED FORMS		NEW FORM
honōs (which plays no active role)	*honōrem* *ōrātor*, *ōrātōrem*, etc. (sponsoring group)	→ *honor*

It is clear that this is a case of 'paraplasm', of the installation of a rival alongside the traditional form – in short, of creation. Whereas sound change introduces nothing new without eliminating what formerly existed (as with *honōrem* replacing *honōsem*, cf. p. [221]), an analogical form does not necessarily eliminate its rival. *Honor* and *honōs* coexisted for a time and were interchangeable. However, since a language dislikes maintaining two signals for a single idea, it usually turns out that the primitive, less regular form falls into disuse and disappears. It is this outcome which makes it look as if a change of form has taken place: once the analogical process is completed, the old state of affairs (*honōs* : *honōrem*) and the new (*honor* : *honōrem*) appear to be opposed in the same way as would have resulted from sound change. But at the stage when *honor* first appears nothing is [225] changed, because *honor* does not replace anything. Nor is the disappearance of *honōs* a change either, since it is quite independent of the appearance of *honor*. Wherever we can follow the course of linguistic events in detail, we find that analogical innovation and elimination of the old form are two separate events. Nowhere does one discover a change in process.

Analogy has nothing to do with replacing one form by another: often, indeed, it produces forms which replace nothing. In German, one can form a diminutive from any noun with a concrete meaning by adding the diminutive suffix *-chen*. But if a form *Elefantchen* ('little elephant') gained acceptance in the language, it would supplant nothing already in existence. Similarly in French on the model of *pension* : *pensionnaire* ('pension : pensioner'), *réaction* : *réactionnaire* ('reaction : reactionary'), etc. someone could invent *interventionnaire* meaning 'in favour of intervention', or *répressionnaire* meaning 'in favour of repression'. The process is clearly the same as that involved in the genesis of *honor*. Both fit the same formula:

réaction : *réactionnaire* = *répression* : *x*
x = *répressionnaire*.

In neither case is there the least pretext for speaking of a 'change'. The word *répressionnaire* replaces nothing. Another example of this kind would be the following. For the plural of the French adjective *final* ('final'), one hears the analogical form *finaux*, which is said to be more regular than *finals*. Now suppose someone invented the adjective *firmamental* ('of the firmament') and gave it a plural *firmamentaux*. Would one say that *finaux* is an example of change, but *firmamentaux* an example of creation? Both cases involve creation. On the model of *mur* : *emmurer* ('wall : immure'), there were formed *tour* : *entourer* ('circuit : surround') and *jour* : *ajourer* ('daylight : perforate (as in fretwork)'). These derivatives, being relatively recent, strike us as creations. But if I discover that French of an earlier period also had the verbs *entorner* and *ajorner*, based on the same nouns *torn* and *jorn* (= modern French *tour* and *jour*), should I now change my mind and declare that *entourer* and *ajourer* are modifications of the earlier [226] forms? The illusion of analogical 'change' comes from a relation established with the term which has been ousted by the new one. But this is a mistake, because these so-called 'changes' (like *honor*) are the same as what we call 'creations' (like *répressionnaire*).

§3. Analogy as the creative principle in languages

If, having demonstrated what analogy is not, we now study it from a positive point of view, it becomes immediately apparent that its principle is simply identical with that of linguistic creation in general. What is this principle?

Analogy is a psychological phenomenon. But that alone does not suffice to distinguish it from sound change, which may also be considered as such (cf. p. [208]). One must take a step further, and say that analogy is a grammatical phenomenon. It presupposes awareness and grasp of relations between forms. Where sound is concerned, ideas count for nothing; whereas they necessarily intervene in the case of analogy.

In the change of intervocalic *s* to *r* in Latin (cf. p. [201]), as in *honōsem* → *honōrem*, no part is played by comparison with other forms, nor by the meaning of the word. It is the corpse of the form *honōsem* which survives as *honōrem*. On the contrary, to account for the appearance of *honor* beside *honōs* we have to appeal to other forms, as indicated in the formula of the four-term proportion:

ōrātōrem : *ōrātor* = *honōrem* : x.
x = *honor*.

This combination would have no rationale if the mind did not associate the forms involved on the basis of their meanings.

So in analogy, everything is grammatical. But to this it must im-
[227] mediately be added that the creation which results can only belong at first to speech. It is the work of a single speaker. This is the sphere, on the fringe of the language, where the phenomenon must first be located. None the less, two things must be distinguished: (1) grasping the relation which connects the sponsoring forms, and (2) the result suggested by this comparison, i.e. the form improvised by the speaker to express his thought. The latter alone belongs to speech.

Analogy teaches us once again, then, to distinguish between the language itself and speech (cf. p. [36] ff.). It shows us how speech depends on the language, and allows us to put our finger on the operational linguistic mechanism, as earlier described (cf. p. [179]). Any creation has to be preceded by an unconscious comparison of materials deposited in the store held by the language, where the sponsoring forms are arranged by syntagmatic and associative relations.

So one whole part of the phenomenon has already been completed before the new form becomes visible. The continual activity of language in analysing the units already provided contains in itself not only all possibilities of speaking in conformity with usage, but also all possibilities of analogical formation. Thus it is a mistake to suppose that the generative process occurs only at the moment when the new creation emerges: its elements are already given. Any word I improvise, like *in-décor-able* ('un-decorat-able') already exists potentially in the language. Its elements are all to be found already in syntagmas like *décor-er* ('to decorate'), *décor-ation* ('decor-ation'), *pardonn-able* ('pardon-able'), *mani-able* ('manage-able'), *in-connu* ('un-known'), *in-sensé* ('in-sane'), etc. Its actualisation in speech is an insignificant fact in comparison with the possibility of forming it.

To summarise, analogy in itself is simply one aspect of the phenomenon of interpretation, a manifestation of the general activity which analyses units in order then to make use of them. That is why we say [228]
that analogy is entirely grammatical and synchronic.

This characteristic of analogy prompts two observations which support our views on absolute and relative arbitrariness (cf. p. [180] ff.).

1. One could classify words according to their relative capacity for giving rise to others, depending on the extent to which they are themselves analysable. A simple word is, by definition, unproductive: e.g. *magasin* ('shop'), *arbre* ('tree'), *racine* ('root'). The word *magasinier* ('store-keeper') was not engendered by *magasin*: it was formed on the model of *prisonnier* : *prison* ('prisoner : prison'), etc. Similarly *emmagasiner* ('to store') owes its existence to the analogy of *emmailloter*: *maillot* ('to swaddle : swaddling clothes'), *encadrer* : *cadre* ('to frame: frame'), *encapuchonner* : *capuchon* ('to hood : hood'), etc.

So in every language there are productive words and sterile words. But the proportions vary. What this comes down to is the distinction previously drawn (cf. p. [183]) between 'lexicological' and 'grammatical' languages. In Chinese, the majority of words are unsegmentable; whereas in artificial languages they are nearly all segmentable. An Esperantist is fully at liberty to construct new words on any given root.

2. We have already noted (p. [222]) that any analogical creation can be represented as an operation like the computation of the fourth term of a proportion. Very often this formula is used to explain the phenomenon itself, whereas we have sought its rationale in the analysis and reconstruction of elements supplied by the language.

There is a conflict between these two conceptions. If the proportion is a sufficient explanation, what purpose is served by the hypothesis which appeals to analysis of the elements? To form *indécorable*, there is no need to extract its elements (*in-décor-able*): it suffices to take [229]
the whole and place it in the equation:

pardonner : *impardonnable*, etc. = *décorer* : *x*.
x = *indécorable*.

In that way there is no need to credit the speaker with a complicated operation too much like the conscious analysis of the grammarian. In a case like *Krantz* : *Kräntze* (cf. p. [222]), based on *Gast* : *Gäste*, decomposition seems less plausible than the proportion, since in the model the stem is *Gast-* in one case and *Gäst-* in the other; it looks as though a phonetic feature of *Gäste* has simply been replicated on *Kranze*.

Which of these theories corresponds to the reality? Let us note first of all that the case of *Kranz* does not necessarily preclude analysis. We have seen alternation operative in roots and prefixes (cf. p. [216]), and a feeling for alternation may exist alongside a positive analysis.

These two conflicting conceptions are reflected in two different grammatical doctrines. Our European grammars operate with the proportion. They explain the formation of a preterite in German, for example, on the basis of complete words: the pupil is told to form the preterite of, say, *lachen* ('to laugh') on the model of *setzen* : *setzte* ('to sit : sat'). A Hindu grammar, on the contrary, would devote one chapter to the study of the roots (*setz-*, *lach-*, etc.), and a different chapter to the endings of the preterite (*-te*, etc.). It would give the elements resulting from the analysis, and one would then have to recombine them to form whole words. In any Sanskrit dictionary, the verbs are arranged in an order determined by their root.

Depending on the predominant tendency in each linguistic group, the grammatical theorists will incline to the one or the other of these methods.

Early Latin seems to favour the analytic procedure. Here is a clear
[230] demonstration of the fact. The vowel length of *a* is not the same in *făctus* ('made') and *āctus* ('done'), although it is in *făciō* ('I make') and *ăgō* ('I do'). One must suppose that *āctus* goes back to **ăgtos* and attribute the lengthened vowel to the voiced consonant which follows. This hypothesis is fully confirmed by the Romance languages. The opposition *spĕciō* : *spĕctus* ('I see : seen') vs. *tĕgō* : *tēctus* ('I cover : covered') is reflected in French *dépit* ('spite': Latin *despĕctus*) vs. *toit* ('roof': Latin *tēctum*). Cf. also Latin *confĭciō* : *confĕctus* ('I complete : completed') vs. *rĕgō* : *rēctus* ('I rule : ruled') : whereas *confĕctus* gives French *confit*, *dīrēctus* gives French *droit*. But **agtos*, **tegtos*, **regtos* were not inherited from Proto-Indo-European, where the corresponding forms were certainly **ăktos*, **tĕktos*, etc. It was prehistoric Latin which introduced **agtos*, **tegtos*, **regtos*, in spite of the difficulty of pronouncing a voiced consonant immediately before a voiceless one. This could only have been done if there was a strong consciousness of the stem units *ag-*, *teg-*, etc. Early Latin thus possessed a high degree of awareness of the constituent parts of a word (stems, suffixes, etc.) and of their fitting together. It is probable that in our modern languages it is not felt so acutely. But German probably has it more than French (cf. p. [256]).

CHAPTER V [231]

Analogy and Evolution

§1. How an analogical innovation enters the language

Nothing enters the language before having been tried out in speech. All evolutionary phenomena have their roots in the linguistic activity of the individual. This principle, already stated earlier (p. [138]), applies particularly to analogical innovations. Before Latin *honor* (cf. p. [223] ff.). could become a rival able to replace *honōs*, a speaker had first to improvise it, and others to imitate it and repeat it, until it became accepted usage.

Far from all analogical innovations are so successful. One constantly comes across combinations with no future which will never probably gain acceptance in the language. Children's language is full of them, because children are poorly acquainted with usage and are not as yet restrained by it. They say *viendre* for *venir* ('to come'), and *mouru* for *mort* ('dead').[1] But adult speech contains examples too. Many people say *traisait* (which is found indeed in Rousseau) instead of *trayait* ('(he) milked'). All these innovations are in themselves perfectly regular. They can be explained in the same way as we explain those the language has accepted. *Viendre*, for instance, is based on the proportion:

éteindrai : *éteindre* = *viendrai* : *x*
('(I) will extinguish : to extinguish') = ('(I) will come : *x*)
x = *viendre*.[1]

Likewise, *traisait* was formed on the model of *plaire* : *plaisait* ('to please : (he) pleased'), etc. [232]

The language retains only a very small proportion of the creations of speech. But those which last are numerous enough to enable the

[1] English children likewise produce *goed* for *went*, and *comed* for *came*. (Translator's note)

sum total of new forms, from one period to the next, to give quite a new look to vocabulary and grammar.

The whole of the preceding chapter shows clearly that analogy alone cannot be a factor in evolution. It is none the less true that this constant substitution of new forms for old is one of the most striking aspects of linguistic change. Every time a new creation is definitely accepted and ousts its rival, there is truly something created and something abandoned. On this score, analogy occupies a preponderant place in the theory of linguistic evolution.

This is the point we wish to emphasise.

§2. Analogical innovations as symptoms of changes in interpretation

The process of interpreting and analysing linguistic units never ceases. But how is it that this interpretation constantly changes from one generation to another?

The cause of this change is to be sought in the enormous mass of factors which constantly threaten the analysis adopted in a given linguistic state. We will review some of these factors.

The first and most important is sound change (cf. Chapter II). By rendering certain analyses ambiguous and others impossible, it alters the conditions governing segmentation, and hence the results of segmentation. From this there ensues a shift in the limits of units and a modification of their nature. (Cf. earlier remarks on p. [195] concerning compounds like *beta-hūs* and *redo-līch*, and on p. [213] about Proto-Indo-European noun flexion.)

[233] But sound change is not all. There is also agglutination, which will be considered below (p. [242] ff.). This has the effect of reducing a combination of elements to a single unit. Then there are all kinds of circumstances external to the word, but liable to affect its analysis. For since word analysis is the result of a set of comparisons, it is clear that it depends constantly upon the associative environment of the word. Thus the Proto-Indo-European superlative **swād-is-to-s* contained two independent suffixes: *-is-* expressing the idea of the comparative (cf. Latin *mag-is* 'more'), and *-to-* designating the fixed place of an object in a sequence (cf. Greek *trí-to-s* 'third'). These two suffixes became agglutinated (cf. Greek *hḗd-isto-s*, or rather *hḗd-ist-os* 'sweetest'). But this agglutination was in turn favoured greatly by a fact unconnected with the superlative: comparatives in *-is* fell out of use, and were replaced by formations in *-jōs*. Thus *-is-*, no longer being recognised as an autonomous element, was not distinguished in *-isto-*.

It should be noted in passing that there is a general tendency to diminish the stem element in favour of the formative element, especially when the stem ends in a vowel. Thus in Latin the suffix *-tāt-* (e.g. *vēri-tāt-em* 'truth', for **vēro-tāt-em*; cf. Greek *deinó-tēt-a* 'harshness') took over the *i* of the stem: hence the analysis *vēr-itāt-em*. Likewise *Rōmā-nus* ('Roma-n'), *Albā-nus* ('*Alba-n*') – cf. *aēnus* 'bronze' for **aes-no-s* 'copper-ness' – became *Rōm-ānus* ('Rom-an'), *Alb-ānus* ('Alb-an').

Now, whatever may be the origin of these changes of interpretation, they are always signalled by the appearance of analogical forms. For if the units which are alive, and recognised as such by speakers at a given period, are alone capable of giving rise to analogical formations, by the same token any given distribution of units implies the possibility of extending its usage. Analogy is thus the decisive argument which shows that a formative element exists at a given time as a significant unit. The form *merīdiōnālis* ('southern') in Lactantius (for *merīdiālis*) shows that at that period the word for 'northern' was segmented as *septentri-ōnālis*, and likewise *regi-ōnālis* ('regi-onal'). [234]
To demonstrate that the suffix *-tāt-* had acquired an *i* from the stem, it suffices to point to *celer-itātem* ('swift-ness'). *Pāg-ānus* ('rural'), formed from *pāg-us* ('village'), demonstrates how speakers of Latin analysed *Rōm-ānus*. The analysis of German *redlich* (p. [195]) is confirmed by the existence of *sterblich* ('mortal'), formed with a verb root (*sterben* 'to die').

A particularly curious example shows how, from one age to the next, analogy operates upon new units. In modern French *somnolent* ('sleep-y') is analysed *somnol-ent* as if it were a present participle. The proof of this is the creation of a verb *somnoler* 'to drowse'. But in Latin the corresponding adjective was segmented *somno-lentus*, like *succu-lentus* ('succulent'), and at an earlier period still *somn-olentus* (i.e. 'smelling of sleep', from *olēre* 'to smell of', as *vīn-olentus* 'smelling of wine': cf. *vīnum* 'wine').

Thus the most evident and most important effect of analogy is to replace old, irregular and ailing formations by new ones of greater regularity, composed of living elements.

Doubtless it does not always happen as simply as this suggests. The action the language takes is interrupted by countless hesitations, approximations, and incomplete analyses. At no one time does a language possess an entirely fixed system of units. Here one should recall what has already been said (p. [213]) about the flexion of Proto-Indo-European **ekwos* as compared with **pods*. These imperfect analyses sometimes give rise to confused analogical creations. The Proto-Indo-European forms **geus-etai, *gus-tos, *gus-tis* allow us to extract a root *geus-, gus-*, ('to taste'). But in Greek intervocalic *s* falls, and the analysis of *geúomai, geustós* (forms of the verb *geúo* 'taste') becomes uncertain. There is hesitation: sometimes *geus-* is identified as the root, and sometimes *geu-*. Analogy in turn bears witness to this fluctuation. One even sees stems in *eu-* take the final *s*: e.g. *pneu-*, *pneûma* ('wind, air'), verbal adjective *pneus-tós*.

Even in these hesitations analogy exercises an influence upon the [235] language. Thus, although not itself a process of change, analogy reflects constantly the changes which have occurred in the linguistic economy, and exemplifies them in new combinations. It collaborates effectively with all the forces which are constantly modifying the architecture of a language. On this ground, analogy counts as a powerful factor in linguistic evolution.

§3. *Analogy as a principle of renovation and conservation*

One is sometimes tempted to ask whether analogy really has the importance seemingly indicated by the developments illustrated above, and whether its effects are as widespread as those of sound change. In fact the history of every language reveals an accumulation of analogical developments, piled one on top of another. Taken all together, these continual readjustments play an even more important role in the evolution of the language than sound change.

But there is one thing of particular interest to the linguist. In spite of the enormous number of analogical changes over the course of several centuries, there is a very high survival rate for the linguistic elements involved: they are merely distributed differently. Analogical innovations are more apparent than real. A language is a dress patched with pieces of its own material. Four fifths of French comes from Proto-Indo-European, if one thinks of the substance from which French sentences are composed: but words carried through as a whole without analogical change, from the parent language down to modern French, could be listed on a single page (e.g. *est* ('is') from **esti*, numerals, and certain words like *ours* ('bear'), *nez* ('nose'), *père* ('father'), *chien* ('dog')). The immense majority of French words, in one way or another, are new combinations of sounds wrenched from older [236] forms. In this sense, one can say that analogy, precisely because it always utilises old material for its innovations, is eminently conservative.

But analogy is no less basically a conservative influence pure and simple. One can say that it intervenes not only when pre-existing materials are distributed into new units, but also when forms remain identical and unchanged. In both cases the same psychological process is at work. To realise this, it is sufficient to recall that its principle is ultimately identical with that of the mechanism of language[1] (cf. p. [226]).

[1] Again the term used is *langage*, not *langue*. (Translator's note)

Latin *agunt* ('they do') came down more or less intact from the prehistoric period, when it was **agonti*, right down to proto-Romance. During that time, successive generations used it and no rival form appeared to challenge it. Did analogy play no part in this conservation? Indeed, analogy is just as responsible for the stability of *agunt* as for any analogical innovation. *Agunt* is set in a system, interdependently related to forms like *dīcunt* ('they say'), *legunt* ('they read'), and others such as *agimus* ('we do'), *agitis* ('you do'). Without this framework, it might well have been replaced by a form composed of new elements. What was handed down was not *agunt* but *ag-unt*. The form survived unchanged because *ag-* and *-unt* occurred regularly in other series, and it was this procession of associated forms which protected *agunt* along the way. Similary Latin *sex-tus* ('sixth') is supported by compact series of forms: *sex* ('six'), *sex-āginta* ('sixty'), etc. on the one hand, and on the other *quar-tus* ('fourth'), *quin-tus* ('fifth'), etc.

Thus forms are kept because they are ceaselessly remade analogically. A word is understood simultaneously as a unit and as a syntagma, and is maintained insofar as its elements do not alter. Correspondingly, its existence is threatened only to the extent that its elements fall out of use. That is what is happening in French to *dites* ('(you) [237]
say') and *faites* ('(you) make'), which descend directly from Latin *dic-itis* and *fac-itis*, but no longer have any support in present-day verb flexion. The language is seeking to replace them. We hear *disez* and *faisez*, on the model of *plaisez* ('(you) please'), *lisez* ('(you) read'), etc., and these new endings are already normal in the majority of compounds, e.g. *contredisez* ('(you) contradict').

The only forms over which analogy exercises no power are naturally isolated words, such as proper names, especially place names (*Paris, Genève, Agen*, etc.). These admit of no analysis and consequently no interpretation of their elements. No rival creation emerges to challenge them.

Thus the conservation of a form may depend on two quite opposite factors: complete isolation, or fitting tightly into the framework of a system which remains intact in its essential parts and so provides constant support. It is in the intermediate domain of forms inadequately supported by their neighbours that analogy is able to introduce innovations.

But whether it is a question of the conservation of a form composed of several elements, or the redistribution of linguistic material in new constructions, the role of analogy is immense. It is always at work.

[238] CHAPTER VI

Popular Etymology

It sometimes happens that we get a word wrong when we are not very sure of its form and meaning: and sometimes these deformations pass into common usage. Old French *coute-pointe*, from *coute* (variant of *couette* 'cover') and *pointe* (past participle of *poindre* 'to stitch, quilt'), was changed to *courte-pointe* ('counterpane') as if it were composed of an adjective *courte* ('short') and a noun *pointe* ('point'). However bizarre such innovations may be, they do not occur haphazardly. They are attempts to make some kind of sense of an embarrassing word by connecting it with something known.

This phenomenon is called 'popular etymology'. At first sight it hardly seems to differ from analogy. When a speaker, forgetting the existence of the word *surdité* ('deafness'), creates analogically the form *sourdité* from *sourd* ('deaf'), the result is the same as if, mishearing *surdité*, he had distorted it by associating it with the adjective *sourd*. Thus the only difference would be that analogical constructions are rational, whereas popular etymology proceeds randomly and merely produces howlers.

However, this difference applies only to the results and is not an essential difference. The real difference in fact goes deeper than that. To see what it is, let us begin by taking a few examples of the main types of popular etymology.

[239] First, there is the case in which the word receives a new interpretation but its form remains unchanged. In German *durchbläuen* ('to thrash') goes back etymologically to *bliuwan* ('to beat'), but is connected with *blau* ('blue') by reason of the bruises caused by beating. In the middle ages, German borrowed from French the word *aventure* ('adventure'), which gave quite regularly *ābentüre*, and then *Abenteuer*. Without any distortion, the word thus became associated with *Abend* 'evening' ('story told of an evening'), with the result that in the eighteenth century it came to be spelt *Abendteuer*. Old French *souf-*

raite 'hardship' (from Latin *suffracta*, past participle of *subfrangere* 'break in pieces') gave rise to the adjective *souffreteux* ('destitute'), which is nowadays associated with the verb *souffrir* ('suffer'), although the two are etymologically unconnected. French *lais* ('legacy') is the verbal noun from *laisser* ('to leave'), but it is nowadays linked to *léguer* ('bequeath') and spelt *legs*. There are even those who pronounce it *le-g-s*. Although that may seem like a change of form brought about by the new interpretation, it was in fact an influence from the written language: the intention was to indicate the supposed origin of the word, not to alter its pronunciation. In a similar manner *homard* ('lobster'), borrowed from the Old Nurse *humarr* (*hummer* in Danish), acquired a final *-d* by analogy with French words ending in *-ard*. But in this instance the error of interpretation reflected in the spelling affects the end of the word, which has been confused with a common French suffix (cf. *bavard* 'gossip', etc.).

But usually a word is distorted in order to accommodate it to elements supposedly recognised in it. This is the case of French *choucroute* ('sauerkraut'), a distortion of German *Sauerkraut* (cf. French *chou* 'cabbage'). In German, Latin *dromedārius* ('dromedary'), became *Trampeltier*, i.e. 'animal that tramples': the compound is new, but contains already existing German words, *trampeln* ('trample') and *Tier* ('animal'). In Old High German, the Latin *margarita* ('pearl') was made into *mari-greoz* ('sea-pebble'), by combining two existing German words.

Finally, a particularly instructive example is that of Latin *carbunculus* ('little coal') which in German turns up as *Karfunkel* (through association with *funkeln* 'to sparkle'), and in French as [240]
escarboucle (through association with *boucle* 'buckle'). In French the verb *calfeter* or *calfetrer* ('block up') became *calfeutrer*, under the influence of *feutre* ('felt'). What is striking at first sight about these examples is that each of them includes, in addition to an intelligible element which exists in other forms, a part which represents no older form: *Kar-*, *escar-*, *cal-*. But it would be a mistake to think that there is any creative element involved here, anything which arose out of the phenomenon in question. The opposite is true. These are fragments which the interpretation has failed to deal with. They are, if you like, popular etymologies which got stuck half way. *Karfunkel* is on the same footing as *Abenteuer* (granted that *-teuer* is a left-over which has no explanation). It is also comparable to *homard*, in which *hom-* is meaningless.

The degree of distortion thus creates no essential differences between words maltreated by popular etymology: what they all have in common is that they are purely and simply misunderstood forms which have been reinterpreted in terms of known forms.

It now becomes apparent in what respects popular etymology resembles analogy and in what respects it differs.

The two phenomena have only one thing in common: both utilise significant elements provided by the language. But otherwise they are diametrically opposed. Analogy always presupposes that the earlier form has been forgotten. Behind the analogical form *traisait* (cf. p. [231]) there is no analysis of the old form *trayait*: the old form has to be forgotten in order for its rival to appear. Analogy does not draw upon the substance of the signs it replaces. Popular etymology, on the contrary, reduces to an interpretation of the old form: it is the memory of the old form, confused though it may be, which is the point of departure for the distortion it undergoes. So in one case it is remem-
[241] bering and in the other case forgetting which is at the basis of the analysis, and this difference is fundamental.

Popular etymology, then, acts only under specific conditions and affects only rare, technical or foreign words which speakers have not thoroughly mastered. Analogy, on the contrary, is an entirely general phenomenon, which belongs to the normal functioning of a language. These two phenomena, so alike in certain respects, are essentially different, and must be carefully distinguished.

CHAPTER VII [242]

Agglutination

§1. Definition

Beside analogy, the importance of which has just been noted above, another factor intervenes in the production of new units. This is agglutination.

No other mode of formation need be taken seriously into consideration. Onomatopoeia (cf. p. [101]), the creation of whole words invented by a particular individual without recourse to analogy (e.g. *gaz* 'gas'), and even popular etymology, are of comparatively little or no importance.

Agglutination occurs when two or more terms originally distinct, but frequently joined together syntagmatically in sentences, merge into a single unit which is either unanalysable or difficult to analyse. Such is the agglutination process: we say 'process' and not 'procedure', since the latter term implies will and intention. But the involuntary nature of agglutination is one of its essential characteristics.

Here are some examples. In French, *ceci* ('this') was originally two words, *ce* ('this') and *ci* ('here'): the single word *ceci* was new, even though its material and constituent elements had not altered. Cf. French *tous* ('all') *jours* ('days') → *toujours ('always'); au jour d'hui* ('on the day of today') → *aujourd'hui* ('today'); *dès* ('from') *jà* ('now') → *déjà* ('already'); *vert* ('green') *jus* ('juice') → *verjus* ('verjuice'). Agglutination may also join together smaller units within a word, as [243] we have seen (p. [233]) in connexion with the Proto-Indo-European superlative **swād-is-to-s* and the Greek superlative *hḗd-isto-s*.

Closer examination reveals three phases:

(1) The combination of two or more terms in a syntagma, comparable to any other.

(2) The agglutination proper: that is, the synthesis of syntagmatic

elements into a new unit. This synthesis occurs of its own accord, in conformity with an automatic tendency. When a compound concept is expressed by a very familiar sequence of significant units, the mind takes a short cut, as it were, and dispenses with analysis: it applies the concept as a whole to the sequence of signs as a whole. The sequence thus becomes a single unit.

(3) Any other changes tending to assimilate the former group to a single word, e.g. unification of stress (*vért–jús* → *verjús*), special phonetic changes, and so on.

It is often held that (3) precedes (2), i.e. phonetic and stress changes precede conceptual changes, so that semantic synthesis is to be explained by material synthesis and unification. It probably does not work like that. Rather, because a single idea was perceived in *vert jus*, *tous jours*, etc. these were made into single words. It would be a mistake to reverse the connexion.

§2. *Agglutination and analogy*

The contrast between analogy and agglutination is striking.

(1) In agglutination, two or more words merge into one by synthesis (e.g. French *encore* ('yet') from Latin *hanc horam* ('this hour')), or else
[244] two smaller units do likewise (cf. p. [233]. Greek *hḗd-isto-s* from **swād-is-to-s*). Analogy, on the contrary, starts with smaller units and uses them to make a larger unit. To form Latin *pāg-ānus*, a stem *pāg-* and a suffix *-ānus* were joined together.

(2) Agglutination operates solely in the syntagmatic sphere. Its action affects a given group: nothing else is involved. Analogy, on the contrary, involves associative series as well as syntagmas.

(3) In particular, agglutination is totally involuntary. It is not a positive action, but merely a mechanical process, in which the blending takes place of its own accord. Analogy, on the contrary is a procedure, presupposing analyses and combinations, an activity of the intelligence, an intention.

The terms *construction* and *structure* are often used of word formation. But these terms have different meanings, depending on whether they apply to agglutination or to analogy. In the former case, they evoke the slow cementing together of elements in contact in a syntagma, leading to a synthesis which may go as far as complete obliteration of the original units. In the case of analogy, on the contrary, construction implies an arrangement completed at one stroke, in a single speech act, by bringing together a number of elements taken from various associative series.

It is clear how important it is to distinguish the two modes of formation. Latin *possum* ('I can') is nothing other than the merging of the two words *potis sum* ('I am the master'): it is an agglutination. Latin *signifer* ('standard bearer') and *agricola* ('farmer', 'land-cultivator'), on the contrary, are products of analogy. They are constructions based on models supplied by the language. The terms *composition* and *derivation* should be reserved for analogical creations only.[1]

It is often difficult to say whether an analysable form began with [245] agglutination, or whether it arose as an analogical construction. Linguists have engaged in endless discussion about Proto-Indo-European forms like **es-mi, *es-ti, *ed-mi*, etc. Were the elements *es-*, *ed-*, etc. separate words at some very early period, which later became agglutinated with others (*mi, ti*, etc.)? Or were **es-mi, *es-ti*, etc. combinations using elements drawn from other complex units of the same kind (which would mean that agglutination was prior to the formation of endings in Proto-Indo-European)? In the absence of historical evidence, the question is probably insoluble.

Only history can tell us about such matters. Every time history allows us to say that a single element was once two or more consecutive elements we are dealing with agglutination. E.g. Latin *hunc* goes back to *hom ce*, (*ce* is attested by inscriptions). But when historical evidence is lacking, it is very difficult to determine what is agglutination and what is the work of analogy.

[1] This amounts to saying that these two phenomena combine their action in the history of the language: but agglutination always comes first, and provides the models for analogy. The type of composition which resulted in Greek *hippó-dromo-s* ('hippo- [245] drome') originated in partial agglutination at a period of Proto-Indo-European when endings were unknown (so *ekwo dromo* was equivalent to an English compound like *country house*). But it was analogy which made this a productive formation before the indissoluble merging of the two elements. Similar is the French future tense (*je ferai* 'I will do'), originating in Vulgar Latin with the agglutination of the infinitive with the present tense of the verb 'to have' (*facere habeō* = 'I have to do'). Thus it is through the intervention of analogy that agglutination creates syntactic types and works on behalf of grammar. Left to its own devices, agglutination carries the synthesis of elements to the point of absolute unity, and produces only unanalysable, unproductive words (e.g. *hanc hōram* → *encore*): in other words it works on behalf of vocabulary. (Editorial note)

[246] CHAPTER VIII

Diachronic Units, Identities and Realities

Static linguistics operates with units which are synchronically linked together. Everything said in the previous chapters shows that in a diachronic sequence we are not dealing with elements delimited once and for all, as might be represented in the following diagram:

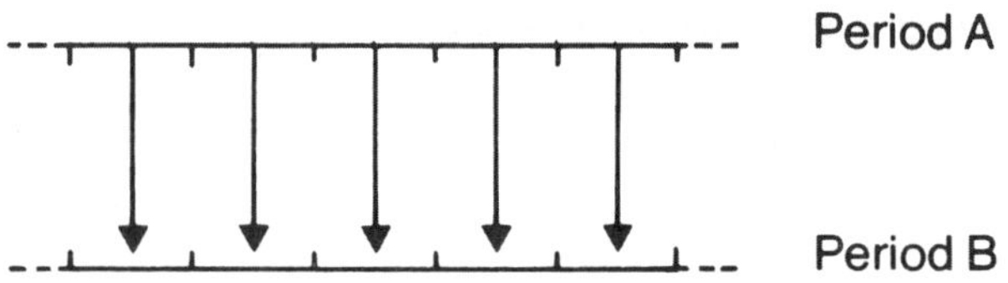

On the contrary, their correlation is constantly changing, because of events taking place in the language. So they might be more appropriately represented as follows:

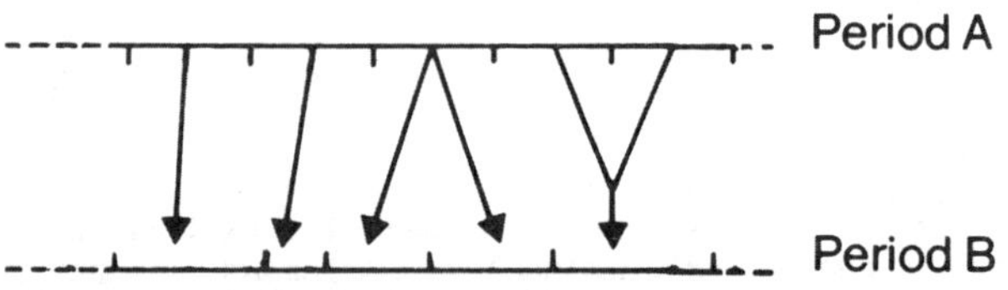

This is the outcome of all the factors discussed above – sound change, analogy, agglutination, etc.

[247] Almost all the examples so far cited relate to word formation. The following example is syntactic. Proto-Indo-European had no prepositions. It marked relations by its numerous case flexions, which had very specific meanings. Nor did Proto-Indo-European have verbs with prefixes. It had only particles, i.e. little words added to a verb phrase to add some specification or nuance of meaning to the verb. So

Proto-Indo-European had nothing corresponding either to Latin *īre ob mortem* ('to go to meet one's death'), or to *obīre mortem*: instead it would have used the equivalent of *īre mortem ob*. This is still the stage we find in early Greek. In (i) *óreos baínō káta* ('I come down from the mountain'), *óreos baínō* alone means 'I come from the mountain' (the genitive *óreos* having the value of an ablative), while *káta* adds the qualification 'descending'. At a later stage, Greek has (ii) *katà óreos baínō*, with *katà* functioning as a preposition, or (iii) *kata-baínō óreos*, with agglutination of the participle as a prefix.

Here there are two or three distinct phenomena, but all are based upon an interpretation of units. (1) There is the creation of a new class of words – prepositions – by a simple redistribution of units given. One particular order, without significance originally, perhaps due to some fortuitous circumstance, gave rise to a new grouping: *kata*, originally independent, attaches itself to the noun *óreos*, and this pair acts as the complement of the verb *baínō*. (2) There is the appearance of a new type of verb, *katabaínō*. This is a different psychological grouping, also favoured by a special distribution of units and consolidated by agglutination. (3) As a natural consequence, there is a weakening of the sense of the genitive ending (*óre-os*). It is *katà* which now takes over the role of expressing the principal idea which formerly the genitive alone expressed. The importance of the ending *-os* is thereby diminished. This development paves the way for its future disappearance.

In all three cases, then, there is indeed a new distribution of units. The same substance is retained, but with different functions. It should [248] be noted that no sound change has intervened to induce any of these shifts. Moreover, although the material has not altered, it is not to be supposed that the change is restricted to the domain of meaning. There is no syntactic phenomenon which does not involve the correlation of a certain sequence of concepts and a certain sequence of phonetic units (cf. p. [191]): it is precisely this correlation which has altered. The sounds remain, but the significant units are no longer the same.

As stated previously (p. [109]), an alteration in the linguistic sign is a shift in the relation between signal and signification. This definition applies not only to changes in individual items, but to the evolution of the whole system. Diachronic development in its entirety is just that.

However, when one has noted a certain shift in synchronic units, one is still a long way from accounting for what has taken place in the language. There is the problem of the *diachronic unit* itself: it arises when we ask, of each event, which is the element directly subject to change. We have already encountered a problem of this kind in connexion with sound change (cf. p. [133]). Sound change affects only individual sounds: words as such are not units affected by it.

Since there are many kinds of diachronic change, there will be many analogous questions to be answered. The units identified for these purposes will not necessarily correspond to the units recognised in the synchronic domain. In conformity with the principle laid down in Part One, the notion of a unit cannot be the same for both synchronic and diachronic studies. In any case, it will not be fully elucidated as long as it has not been studied from both static and evolutionary points of view. Only the solution of the problem of the diachronic unit will
[249] enable us to penetrate beyond the superficial appearance of linguistic evolution and grasp its essence. Here, as in synchrony, understanding what the units are is indispensable in order to distinguish illusion from reality (cf. p. [153]).

But another question, and a particularly delicate one, is that of *diachronic identity*. For in order to be able to say that a given unit has remained the same over time, or that, while remaining a distinct unit, it has changed in form or meaning – any of which is possible – I must know on what I base the claim that an element taken from one period – e.g. the French word *chaud* ('hot') – is the same as an element taken from another period – e.g. the Latin *calidum*.

To this question it will doubtless be replied that *calidum* became *chaud* through the regular operation of phonetic laws, and that therefore the equation *calidum* = *chaud* is correct. This is what is called a 'phonetic identity'. Another would be Latin *sēparāre* and French *sevrer*. French *fleurir*, on the other hand, would not thus be equated with Latin *flōrēre*, since the latter by regular phonetic change should have produced **flouroir*.

This type of correspondence seems at first sight to cover the notion of diachronic identity in general. But in fact historical phonetics alone does not suffice to account for it. It is doubtless correct to say that Latin *mare* ('sea') ought to appear in French in the form *mer* on the grounds that Latin *a* became *e* in French under certain conditions, that final unstressed *e* fell, etc. But to state that these connexions *a* → *e*, *e* → zero, etc. constitute the identity in question is to put the cart before the horse. On the contrary, one judges that *a* became *e*, that final *e* fell, etc. in the light of the correspondence *mare* : *mer*.

If two people from different regions of France say *se fâcher* ('become angry') and *se fôcher* respectively, the difference is very minor in comparison with the grammatical facts which allow us to recognize in
[250] these two different forms one and the same linguistic unit. The diachronic identity of two words as different as *calidum* and *chaud* simply means that the transition from one to the other was via a series of synchronic identities in speech, without the link between them ever being broken by successive sound changes. That is why we could say (p. [150]) that it is just as interesting to know how *Messieurs!* ('Gentlemen!') repeated several times in succession in the same speech is one

and the same as it is to know how the negation *pas* ('not') is the same as the noun *pas* ('pace'), or why *chaud* is the same as *calidum*, which comes to the same thing. The second problem is no more than an extension and complication of the first.

[251] Appendices to Parts Two and Three

A. Subjective and Objective Analysis

The analysis of linguistic units, constantly being made by the speakers of a language, may be called *subjective analysis*. It must not be confused with *objective analysis*, based on history. In a form such as Greek *híppos* 'horse', the grammarian distinguishes three elements: a root, a suffix and an ending (*hípp-o-s*). Greeks themselves recognised only two (*hípp-os*: cf. p. [213]). Objective analysis distinguishes four smaller units in Latin *amābās* 'you were loving' (*am-ā-bā-s*): but speakers of Latin segmented the form as *amā-bā-s*, or probably even treated *-bās* as a single flexion, as distinct from the stem. In the French words *entier* 'entire' (Latin *in-teger* 'intact'), *enfant* 'child' (Latin *in-fans* 'not speaking'), *enceinte* 'pregnant' (Latin *in-cincta* 'un-girdled'), the historian will detect a prefix *en-*, identical with the privative *in-* of Latin. But the subjective analysis of French speakers fails to recognise it altogether.

The grammarian is often tempted to see mistakes in these spontaneous linguistic analyses. But subjective analysis is no more in error than is 'false' analogy (cf. p. [223]). The language does not make mistakes. Its point of view is a different one, that is all. There is no common measure between the analysis of speakers and the analysis of historians, even though both proceed in the same way, i.e. by correlating series containing a common element. Both can be justified.
[252] Each has its own value. But in the last resort the only one that matters is the speakers', for it is based directly on the facts of linguistic structure.

Historical analysis is only a derivative form of analysis. In the end, it comes down to a projection of constructions taken from different periods on to a single plane. Like spontaneous segmentation, its aim is to identify the smaller units which go to make up a word. But it brings together the various segmentations made over a period of time, with a view to determining the oldest of these. A word is like a house of which the internal arrangement and purpose have been changed on various occasions. None the less, for those who live in it, there is only ever one. The analysis *hípp-o-s* examined above is not false, for it reflects facts that speakers were at some time aware of: it is simply 'anachronic', relating to a different period from that from which the word is taken. This *hípp-o-s* is not in contradiction with the *hípp-os* of Classical Greek; but it must be judged differently. Which once more comes back to the intrinsic difference between the diachronic and the synchronic.

Moreover, this allows us to deal with a methodological question still unresolved in linguistics. The comparative philologists divided words into roots, themes, suffixes, etc. and treated these distinctions as having an absolute value. To read Bopp and his disciples, one would think that the Greeks had brought with them from time immemorial a whole outfit of roots and suffixes, and that they put their words together as they went along; so that *patḗr*, for example, was as far as they were concerned a root *pa* plus a suffix *ter*, and *dṓsō* was the sum total of *dō+so+* a personal ending.

It was inevitable that there should come a reaction against these aberrations, and the watchword became – quite rightly – 'look at what happens in present-day languages, in everyday speech, and do not attribute to earlier periods any process or phenomenon which cannot [253]
be observed nowadays'. And since very frequently it is not possible to foist on modern languages analyses of the kind Bopp made, the Neogrammarians declare in accordance with this principle that roots, themes, suffixes, etc. are pure abstractions of the mind: if we make use of these abstractions, it is solely for convenience of exposition. But if there is no justification in the establishment of these categories, why establish them? And when they are established, on what ground is it claimed that a segmentation like *hípp-o-s*, for example, is prefertable to *hípp-os*?

The new school, after pointing out the defects of the old doctrine – which was easily done – was content with rejecting it in theory, while in practice remaining encumbered with a scientific apparatus which it could not dispense with after all. As soon as one examines these 'abstractions' rationally, one sees to what extent they do correspond to reality, and a very simple qualification is all that is needed to give these grammarian's devices an interpretation which is both valid and precise. An attempt has been made to do this above, by showing that objective analysis, being linked internally to subjective analysis of the living language, has a legitimate and clearly defined place in linguistic method.

B. Subjective Analysis and Determination of Units Smaller than the Word

As regards linguistic analysis, one cannot establish a method or formulate definitions except by approaching the task synchronically. This we should now like to demonstrate by commenting on the parts of the word: prefixes, roots, stems, suffixes, endings.[1]

Let us first consider *endings*: that is to say, the characteristic flexions or variable elements at the end of a word which distinguish the forms of a noun or verb paradigm. In the Greek verb 'to harness', *zeúgnū-mi*, *zeúgnū-s*, *zeúgnū-si*, *zeúgnu-men*, etc., the endings *-mi*, *-s*, *-si*, etc. are delimited simply by contrast with one another and with the preceding part of the word (*zeugnū̆-*). It has already been noted (pp. [123] and [163]) in connexion with the Czech genitive *žen*, as opposed to the nominative *žena*, that the absence of an ending may play the same role as an ending itself does. Thus in Greek the singular *zeúgnū!* ('harness!') contrasts with the plural *zeúgnu-te!* ('harness!'), and the vocative *rhêtor*! ('O speaker!') contrasts with *rhḗtor-os*, etc. In French *marš* (written *marche!* 'march!') contrasts with *maršõ* (written *marchons!* 'let us march!'). These are examples of inflected forms with a zero ending.

By discarding the ending, one obtains the *theme* or *stem*. This is, generally speaking, the common element which can be identified spontaneously by comparison of a series of related words, whether inflected or not, and which carries the idea common to the whole series. Thus in French in the series *roulis* ('rolling'), *rouleau* ('roller'), *rouler* ('to roll'), *roulage* ('rolling'), *roulement* ('rolling'), it is easy to identify a stem *roul-*. But the analysis made by speakers often distinguishes stems of various kinds within the same family of words; or more exactly, stems of various grades. The element *zeugnū̆-*, identified above in *zeúgnū-mi*, *zeúgnū-s*, etc., is a first-grade stem. It is not unanalysable: for if one compares other series (*zeúgnūmi* ('I harness'), *zeuktós* ('yoked'), *zeûksis* ('a joining'), *zeuktḗr* ('one who harnesses'), *zugón* ('yoke'), etc. vs. *zeúgnūmi* ('I harness'), *deíknūmi* ('I show'), *órnūmi* ('I stir'), etc.) the segmentation *zeug-nu* becomes obvious. So
[255] *zeug-* (with its variants *zeug-*, *zeuk-*, *zug-*, cf. p. [220]) is a second-grade stem. This stem is irreducible, for by comparing related forms it is impossible to take its segmentation any further.

This irreducible element common to all the words of one family is called a *root*. Since any subjective synchronic segmentation can only separate out different material elements by attaching some fragment of meaning to each, the root is in this respect the element where the meaning common to the whole series of related words reaches a maximum of abstraction and generality. Naturally, this vagueness varies

[1] Saussure did not deal with the question of compound words, at least from a syn-
[254] chronic viewpoint. Consequently, judgment must be suspended on this topic. What is clear enough is that the diachronic distinction earlier drawn between compounds and agglutinated forms cannot simply be carried over here, where one is dealing with the analysis of a linguistic state. It need hardly be added that this discussion of smaller units is not intended to resolve the more ticklish question raised on pp. [147] and [154] concerning the definition of the word as a unit. (Editorial note)

from one root to another, but it also depends to some extent upon the grade of the stem in question. The more segmentations involved, the more abstract the residual meaning is likely to be. Thus *zeugmátion* means 'little yoke', *zeûgma* 'yoke, band' (of no special kind), and *zeug-* expresses the general idea of 'joining together'.

It follows that a root, as such, cannot constitute a word and have endings directly added to it. A word always represents a relatively specific idea, at least from a grammatical point of view, and this is incompatible with the generality and abstractness characteristic of roots. But what then is to be made of the type of case which arises very frequently, where root and stem appear to be identical? For example, the Greek word for 'flame' *phlóks* (genitive *phlogós*) has a root *phleg-* or *phlog-*, which is found in all words of this family (*phlég-ō* 'I burn', etc.). Is this not counterevidence to the distinction laid down above? No; for we must here distinguish the root *phleg-* or *phlog-* in its general sense from *phlog-* with a particular meaning. Otherwise we shall be considering just the material form and ignoring the meaning. In this case the same phonetic element has two different values, and thus constitutes two distinct linguistic elements (cf. p. [147]). Just as previously *zeúgnū!* ('harness!') was seen to be an inflected form with a zero ending, we can say that *phlóg-* ('flame') is [256]
a stem with a *zero suffix*. Thus any confusion is avoided: the stem is kept distinct from the root, even if the two are phonetically identical.

The root, then, is a reality which speakers of a language recognise. They do not always, it is true, identify it equally clearly in all cases. There are differences in this respect from one language to another, as well as within individual languages.

In certain languages, specific features make speakers aware of roots. This is the case in German, where the root tends to take a regular form. It is nearly always monosyllabic (e.g. *streit-*, *bind-*, *haft-*, etc.), and conforms to certain rules of structure. There are restrictions on the order of sounds. Certain combinations, such as stop + liquid, are not allowed in final position. Thus *werk-* is a possible root, but not *wekr-*. Similarly *helf-* and *werd-* are found, but not *hefl-* or *wedr-*.

It will be recalled that regular alternations, especially between vowels, reinforce much more than they weaken a feeling for roots and smaller units in general. In this respect too, German with its *Ablaut* variations (cf. p. [217]) differs profoundly from French. Semitic roots have similar characteristics to an even higher degree. There the alternations are very regular, and form the basis of a large number of complex oppositions (e.g. Hebrew *qāṭal*, *qṭaltem*, *qṭōl*, *qiṭlū*, etc., – all forms of the same verb 'to kill'). Moreover, they show a feature reminiscent of the monosyllabic character of roots in German, but more striking; namely, they invariably have three consonants (cf. p. [315] ff.).

From this point of view, French is quite different. It has few alternations, and many two- or three-syllable roots, such as *commenc-*, *hésit-*, *épouvant-*, in addition to monosyllabic ones like *roul-*, *march-*, and *mang-*. Furthermore, French roots are too diverse in the
[257] combinations of sounds they allow, especially in final position, to be reduced to rules (cf. *tu-er*, *régn-er*, *guid-er*, *grond-er*, *souffl-er*, *tard-er*, *entr-er*, *hurl-er*). Thus it is not surprising that in French a feeling for roots is relatively weak.

If roots can be identified, so too can prefixes and suffixes. The *prefix* precedes that part of the word recognised as its stem: e.g. *hupo-* 'under' in Greek *hupo-zeúgnūmi* ('bring under (the yoke)'). The *suffix* is the element added to the root in order to form a stem (e.g. Greek *zeug-mat-*), or to one stem in order to form a second-grade stem (e.g. *zeugmat-io-*).[1] This element, as already noted above, may be represented by zero, just as an ending may. Identifying the suffix is thus simply another facet of the analysis of stems.

Sometimes the suffix has a concrete meaning, a semantic[2] value, as in *zeuk-tēr-*, where *-tēr-* designates the agent or instigator of the action ('one who, or that which (yokes)'). Sometimes it has a purely grammatical function, as in *zeúg-nū-(mi)*, where *nū* marks the notion of present tense. The prefix may also play either role, although it is rare for it to have a grammatical function in Indo-European languages, as it does in the *ge-* of the German past participle (*ge-setzt* from *setzen* 'to put, place'), or the perfective prefixes of Slavic (Russian *na-pisát'*, etc.).

The prefix also differs from the suffix in another respect, which is not universal but very common nevertheless: namely, it is more easily identifiable because it stands out more clearly from the word as a whole. This has to do with the nature of the prefix as a linguistic element: for in most cases when a prefix is removed from a form, what is left over itself appears as a complete word (e.g. in French *recommencer* ('begin again') vs. *commencer* ('begin'), *indigne* ('unworthy') vs. *digne* ('worthy'), *maladroit* ('unskilful') vs. *adroit* ('skilful'), *contrepoids* ('counterweight') vs. *poids* ('weight')). This feature is even more striking in Latin, Greek and German. It should be added that a prefix may

[1] In the example previously given (p. [254]), *zeug-* itself was described as a 'second-grade' stem. The discussion throughout this section bears witness to a failure to distinguish consistently between the type of relationship which links a root to the word forms based upon that root, on the one hand, and the quite different type of relationship which links the stem of any given word form with its ending, on the other. (Translator's note)

[2] The distinction here between what is 'semantic' and what is 'purely grammatical' is unfortunate in view of the sense given elsewhere in the text to the term 'grammatical'. Saussurean linguistics, as expounded in the *Cours*, lays no foundation for a distinction between meanings like 'instigator of action' and meanings like 'present tense'. On the contrary, it is difficult to see how such a distinction could be validated other than by reference to strictly non-linguistic factors. (Translator's note)

often function as an independent word: e.g. French *contre*, *mal*, *avant*, *sur*, German *unter*, *vor*, Greek *katá*, *pró*.[1] But this is not the case with suffixes. If a suffix is removed, what is left is an incomplete word: [258]
e.g. French *organisation* – *organis-*, German *Trennung* – *trenn-*, Greek *zeûgma* – *zeug-*.[2] Furthermore, the suffix has no independent existence as a form.

Thus it comes about that the stem usually has its starting point clearly marked out. Before there is any comparison with other forms, the speaker knows where to place the boundary between the prefix and what follows it. But it is not the same at the end of a word. No boundary emerges except as the result of comparison between forms having the same stem or the same suffix, and such comparisons will give different results depending on the kinds of forms compared.

From the point of view of subjective analysis, suffixes and stems exist only in virtue of syntagmatic and associative oppositions. It is possible in some cases to find a formative element and a stem in two different parts of a word, whatever they may be, provided they give rise to an opposition. In the Latin accusative *dictātōrem* ('dictator'), for instance, comparison with accusatives like *consul-em* ('consul'), *ped-em* ('foot'), etc. suggests a stem *dictātōr-*: whereas comparison with *lic-tō-rem* ('lictor'), *scrip-tōrem* ('writer') etc. suggests a stem *dictā-*, and comparison with *pō-tātōrem* ('drinker') and *can-tātōrem* ('singer') suggests a stem *dic-*. Given the right circumstances, the speaker may be led to segment forms in any or all of a number of conceivable ways, e.g. *dictāt-ōrem* on the model of *am-ōrem* ('love'), *ard-ōrem* ('flame'), or *dict-ātōrem* on the model of *ōr-ātōrem* ('orator'), *ar-ātōrem* ('ploughman'). As we know (cf. p. [233]), the results of these spontaneous analyses can be seen in analogical formations of every period. These formations allow us to identify the smaller units (roots, prefixes, suffixes, endings) which the language recognises, and the values it attaches to them.

C. Etymology [259]

Etymology is neither a separate discipline nor a part of evolutionary linguistics. It is only a special application of principles relating to synchronic and diachronic facts. It traces back the past history of words until it finds something that explains them.

When one speaks of the origin of a word and says that it 'comes from' another word, there are several things that may be meant. French *sel* ('salt') comes from Latin *sal* ('salt') by simply a change of

[1] English examples would be *in*, *over*, *under*. (Translator's note)

[2] English examples would be *eld-est*, *wid-th*, *burgl-ar*. But English also provides counterinstances. (Translator's note)

sound. French *labourer* ('to plough') comes from Old French *labourer* ('to work') simply by a change of meaning. French *couver* ('to hatch') comes from Latin *cubāre* ('to lie down') by changes of both meaning and sound. Finally, to say that French *pommier* ('apple tree') comes from *pomme* ('apple') is to state a relationship of grammatical derivation. In the first three cases we are dealing with diachronic identities, whereas the fourth is based on a synchronic relation between various different terms. This latter is the most important part of etymological research, as is shown by everything which has been said above in connexion with analogy.

The etymology of Latin *bonus* ('good') is not established simply by the discovery of an earlier form *dvenos*. But if one finds that Latin *bis* ('twice') goes back to *dvis*, thus uncovering a connexion with *duo* ('two'), that is what may be called an etymological operation. The same applies to tracing French *oiseau* ('bird') back to Latin *avicellus* ('little bird'), which brings to light the connexion between the French word and the Latin word for 'bird' (*avis*).

Etymology is thus first and foremost the explanation of words by investigating their connexions with other words. Explaining means relating to terms already known. In linguistics, to *explain a word is to relate it to other words*: for there are no necessary relations between sound and meaning. (Cf. p. [100] on the arbitrary nature of the linguistic sign.)

[260] Etymology is not satisfied with explaining isolated words. It traces the history of word families, and also of formative elements (prefixes, suffixes, etc.).

Like static and evolutionary linguistics, etymology describes facts: but the description is not methodical, since it follows no particular direction. In investigating a word, etymology may take its information from phonetics, morphology, semantics, etc. as the need arises. To achieve its aims, etymology makes use of all the means which linguistics makes available, but does not scrutinise the nature of the processes it is obliged to engage in.

PART FOUR [261]

Geographical Linguistics

CHAPTER I

On the Diversity of Languages

Approaching the question of relations between linguistic phenomena and their geographical distribution involves leaving internal linguistics and entering the domain of external linguistics. Chapter V of the Introduction has already given some indication of the extent and variety of this domain.

The first thing that strikes one in studying languages is their diversity, the differences as between one country and another, or even one district and another. Whereas divergences over time often do not come to the notice of the observer, territorial divergences leap immediately to the eye. Even savages grasp them, through contact with other tribes speaking other languages. It is even by means of such comparisons that a people becomes aware of its own language.

It may be noted in passing that this is what gives rise to the notion primitive peoples have that a language is a habit, a custom analogous to dress or weaponry. The term *idiom* itself designates, most appropriately, the language as a reflection of the individual characteristics of a community. (The Greek word *idíōma* already had the meaning 'special custom'.) This notion contains an element of truth, but one
which easily turns into error when it is taken so far that a language [262]
is seen as the attribute not of a nation but of a race, on a par with the colour of the skin or the shape of the head.

It may be added that each people believes its own language to be superior to others. Someone speaking another language is often regarded as someone incapable of speaking. The Greek word *bárbaros* ('barbarian') appears to have meant 'stutterer, stammerer' and to be related to Latin *balbus* ('stuttering, stammering'). In Russian, Germans are called *Nêmtsy*, i.e. 'dumb, mute'.

So geographical diversity was the first observation ever made in linguistics, and determined the initial form taken by scientific research into linguistic matters, even by the Greeks. They, it is true, simply fastened upon the differences between various Greek dialects; but this was because they took little interest in general in what went on outside Greece itself.

After recognising that two languages differ, one is instinctively led to discover analogies between them. This is a natural tendency among language-users. Country people like to compare their own local speech with that of a neighbouring village. People who know several languages notice features they have in common. But it is a curious fact that science took an extremely long time to make use of observations of that kind. The Greeks, who had noticed many resemblances between Latin vocabulary and their own, drew no linguistic conclusion from this.

Scientific observation of these analogies allows us to state in certain cases that two or more languages are related: that is to say, they have a common origin. A group of languages thus related is called a 'family'. Modern linguistics has recognized one after another the Indo-European family, the Semitic family, the Bantu[1] family, and so on. These
[263] families may in turn be compared, and sometimes broader and older affiliations come to light. Analogies have been sought between Finno-Ugrian[2] and Indo-European, between Indo-European and Semitic, and so on. But comparisons on this scale soon encounter insurmountable barriers. One must not confuse what might be with what demonstrably is the case. It is not probable that all languages are phylogenetically related; but even were it so – as held by Trombetti[3] – it would not be provable because too many changes have taken place.

So beside diversity of relationship, there is also absolute diversity between languages, where no relationship is recognisable or demonstrable. What methods should linguistics adopt in these two cases? Let us take the latter first, for it is the commoner. As has just been observed, there are countless languages and language families which cannot be treated as identical. One example would be Chinese and the Indo-European languages. This does not mean that comparison is ruled out. Comparison is always possible and useful. Comparison can

[1] Bantu is a group of languages spoken by the populations of southern equitorial Africa. (Editorial note)

[2] Finno-Ugrian, which includes among other languages Finnish proper (or Suomi), Mordvin, Lappish, etc., is a family of languages spoken in northern Russia and Siberia, going back certainly to some common ancestral language. It is regarded as part of a vast group of languages called 'Ural-Altaic', which have not been proved to have a common origin, although they all share certain features in common. (Editorial note)

[3] *L'unità d'origine del linguaggio*, Bologna, 1905. (Editorial note)

be made of grammatical systems and of general ways of expressing ideas, as well as of sound systems. Similarly, comparisons involving diachronic facts can be made, comparisons of the phonetic evolution of two languages, etc. In this respect, although the possibilities are infinite, they are limited by certain constant phonetic and psychological facts which circumscribe the establishment of any language. At the same time, it is the discovery of these constant factors which is the main aim of any comparison between languages unrelated to one [264]
another.

As for the other category of variations, those occurring within a language family, it offers endless scope for comparison. Two related languages may differ in any degree. They may be surprisingly similar, like Zend and Sanskrit; or they may appear entirely dissimilar, like Sanskrit and Irish. All intermediate degrees are possible. Greek and Latin, for example, are closer to each other than either is to Sanskrit. Languages differing only slightly are called *dialects*: but this term is not to be given a rigorously exact interpretation. As we shall see (p. [278]), between dialects and languages there is a difference of quantity, not of nature.

[265]

CHAPTER II

Geographical Diversity: Its Complexity

§1. Coexistence of several languages in the same place

Geographical diversity we have thus far considered in its ideal form, where different areas correspond to different languages. This was perfectly justifiable, in that geographical separation is the most general of the factors involved in linguistic diversification. We must now consider secondary facts which may disturb this correlation, resulting in the coexistence of two or more languages in the same area.

This is not a question of an actual, organic mixture or interpenetration of two languages, bringing about a change of system (as e.g. with English after the Norman conquest). Nor is it a question of several languages clearly separated territorially, but included within the political boundaries of a single state (as e.g. in Switzerland). We shall be concerned only with the fact that two languages may live side by side in the same place, and coexist without merging. This frequently occurs; but two types of case must be distinguished.

First, it may happen that the language of a new population is added to the already existing language of an indigenous population. Thus in South Africa, alongside several African dialects, we have Dutch and
[266] English from two successive colonisations. In the same way, Spanish has taken root in Mexico. It must not be supposed that linguistic encroachments of this kind are peculiar to the modern period. At all times nations have mingled without merging languages. To realise this, it suffices to take a look at a map of modern Europe. In Ireland, Celtic and English are spoken: many Irish people know both languages. In Brittany, Breton and French are in use. In the Basque country, French or Spanish are used along with Basque. In Finland, Swedish and Finnish have coexisted for a long time, and Russian has arrived more recently. In Courland and Livonia, Lettish, German and

Russian are spoken. German, imported during the Middle Ages by colonists coming under the auspices of the Hanseatic league, is confined to a certain class of the population, and Russian was subsequently brought in by conquest. In Lithuania, which was formerly united with Poland, Polish has become established alongside Lithuanian, and there is also Russian, the outcome of incorporation in the Muscovite empire. Until the eighteenth century, Slavic and German were in use throughout the region of Germany east of the Elbe. In some countries, the linguistic hotchpotch is even more varied. In Macedonia one finds any number of languages – Turkish, Bulgarian, Serbian, Greek, Albanian, Rumanian, etc. – mingling in various ways in different regions.

In the cases we are considering, the languages in question are not always uniformly distributed: their coexistence in a given area does not rule out the possibility of certain territorial distinctions. For example, it may happen that one language is spoken predominantly in the towns and another in the country; but the relative distribution may not always be clear-cut.

In antiquity, similar phenomena are to be found. If we had a linguistic map of the Roman Empire, it would show facts quite similar [267] to those of more recent times. In Campania, for example, towards the end of the Roman republic, the languages in use included Oscan (as the inscriptions of Pompeii bear witness), Greek (the language of the colonists who founded Naples and other towns), Latin, and perhaps even Etruscan (which had been spoken predominantly in this region before the arrival of the Romans). In Carthage, Punic or Phoenician had survived beside Latin and was still alive at the time of the Arab invasion, while Numidian was also certainly spoken on Carthaginian territory. It would hardly be going too far to say that in antiquity one-language countries were the exception rather than the rule around the Mediterranean.

Usually this superimposition of languages is the result of invasion by a stronger people. But there is also colonisation, a form of peaceful penetration, as well as wandering peoples bringing their language with them. This happened in the case of the gipsies, who settled mainly in Hungary, where they have established compact communities; but a study of their language shows that they must have come from India at some unknown time in the past. In Dobrudja at the mouth of the Danube one finds a number of Tartar villages scattered here and there, small specks on the linguistic map of the region.

§2. Literary language and local dialect

There remains to consider the fact that linguistic unity may disintegrate when a spoken language undergoes the influence of a literary

language. That happens without fail whenever a people reaches a certain level of civilisation. By 'literary language' is here to be understood not only the language of literature but also in a more general sense every variety of cultivated language, whether official or not, which is at the service of the entire community. Left to its own devices,
[268] a language has only dialects, which do not overlap. Thus it is destined to infinitesimal subdivision. But as civilisation in the process of development increases communication, a kind of tacit convention emerges by which one of the existing dialects is selected as the vehicle for everything which is of interest to the nation as a whole. The choice depends on a variety of factors. Sometimes preference is given to the dialect of the region where civilisation has progressed further than elsewhere. Sometimes a court imposes its speech upon the nation. Once promoted to the rank of a common, official language, the privileged dialect rarely remains what it was. It assimilates dialect features from other regions. It becomes increasingly composite, yet without entirely losing its original character. Thus in literary French one can recognise still the dialect of the Ile-de-France, and likewise Tuscan in common Italian. In any event, a literary language does not become established overnight, and a large proportion of the population finds itself bilingual, speaking the common language as well as the local dialect. This can be seen in many regions of France, such as Savoy, where French is an imported language and has not yet stifled the country dialects. It is also a common state of affairs in Germany and Italy, where dialects survive everywhere alongside the official language.

The same thing has happened at all times whenever a people reaches a certain level of civilisation. The Greeks had their *koinè* or common language, based on Attic and Ionic, with local dialects continuing alongside it. Even in ancient Babylon it is thought to be demonstrable that there was an official language as well as regional dialects.

Does a general language of this kind necessarily presuppose writing? The Homeric poems appear to prove the contrary: for although
[269] they emerged at a period when there was little or no writing, their language is conventional and exhibits all the characteristics of a literary language.

The facts discussed in this chapter are so common that they might seem to be normal in the history of languages. However, we shall here set aside everything that obscures a clear view of natural geographical diversity, in order to consider the basic phenomenon unalloyed by any importation of foreign languages or formation of a literary language. This schematic simplification may seem to distort reality; but the natural state of affairs must first be studied in its own right.

In accordance with the principle to be adopted here we shall, for example, say that Brussels is Germanic, because it is situated in the

Flemish part of Belgium, and although French is spoken there, all that matters from our point of view is the line of demarcation separating Flemish from Walloon. On the other hand, from the same point of view Liège will be Romance because it is in Walloon territory: the French spoken there is a foreign language superimposed upon a dialect of the same family. Brest likewise belongs linguistically to Breton: the French spoken there has nothing in common with the indigenous language of Brittany. Berlin, where High German is spoken almost exclusively, will be assigned to Low German.

[270]
CHAPTER III

Causes of Geographical Diversity

§1. Time, the essential cause

Absolute diversity (cf. p. [263]) poses a purely speculative problem. Diversity of relationship, on the other hand, is amenable to observation and can be reduced to unity. French and Provençal, for example, both go back to Vulgar Latin, which evolved differently in northern and southern Gaul, and there is concrete evidence for their common origin.

In order to understand what happens, let us imagine theoretical conditions as simple as possible, which will allow us to identify the essential cause of territorial differentiation. Let us ask what would happen if a language spoken at one clearly delimited place – a small island, for example – was taken by colonists to some other place, also clearly delimited – say another island. After a certain time, it will be possible to detect various differences of vocabulary, grammar, pronunciation, etc. between the language of the first location (1) and the language of the second location (2).

It must not be supposed that the language taken to 2 will change while the language of 1 remains stationary, or the reverse. Innovation
[271] may occur in either or in both. Given a linguistic feature *a* which may be replaced (by *b*, *c*, *d*, etc.), the differentiation can occur in three different ways:

$$\frac{a\ (1)}{a\ (2)} \left\{ \begin{array}{l} \rightarrow \dfrac{b}{a} \\[2ex] \rightarrow \dfrac{a}{c} \\[2ex] \rightarrow \dfrac{b}{c} \end{array} \right.$$

A study of differentiation thus cannot be unilateral: innovations in both languages are of equal importance.

What brings about these differences? If anyone believes it is just the distance between 1 and 2, he is the victim of an illusion. Distance alone can have no effect upon a language. The day after their arrival at 2, the colonists from 1 spoke exactly the same language as the day before. One forgets the time factor, because it is less concrete than distance: but in fact it is time on which linguistic differentiation depends. Geographical diversity has to be translated into temporal diversity.

Take two contrasting features *b* and *c*, and let us suppose that *b* has never been known to change to *c*, nor vice versa. In order to trace how unity has given way to diversity, it is necessary to go back to the original feature *a* which *b* and *c* later replaced. Hence the following schema of geographical differentiation will be valid for all such cases.

$$\begin{array}{ccc} 1 & & 2 \\ a & \longleftrightarrow & a \\ \downarrow & & \downarrow \\ b & & c \end{array}$$

The separation of the two languages at 1 and 2 is the tangible form taken by the phenomenon, but not its explanation. Doubtless the
differentiation would not have occurred had it not been for the dis- [272]
tance, however small, between 1 and 2. But distance itself does not give rise to differences. Just as one cannot estimate volume on the basis of a single surface, but only by recourse to a third dimension – depth – so the schema of geographical differentiation is not complete unless it is projected in time.

It may be objected that varying circumstances, climate, topography, ways of life (as between, for instance, mountain dwellers and sea folk) may affect the language, and that in these cases the variations will be geographically conditioned. But these influences are debatable (cf. p. [203]) and even if they were proven there is one further distinction to be drawn. *The direction of change* is attributable to circumstances: it is determined by imponderable factors acting in each particular case, and one can neither prove nor describe their influence. For instance, a *u* becomes *ü* at a given time, in given circumstances. But why did it change at that particular time and place, and why did it change to *ü* and not to *o*? It is impossible to say. But *the change itself*, apart from its specific direction and particular manifestations, – in short, the instability of the language – depends on time alone. Geographical diversity is thus a secondary aspect of the general phenomenon. The unity of related languages is to be traced only through time. Unless the student of comparative linguistics fully realises this, all kinds of misconceptions lie in wait for him.

§2. Linguistic areas affected by time

Let us now take the case of a monoglot country: that is to say, where the same language is uniformly spoken by a stable population. Gaul in 450 A.D., with Latin firmly established everywhere, would be an example. What is going to happen?

[273] (1) Since language is never absolutely stationary (cf. p. [110] ff.), after a certain time has elapsed, the language will no longer be the same.

(2) Evolution will not be uniform over the whole territory, but will vary from place to place. A language has never been found to change in the same way throughout the whole area where it is spoken. So the realistic model is not

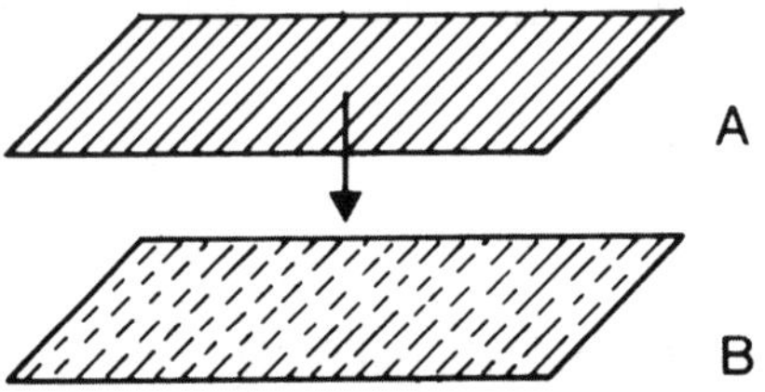

but rather

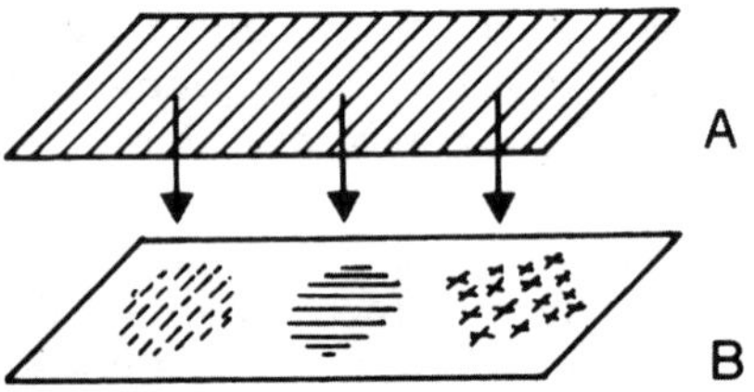

How does the differentiation which will eventually produce dialect forms of all kinds begin and develop? This is more difficult than it might at first sight appear. The phenomenon exhibits two principal features.

(1) Evolution takes the form of successive, specific innovations. These are partial facts that can be enumerated, described and classified by type (phonetic, lexicological, morphological, syntactic, etc.).

[274] (2) Each innovation has its own particular area. Either this area covers the whole territory and so creates no dialect division (which is rare), or else it covers only part of the territory and thus becomes a dialect feature of that part (which is usually the case). Phonetic change will serve as an example, although what follows may be applied to any innovation. Suppose the change from *a* to *e* divides the territory

in one way, and the change from *s* to *z* divides the same territory in another way.

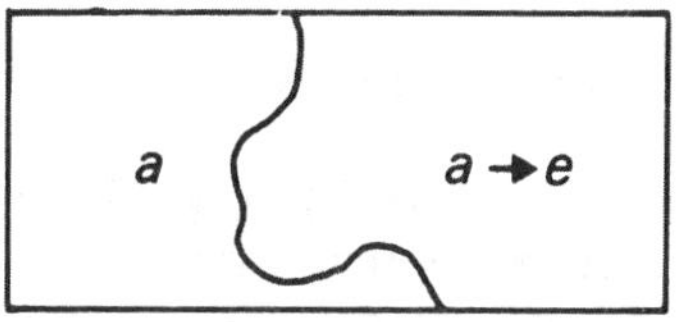

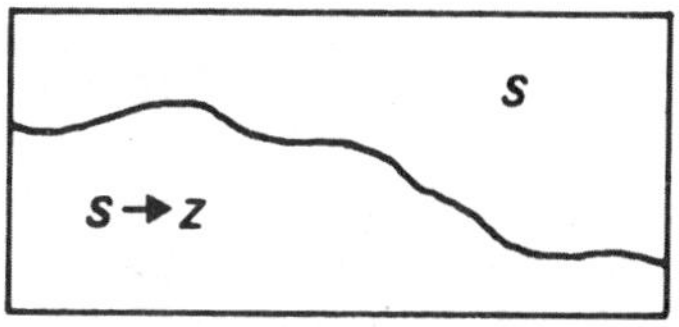

The existence of these different areas explains the differences which are found at all points in the territory over which a language is spoken, assuming the language follows its own natural course of evolution. These areas cannot be predicted. Their extent cannot be determined in advance. All that can be done is to describe them when they are established. Superimposed on a map, they cut across one another and overlap in patterns of great complexity. Sometimes they show surprising configurations. For example, Latin *c* and *g* before *a* became *tš* and *dž* respectively, then *š* and *ž* (e.g. *cantum* → *chant* 'song', *virga* → *verge* 'rod'), over the whole of northern France except Picardy and part of Normandy, where *c* and *g* remained unchanged: cf. Picard *cat* for *chat* 'cat', *rescapé* for *réchappé* 'survivor' (which has recently passed into French), and *vergue* 'rod' from Latin *virga*.

What is bound to be the result when all this is added together? [275] Whereas a single language was formerly in use throughout a given area, after five or ten centuries have elapsed people living at opposite points on the periphery of the area will in all probability no longer understand one another. On the other hand, those living at any given place will still understand the speech of neighbouring regions. A traveller crossing the country from one side to the other will find only slight differences between one locality and the next. But as he proceeds the differences accumulate, so that in the end he finds a language which would be incomprehensible to the inhabitants of the region he set out from. Or starting from the centre and proceeding to the periphery, he will find the divergences progressively increase whichever direction he takes, although in different ways depending on the direction chosen.

The special features noted in the speech of one village will recur in the localities round about, but it will be impossible to predict how far each of them extends. At Douvaine, a town in the Haute-Savoie, the name of the city of Geneva is pronounced *đenva*. This pronunciation is found very far afield to the east and south. But on the other side of Lake Léman the pronunciation is *dzenva*. It is not a question of two clearly distinct dialects: for another feature the boundaries would be different. At Douvaine the word for 'two' in *daue*, but this pronunciation extends over a much smaller area than *đenva*: a few kilometres away, at the foot of the Salève, 'two' is *due*.

§3. *Dialects have no natural boundaries*

The usual conception of dialects nowadays is quite different. They are envisaged as clearly defined linguistic types, determinate in all respects, and occupying areas on a map which are contiguous and distinct (*a, b, c, d*, etc.).

[276]

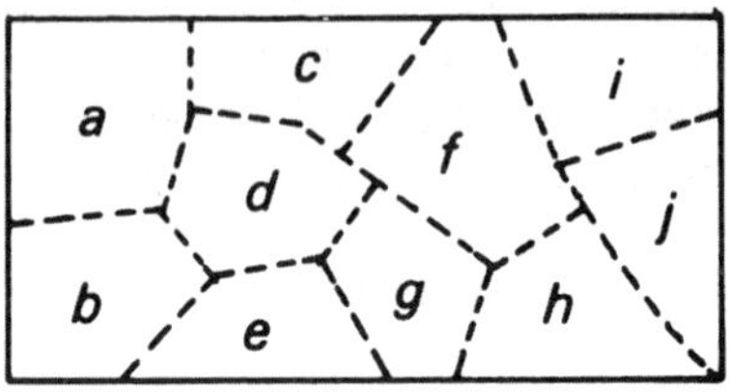

But natural dialect changes give a quite different result. As soon as linguistics began to study each individual feature and establish its geographical distribution, the old notion of a dialect had to be replaced by a new one, which can be defined as follows: there are no natural dialects, but only natural dialect features. Or – which comes to the same thing – there are as many dialects as there are places.

The notion of natural dialects is thus in principle incompatible with the notion of a region. The linguist is faced with a choice. One possibility is to define a dialect by the totality of its features. In this case, one must concentrate on a single locality at a given point on the map. As soon as one moves from this locality, one will no longer be dealing with exactly the same set of dialect features. The other possibility is to define a dialect on the basis of just one feature. In this case, naturally, there will be an area, corresponding to the geographical extension of the feature selected. But it is hardly necessary to point out that this latter procedure is an artificial one, and the boundaries thus established correspond to no dialectal reality.

Research into dialect features was the point of departure for linguistic cartography, of which the model is Gilliéron's *Atlas linguistique de la France*. For Germany, one should mention also Wenker's atlas.[1] The form of such an atlas is determined in advance, for it is
[277] necessary to study the country region by region, and for each region one map can record only a few dialect features. Any region will require a large number of maps to show the various phonetic, lexicological,

[1] Cf. also Weigand's *Linguistischer Atlas des dakorumänischen Gebiets* (1909), and Millardet's *Petit atlas linguistique d'une région des Landes* (1910).

morphological, etc. features superimposed within it. Research of this nature requires careful organisation, with systematic inquiries on the basis of questionnaires, the assistance of local helpers, and so on. In this connexion one may point to the survey of the Romance dialects of Switzerland as an example. One advantage of linguistic atlases is that they provide materials for dialectology: numerous studies recently have been based upon Gilliéron's atlas.

The term 'isogloss lines' or 'isoglosses' has been introduced to designate the boundaries of dialect features. The expression is modelled upon *isotherm*. But it is unclear and inappropriate, for it means 'having the same language'. Granted that *glosseme* means 'linguistic feature', it would be more accurate to call them *isoglossematic lines*, if this term were usable. We would prefer to call them *waves of innovation*, taking up the image originally suggestion by J. Schmidt, which the following chapter will give reasons for adopting.

When one looks at a linguistic map, one sometimes sees two or three of these waves almost coinciding or even merging over a certain distance.

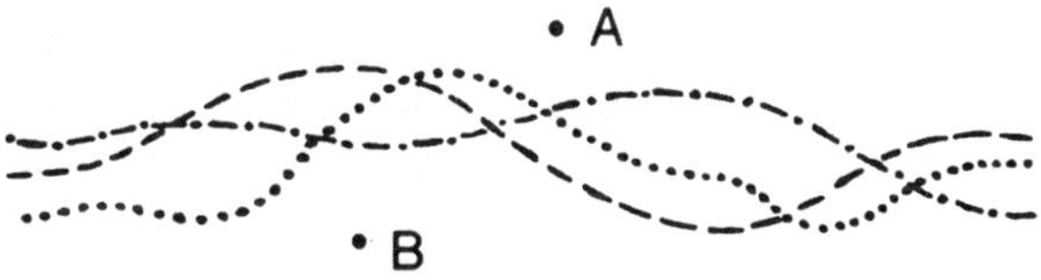

It is evident that two points A and B separated by a zone of this kind will show a certain accumulation of contrasts and constitute two fairly distinct forms of speech. It may also happen that these convergences
are not merely partial, but mark out the entire perimeter of two or [278]
more areas.

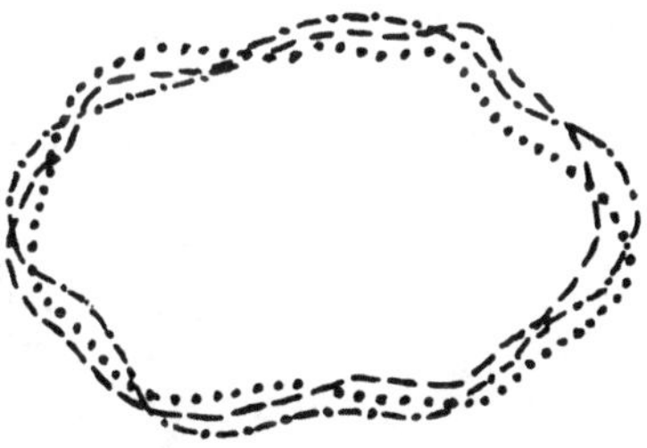

When these convergences are numerous, one can use 'dialects' as a roughly appropriate term. The convergences are explained by social, political, religious, etc. factors, which we are completely ignoring for present purposes. These convergences disguise but never entirely obscure the primary and natural phenomenon of differentiation into independent areas.

§4. Languages have no natural boundaries

It is difficult to say what the difference is between a language and a dialect. Often a dialect is called a language because it has a literature: that is true of Portuguese and Dutch. The question of intelligibility also plays a part. People who cannot understand one another are generally described as speaking different languages. However that may be, languages which have developed in one continuous area with a settled population exhibit the same phenomena as dialects, but on a larger scale. They show waves of innovation over a territory where a number of different languages are spoken.

In the ideal conditions postulated, it is no more feasible to determine boundaries separating related languages than to determine dialect boundaries. The extent of the area involved makes no difference. Just
[279] as one cannot say where High German ends and Low German begins, so also it is impossible to establish a line of demarcation between German and Dutch, or between French and Italian. Taking points far enough apart, it is possible to say with certainty 'French is spoken here; Italian is spoken there'. But in the intervening regions, the distinction becomes blurred. The notion of smaller, compact intermediate zones acting as linguistic areas of transition (for example, Provençal as a half-way house between French and Italian) is not realistic either. In any case, it is impossible to imagine in any shape or form a precise linguistic boundary dividing an area covered throughout by evenly differentiated dialects. Language boundaries, just like dialect boundaries, get lost in these transitions. Just as dialects are only arbitrary subdivisions of the entire surface covered by a language, so the boundaries held to separate two languages can only be conventional ones.

None the less, abrupt geographical transitions from one language to another are very common. How do they arise? They are the outcome of circumstances which have militated against the survival of gradual, imperceptible transitions. Population movement is the most important factor. Throughout history, peoples have migrated. Over the course of centuries, these migrations have complicated the picture and in many instances obliterated the vestiges of linguistic patterns of transition. The Indo-European family is a typical example. Originally these languages must have been very closely connected, forming an uninterrupted chain of linguistic areas. We can reconstruct the main ones in broad outline. In terms of linguistic features, Slavic overlaps with Iranian and Germanic, and this corresponds to the geographical distribution of the languages in question. Similarly, Germanic may be considered as forming a link between Slavic and Celtic, which in turn
[280] is closely related to Italic. Italic is intermediate between Celtic and Greek. Not knowing the geographical location of any of these

languages, a linguist could assign relative geographical positions to them without any trouble. And yet as soon as we consider a boundary between two linguistic groups, such as Slavic and Germanic, we find a clear gap with no transition. The languages do not merge into one another, but stand opposed. This is because the intermediate dialects have disappeared. Neither the Slavs nor the Germans remained settled. They migrated and conquered land from one another. The Slav and Germanic populations who are neighbours today are no longer those formerly in contact. Imagine that Italians from Calabria were to come and settle on the borders of France. This migration would automatically wipe out the imperceptible transition which, as we have noted, links Italian with French. Facts of this kind account for the situation in the Indo-European family.

But other causes also contribute to obliterate transitions; for example, the extension of a common language at the expense of local dialects (cf. p. [267] ff.). Today literary French (the former language of the Ile-de-France) meets official Italian (the generalised dialect of Tuscany) at the frontier. It is only by chance that we can still find transitional dialects in the western Alps. Along many other linguistic borders all trace of intermediate forms of speech has been lost.

[281] CHAPTER IV

Propagation of linguistic waves

§1. *Force of intercourse*[1] *and parochialism*

The propagation of linguistic features is subject to the same laws as any other habit, such as fashion. In any community, there are always two forces simultaneously pulling in opposite directions: particularism or parochialism on the one hand, and on the other the force of 'intercourse', which establishes communication between men.

It is parochialism which accounts for why a linguistic community remains faithful to the traditions it has nurtured. These habits are the ones every individual first acquires as a child: hence their strength and persistence. If they acted alone, they would give rise to endless linguistic diversity.

But their influence is counteracted by the opposite force. If parochialism makes men keep to themselves, intercourse forces them to communicate with others. Intercourse brings a village visitors from elsewhere, brings together people from all around on the occasion of
[282] a celebration or a fair, and unites men from different provinces under the same flag. In short, intercourse is a principle of unification, which counteracts the disuniting influence of parochialism.

It is intercourse which is responsible for the extension and cohesion of a language. It acts in two ways. Negatively, it prevents dialectal fragmentation by suppressing innovations as they emerge at one point or another. Positively, it favours unity by accepting and propagating innovations. It is this latter form which intercourse takes which justifies the term *wave* (cf. p. [277]) as a designation of the geographical boundaries of a dialect feature. The isoglossematic line is like the edge

[1] We have opted for retaining Saussure's vivid term *intercourse*, even though it is borrowed from English (pronounced *interkors* and meaning 'social relations, commerce, communications') and is perhaps better suited to oral exposition than to the requirements of theoretical analysis. (Editorial note)

of a wave advancing or retreating.

Sometimes it is surprising how two dialects of the same language quite far apart geographically share common features. This happens when a development emerging at one point has encountered no obstacles in its way and has progressively extended further and further afield. There is no barrier to intercourse in a linguistic situation where only gradual transitions occur.

This generalisation of a particular feature, whatever its eventual extension, takes time. The time can sometimes be measured. The change from *þ* to *d* which intercourse spread throughout continental Germany was propagated at first in the south, between 800 A.D. and 850 A.D., except in Frankish, where *þ* persists in the form *đ* and does not give way to *d* until later. The change from *t* to *z* (pronounced *ts*) occurred in a more restricted area and began before the period of the earliest written documents. It must have begun in the Alps about 600 A.D. and spread both to the north and also to Lombardy in the south. The *t* is still found in a Thuringian charter of the eighth century. At a later period, Germanic *ī* and *ū* diphthongised (e.g. *mein* for *mīn*, [283]
braun for *brūn*). This began in Bohemia about 1400, taking three hundred years to reach the Rhine and occupy its present-day area.

These linguistic features were spread by contact. It is probable that this is the case with all waves: they start at a given point and radiate. This brings us to a second important consideration.

The time factor, as we have seen, suffices to explain geographical diversity. But this principle does not hold unless one takes into account the place where the innovation originated.

Let us reconsider the case of consonantal mutation in German. If a sound *t* becomes *ts* at one place in the Germanic area, the new sound will tend to radiate outwards from its place of origin, and through this territorial expansion come into conflict with the original *t* or any other sounds which may have emerged elsewhere. At the place where it originated, an innovation of this kind is purely a phonetic change; but elsewhere it becomes established only through geographical contact. So the formula *t*→*ts* is valid in its simplest interpretation only for the place of innovation. Applied to the propagation of the change, it would be misleading.

Historical phonetics must therefore distinguish carefully between areas of innovation, where a sound evolves solely along a temporal axis, and areas of propagation. The latter, where both time and distance are involved, have nothing to do with the theory of sound change as such. When a *ts* originating elsewhere is substituted for a *t*, that is not modification of a traditional prototype but imitation of a neighbouring dialect, regardless of the prototype. When a form *herza* [284]
('heart'), of Alpine origin, replaces the old Thuringian form *herta*, one should speak not of sound change but of sound borrowing.

§2. A single principle underlying both forces

At any given place – by which we mean a location which can be treated as a point on a map (cf. p. [276]), such as a village – it is quite easy to distinguish what is due to each of the two forces, parochialism and intercourse. A feature is due either to one of these or to the other, but not to both. Any feature shared with another dialect is due to intercourse. Any unique feature is due to parochialism.

But where an area is involved – a canton, for example – a new difficulty arises. It is no longer possible to say which of the two factors is responsible for a given feature. For both contribute to every linguistic feature, even though they are in conflict. What is linguistically distinctive for canton A is found throughout that canton. Here we see particularism at work, preventing imitation of the language of canton B, or the imitation of canton A by speakers from canton B. But the unifying force of intercourse is also at work, bringing together the various parts of A (A1, A2, A3 . . . etc.). So where areas are concerned, the two forces operate simultaneously but in varying degrees. The more an innovation is favoured by intercourse, the larger its area grows; while parochialism tends to maintain a feature within the area it has already acquired, and protect it against outside competition. It is impossible to predict what the outcome from the joint action of these two forces will be. As we have seen (p. [282]), in Germanic, extending
[285] from the Alps to the North Sea, the change from *þ* to *d* was general, whereas the change from *t* to *ts* (written *z*) affects only the south. Thus parochialism brought about a division between south and north; but within these limits intercourse promoted linguistic uniformity. So in principle there is no fundamental difference between the latter case and the former. The same forces are operative: all that varies is their effectiveness.

What that means in practice is that in studying linguistic evolution over an area we can leave particularism out of account: or, equivalently, treat it as the negative aspect of the force of unification. If the force of unification is powerful enough, it will establish uniformity over the whole area. If not, the feature will spread only so far and be restricted to one part of the area in question. That part, none the less, will itself form a coherent whole internally. Therefore one can explain everything by reference simply to the force of unification, without appeal to parochialism. Parochialism is nothing other than the force of intercourse characteristic of each individual region.

§3. Linguistic differentiation in separate areas

It is only when one has grasped the facts that in a monoglot community cohesion varies from one feature to another, that not all innovations are generalised, and that geographical continuity does not prevent perpetual differentiation, that one is in a position to examine the case of a language developing in two separate areas independently.

This often happens. When Germanic was imported into the British Isles from the continent, its evolution became twofold. Beside the German dialects there emerged Anglo-Saxon, which later gave birth to English. Another example would be French transplanted to Canada. [286]
Discontinuity is not always the effect of colonisation or conquest. It can result from isolation. Rumanian lost contact with the rest of Latin-speaking Europe, being cut off by the southern expansion of the Slavs. What in particular causes separation makes little difference. The main questions are whether separation does play any role in the history of languages, and if so whether it has different effects from those we have noted where no separation occurs.

In order to bring out the preponderant role of the time factor, we above imagined the case of a language developing simultaneously at two separate locations of no appreciable size, such as two small islands, where propagation from one area to a neighbouring area can be disregarded. But as soon as one is dealing with territories of any size, this phenomenon re-emerges and gives rise to dialect differences. So the problem is in no way simplified by considering separate locations. We must not attribute to geographical separation things which can be otherwise accounted for.

That was the mistake of the early Indo-European scholars (cf. p. [14]). Dealing with an extensive family of languages which had become very different one from another, they supposed that this could only have happened as a result of geographical dispersion. It is easier to imagine separate languages existing in separate places. To a casual observer, that appears to be both a necessary and sufficient explanation of linguistic differentiation. But that was not all. The notion of a language came to be associated with that of a nation, the latter explaining the former. The Slavs, Germans, Celts, etc. were thought of as swarms coming from the same hive. These peoples, having become cut off from their original stock as the result of migration, brought Proto-Indo-European with them into the various countries where they settled.

This error went uncorrected for a long time. Only in 1877[1] did [287]
Johannes Schmidt's *Die Verwandtschaftsverhältnisse der Indogermanen* open the eyes of linguists by putting forward for the first time a theory of continuity, or 'wave theory' (*Wellentheorie*). It was then realised that differentiation in one place suffices to explain the relations obtaining between the Indo-European languages, without any

[1] Schmidt's work was in fact published in 1872. (Translator's note)

need to postulate that the various peoples had left their original home (cf. p. [279]). Dialect differences could and must have arisen before these nations migrated and spread. The wave theory not only gives us a more accurate picture of Indo-European prehistory, but throws light on the basic laws of all linguistic differentiation and on the conditions governing relationships between languages.

The wave theory, however, is not necessarily incompatible with the theory of migration. The history of the Indo-European languages offers many examples of peoples becoming detached from the main family through migration, and this must have had special consequences of some kind. But these consequences are additional to those resulting from differentiation without separation. What exactly they are it is very difficult to say. We find ourselves back with the problem of the evolution of the same language in different locations.

Take Old English, for example. It became separated from Germanic as the result of a migration. In all probability, its present form would be different if the Saxons had remained on the continent in the fifth century A.D. But what were the specific effects of the separation? To assess this, one must first ask whether this change or that might not equally well have taken place if the separation had never taken place. Suppose the Angles had occupied Jutland instead of the British Isles. Can one be sure that one of the features attributed to the separation would not have developed had they remained geographically in contact with other Germanic peoples? When it is said that the separation
[288] enabled English to retain the old *þ*, which everywhere on the continent became *d* (cf. English *thing*, but German *Ding*), that is tantamount to claiming that in continental Germanic the change was generalised owing to the geographical continuity of the languages. But the generalisation could have failed to take place on the continent in spite of that. As usual, the source of the error lies in contrasting the dialect which has become isolated with the dialects which have remained in contact. In fact, there is nothing to prove that a colony of Angles in Jutland would necessarily have acquired the *d*. As we have noted above, *k* before *a* remained intact in France in one corner of Picardy and Normandy, while elsewhere changing to *š* (written *ch*). So appeal to separation is inadequate and superficial. It is never necessary in order to explain differentiation. Whatever separation can bring about can be brought about just as well without separation. If there is a difference between the two cases, it remains elusive.

However, let us now consider the positive rather than the negative side of the matter, and look at the interconnexions between related languages, instead of their differentiation. We observe that when a language becomes geographically isolated all contact is virtually broken off from the moment of separation onwards; whereas geographical continuity promotes continued connexion, even between clearly distinct forms of speech, provided they are linked by intermediate dialects.

Thus in order to assess degrees of relationship between languages, a strict distinction must be drawn geographically between cases of contact and cases of isolation. In the latter, two languages will preserve from their common past a certain number of features bearing witness to their relationship. But as each has evolved independently too, new features will appear which they do not share (unless by
coincidence the same features develop separately in both). What is [289]
ruled out in any case is propagation of new features by contact. Generally speaking, a language which has evolved in geographical isolation will show, in contrast with other members of the same family, a set of characteristics they do not share. When this language in turn splits up, the various dialects which emerge will bear witness to the closer relationship which links them, by sharing common features not shown by dialects from elsewhere. Thus they will constitute a distinct branch separate from the main trunk.

Relations between languages which have remained geographically in contact are quite different. The common features they show are not necessarily older than the disparate features. For at any time an innovation starting in one particular place may have spread and succeeded in becoming general throughout the linguistic area in question. Furthermore, since the spread of innovations varies, two neighbouring dialects may share a special common feature even though they do not form a group apart within the family. Each of them may be linked to other neighbours by sharing other features, as is the case in the Indo-European languages.

PART FIVE [291]

Questions of Retrospective Linguistics
Conclusion

CHAPTER I

The Two Perspectives of Diachronic Linguistics

Whereas synchronic linguistics allows only one perspective, which is that of the language-users, and consequently only one method, diachronic linguistics has both a forward-looking perspective, following the course of time, and a backward-looking perspective, which takes the opposite direction (cf. p. [128]).

The first of these perspectives corresponds to the actual progression of events. This is the perspective necessarily adopted in writing any chapter of historical linguistics, to develop any point in the history of a language. The method is simply a matter of checking the available evidence. But in very many instances this way of going about diachronic linguistics is inadequate or inapplicable.

For in order to set out the history of a language in detail following the chronological sequence, we would have to be in possession of an [292] infinite series of photographs of the language, taken moment by moment. But this condition is never fulfilled. Romance scholars, for example, who have the advantage of knowing Latin, which is the starting point for their investigations, and of having an impressive mass of documents extending over many centuries, constantly find great gaps in their evidence. So the forward-looking method, with its reliance on direct documentation, must be abandoned in favour of going in the opposite direction, proceeding retrospectively against the chronological sequence of events. Adopting this perspective involves selecting a given period and inquiring not what a given form subsequently became, but what earlier form was its parent.

Whereas the forward-looking method involves simple narration of events, based entirely on a critical assessment of evidence, the opposite approach requires a method of reconstruction, based upon comparison. We cannot establish the original form of just one sign in isolation. Two different forms of the same origin, like Latin *pater* ('father') and Sanskrit *pitar-*, or the stems of Latin *ger-ō* ('I bear') and *ges-tus* ('borne'), straight away invite comparison and give a glimpse of the diachronic unity which links both to a prototype which can be reconstructed inductively. The more terms available for comparison, the more exact these inductions will be, and they will result – if sufficient evidence is available – in genuine reconstructions.

The same holds for languages as a whole. We can infer nothing from Basque: its isolation offers no possibility of comparison. But from a set of related languages, like Greek, Latin, Old Slavonic, etc., it has proved possible to identify by comparison the primitive common elements they contain, and so to reconstruct the basis of Proto-Indo-European, as it existed before becoming geographically differentiated. And what was achieved for the family as a whole has been repeated
[293] on a smaller scale – but by the same means – for each individual branch, wherever such a reconstruction was necessary and feasible. Whereas many Germanic languages are directly attested by documentary evidence, the common Germanic from which they came is known to us only indirectly through the retrospective method. The same method has been applied by linguists, with varying success, to establish the original unity of other families (cf. p. [263]).

The retrospective method, then, allows us access to the past history of a language back beyond the time of the earliest documents. Any forward-looking history of Latin could hardly begin at a point earlier than the third or fourth century B.C. But the reconstruction of Proto-Indo-European has enabled us to gain some idea of what must have happened in the period which extends from the time of that original linguistic community and the earliest surviving Latin documents. Only subsequently was it possible to outline a forward-looking sketch of those developments.

In this respect evolutionary linguistics is comparable to geology, another historical science. In geology, too, stable states are described (for example, the present state of the Léman basin) without reference to anything which preceded them; but its main concern is with events and changes which, linked in succession, constitute diachronic facts. In theory, one can imagine a forward-looking geology, but usually in practice the perspective has to be backward-looking. Before describing what happened in any given location, it is necessary to reconstruct the chain of events and find out what brought that particular part of the world to its present state.

It is not only the methods of the two perspectives which differ so strikingly. Even for didactic purposes it is not wise to use both simultaneously in the same survey. A study of sound changes will present a very different picture depending on which perspective is adopted. [294]
Looking forward, it is relevant to inquire what became of Classical Latin *ĕ* in French; and the answer is that this single sound split in the course of time and gave rise to several different sounds: Latin *pĕdem* ('foot')→French *pye* (written *pied*), *vĕntum* ('wind')→*vã* (written *vent*), *lĕctum* ('bed')→*li* (written *lit*), *nĕcāre* ('kill')→*nwayę* (written *noyer*), etc. Looking backwards, on the other hand, if we inquire what sound in Latin lies behind the open *ę* of modern French, we find that this one sound is the end product of what were originally several different sounds: French *tęr* 'earth' (written *terre*)←Latin *tĕrram*, *vęrž* 'rod' (written *verge*)←*vĭrga*m, *fę* 'fact' (written *fait*)←*factu*m, etc. The evolution of formative elements can similarly be presented in these two ways, and equally different pictures will result. All our earlier observations on the subject of analogical formations (p. [232] ff.) demonstrate the point *a priori*. Looking backwards, for example, in search of the origins of the French participial suffix *-é*, we go back to Latin *-ātum*. Latin *-ātum* is originally attached to Latin verbs in *-are* formed from nouns, mainly feminine nouns in *-a* (cf. Latin *plantāre* 'to plant': *planta* 'twig, slip'; Greek *tīmáō* 'I honour': *tīmḗ* 'honour'). But *-ātum* would not have existed if the Proto-Indo-European suffix *-to-* had not been alive and productive in its own right (cf. Greek *klu-tó*-s, Latin *in-clu-tu*-s, Sanskrit *çru-ta*-s, etc.). Latin *-ātum* also includes the formative element *-m* of the accusative singular (cf. p. [212]). Looking forward, on the other hand, if we ask in which French forms the primitive suffix *-to-* is to be found, we can draw up a list which includes not only the various suffixes of the past participle, whether productive or not (*aimé* ('loved')←Latin *amātum*, *fini* ('finished')←Latin *fīnītum*, *clos* ('closed')←Latin *clausum* for **claudtum*), but also many others such as *-u* from Latin *-ūtum* (*cornu* ('horned')←*cornūtum*), the learned suffix *-tif* from Latin *-tīvum* (*fugitif* ('fugitive')←*fugitīvum*, *sensitif* ('sensitive'), *négatif* ('negative'), etc.), and a number of words no longer analysable, like *point* ('point') from Latin *punctum*, *dé* ('die')←*datum*, and *chétif* ('wretched')←*captīvum*.

[295] CHAPTER II

Earliest Languages and Prototypes

In its earliest phase, Indo-European linguistics failed to understand the true objective of comparative studies and the importance of the reconstructive method (cf. p. [16]). This is what explains one of its most striking mistakes: the exaggerated and almost exclusive importance attached to Sanskrit for purposes of comparison. Being the earliest source of evidence about the Indo-European family, Sanskrit was promoted to the status of prototype. But it is one thing to envisage Proto-Indo-European giving rise to Sanskrit, Greek, Slavic, Celtic, Italic – and quite a different thing to put one of these in the place of Proto-Indo-European. The consequences of this gross error were various and serious. The hypothesis was doubtless never formulated as categorically as we have just stated it, but in practice it was tacitly adopted. Bopp wrote that 'he did not believe Sanskrit could be the common ancestor' – as if it were possible to entertain, albeit speculatively, such a theory.

This leads to the question of what is meant when a language is said to be older or more ancient than another. Three interpretations are possible in theory.

(1) Age might be supposed to be measured by reference to the origins or primitive state of a language. But even the most elementary
[296] reasoning must reject the idea that age can be assigned on these grounds, for every language is a continuation of what was spoken earlier. Language in this respect is not like humanity. Its absolute continuity of development precludes distinguishing between generations. Gaston Paris was right to object to speaking of parent languages and daughter languages: for that presupposes breaks in continuity. This is not, then, a sense in which we can say that one language is older than another.

(2) It might also be supposed to refer to the fact that one language

is attested earlier than another. Thus the Persian of the Achaemenian inscriptions would be older than the Persian of Firdousi. When, as in this case, both languages are equally well known and one is a continuation of the other, the earlier attested is the older. But if these two conditions are not fulfilled, priority of attestation is unimportant. Lithuanian, attested only since 1540, is no less valuable on that account than Old Slavonic, which was written down in the tenth century, or even the Sanskrit of the Rig Veda.

(3) The term 'old' may also designate a more archaic linguistic state: that is to say, one in which the forms remain closer to the primitive forms, regardless of date. In this sense, one can say that the Lithuanian of the sixteenth century A.D. is older than the Latin of the third century B.C.

If Sanskrit is said to be older than other languages, it can only be in senses (2) or (3). In fact, it has claims under both heads. On the one hand, the Vedic hymns are accepted as being older than the earliest Greek texts. On the other hand, Sanskrit has a total of archaic features which is considerable in comparison with those maintained in other Indo-European languages (cf. p. [15]).

As a result of this muddled notion of antiquity which makes San- [297]
skrit earlier than the Indo-European family itself, it came about that later on, even when linguists no longer clung to the idea of Sanskrit as the parent language, they continued to attach disproportionate importance to the evidence it provides as a collateral language.

Adolphe Pictet, in his *Origines indo-européennes* (cf. p. [306]), although explicitly recognising the existence of an original Proto-Indo-European community with its own language, remains none the less convinced that we must look first and foremost to Sanskrit, and that the evidence of Sanskrit is more valuable than that of a number of other Indo-European languages put together. This is the illusion which for many years obscured questions of first-rate importance, such as the original vowel system.

The same error was repeated on a smaller scale. In studying individual branches of Indo-European, the earliest attested language was often treated as an adequate and sufficient representative of the whole group, and no serious attempt was made to investigate the primitive state common to all. For example, instead of speaking of Germanic, scholars did not hesitate simply to cite Gothic, Gothic being attested several centuries earlier than the other Germanic dialects. Thus Gothic usurped the place of prototype or source of these other dialects. For Slavic, Old Slavonic, attested in the tenth century, is taken as the sole evidence, the other languages of the group being recorded at a much later date.

In fact it is extremely rare that two forms of a language fixed in writing at different dates turn out to represent exactly the same line

of development caught at two different historical phases. Usually they turn out to be different dialects which are not in the same line of linguistic succession. But exceptions confirm the rule. The best known is that of the Romance languages and Latin. French is in direct line
[298] of descent from Latin. The area occupied by the Romance languages happens to be the same as the area where Latin used to be spoken, and each one of these languages is simply a developed form of Latin. Similarly, as noted above, the Persian of the inscriptions of Darius is the same dialect as the Persian of the Middle Ages. But the other type of case is much more common, the written forms of different periods belonging to different dialects of the same family. Germanic, for instance, is recorded successively in the Gothic of Ulfila (of which no descendant is known), Old High German texts, Anglo-Saxon texts, Norse texts, and so on; but none of these dialects or dialect groups is the direct successor of the one attested previously. This state of affairs can be schematised as follows, with letters representing dialects, and dotted lines periods:

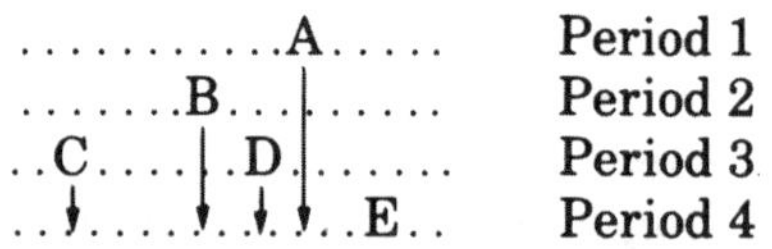

This is fortunate for linguistics. Otherwise the earliest attested dialect (A) would already tell us everything that could be inferred from the analysis of later states. As it is, by tracing back the point of convergence for all these dialects (A,B,C,D, etc.), an older form than A can be determined. This will be the prototype X. Thus no confusion between A and X is possible.

CHAPTER III [299]

Reconstructions

§1. Their nature and purpose

If the only method of reconstruction is the comparative method, by the same token comparison has no other aim than reconstruction. Unless they are to be sterile, correspondences observed between several forms must be placed in a chronological perspective and result in the reconstitution of a unique form, as we have already insisted several times (cf. p. [16] ff., p. [272]). Thus in order to explain Latin *medius* ('middle') beside Greek *mésos* ('middle'), it was necessary to postulate an earlier (though not necessarily Proto-Indo-European) form **methyos*, from which both *medius* and *mésos* could be derived. If the comparison is between two forms belonging to the same language rather than different languages, the same applies: thus Latin *gerō* ('I bear') and *gestus* ('borne') point back to an earlier stem **ges-* once common to both.

It should be noted in passing that comparison based on phonetic changes should always be supported by morphological considerations. In examining Latin *patior* ('I suffer') and its past participle *passus*, one takes into consideration the past participles *factus* ('made'), *dictus* ('said'), etc. because *passus* is a formation of the same kind. On the basis of the morphological connexion between *faciō* ('I make') and *factus* ('made'), *dīcō* ('I say') and *dictus* ('said'), etc., it becomes possible to set up a similar connexion at an earlier period for *patior* and
**pat-tus*. Likewise, if the comparison is morphological, it should be [300]
supported by appeal to phonetics. The Latin comparative *meliōrem* ('better') can be compared to Greek *hēdíō* ('sweeter') because phonetically one goes back to **meliosem*, **meliosm* and the other to **hādioa*, **hādiosa*, **hādiosm*.

Linguistic comparison is not, then, a mechanical operation. It implies bringing together all the information relevant to constructing an explanation. But it should always result in a hypothesis couched in a formula which purports to reconstruct an antecedent. Comparison should always return to the reconstruction of linguistic forms.

But does this investigation of the past aim at the reconstruction of the actual, concrete linguistic forms of an earlier period? Or is it limited merely to abstract and fragmentary claims concerning parts of words; for example, that Latin *f* in *fūmus* corresponds to a Common Italic *þ*, or that the first sound of Greek *állo* and Latin *aliud* was already an *a* in Proto-Indo-European? Its task may well be limited to the latter; we might even say that its analytic method has no other aim than establishing these partial connexions. However, from a number of isolated facts of this kind it is possible to draw more general conclusions. For example, a series of cases like Latin *fūmus* allows us to say with certainty that *þ* occurred in the sound system of Common Italic. Similarly, we can say that Proto-Indo-European had in what is called pronominal flexion a neuter singular ending *-d*, which was different from the adjectival ending *-m*; and that again is a general morphological fact inferred from a collection of isolated cases (cf. Latin *istud*, *aliud*, vs. *bonum*; Greek *tó* ← _*tod_, *állo* ← _*allod_ vs. *kalón*; English *that*, etc.). But we can go further. Having reconstructed these various correspondences, it is possible to synthesise all those which
[301] bear upon a form in its entirety. Thus we can reconstruct whole words (e.g. Proto-Indo-European _*alyod_), flexional paradigms, etc. In order to do this, one must take various independent facts and group them together. If, for example, one compares the various parts of a reconstructed form like _*alyod_, one notices a great difference between the *-d*, which raises a question of grammar, and the *a-*, which raises no such question. A reconstructed form is not given as a whole. It is a sum total of historical phonetic arguments which can always be broken down into its constituents. Each part of the reconstruction can be called in question and remains open to examination. Hence reconstructed forms have always provided a faithful reflection of the general conclusions which are applicable to their particular case. The Proto-Indo-European word for 'horse' has at different times been held to be _*akvas_, _*ak_$_1$_vas_, _*ek_$_1$_vos_, and finally _*ek_$_1$_wos_: only the *s* has remained uncontroversial, and the total number of sounds in the word.

The aim of reconstruction is thus not to restore a form for its own sake, which would be in any case rather ridiculous, but to crystallise and condense a series of conclusions which are held to be correct in the light of the evidence currently available. In a word, it records the progress made to date in our science. Linguists have no need to be defended against the bizarre accusation of attempting to reconstruct Proto-Indo-European in its entirety, as if they intended to use it as a language. Since that is not what they have in mind when studying historically attested languages (for they do not study Latin linguistically in order to be able to speak it well), it is even less plausible in the case of isolated words in prehistoric languages.

Moreover, although reconstructions remain open to correction, they cannot be dispensed with if one hopes to gain some idea of the language as a whole, and to what linguistic type it belongs. It is an indispensable way of representing in a relatively simple form a host of general facts, both synchronic and diachronic. The general outlines of Proto-Indo-
European immediately become apparent from the reconstructions as [302]
a whole. For example, it is clear that the suffixes were formed from certain elements (*t*, *s*, *r*, etc.) and not others, and that the complications of vowels in German verbs (cf. *werden*, *wirst*, *ward*, *wurde*, *worden*) conceal in the main the same original alternation: *e* — *o* — *zero*. Furthermore the study of the history of later periods is much easier as a result. Without reconstructions to begin with, it would be much more difficult to explain changes that have taken place since the prehistoric period.

§2. *Degree of certainty of reconstructions*

There are some reconstructed forms which are quite certain, and others which are disputable or clearly problematic. As we have just seen, the degree of certainty to be attached to a reconstructed form as a whole depends on the relative certainty attributable to the partial reconstructions involved in the synthesis. In this respect, two words are hardly ever comparable. There is a difference between two such informative Proto-Indo-European reconstructions as *esti ('he is') and *didōti ('he gives'); for in the latter the vowel of the reduplication is open to doubt (cf. Sanskrit *dadāti*, Greek *dídōsi*).

In general, more doubt is cast upon reconstructions than is warranted. There are three facts which should boost confidence in them.

The first, which is of capital importance, has already been indicated earlier (p. [65] ff.). Given any word, one can distinguish clearly its constituent sounds, how many of them there are, and where they begin and end. The objections raised by linguists given to peering into their phonetic microscopes have been dealt with previously (p. [83]). Doubtless in a group like *-sn-* there are fleeting transitional sounds present; but it is antilinguistic to bother about them. The ordinary ear does
not catch them. Above all, speakers are invariably in agreement about [303]
how many sounds there are. We can say, then, that in the Proto-Indo-European *ek_1wos there were just five distinct differential elements which speakers recognised.

The second fact has to do with the sound system of each language. Every language has an inventory of sounds fixed in number (cf. p. [58]). In Proto-Indo-European, each element in the system appears in at least a dozen reconstructed forms, and sometimes in thousands. So we can be sure we have identified the whole inventory.

Finally, in order to identify the sound units of a language it is not necessary to be able to characterise them positively. They are to be considered differential entities having the property of not being confused with one another (cf. p. [164]). That is what is essential: so much so that one could designate the phonetic elements of a reconstructed language simply by figures or symbols of any kind. In Proto-Indo-European **ĕ*k_1*wŏs*, it is useless to inquire about the exact quality of the *ĕ*, whether it was open or close, how fronted it was, etc. As long as there are not various kinds of *ĕ*, that is unimportant, provided *ĕ* cannot be confused with any other distinct phonetic element in the language (*ă*, *ŏ*, *ē*, etc.). This amounts to saying that the first sound of **ĕ*k_1*wŏs* did not differ from the second sound of **mĕdhyŏs*, or the third sound of **ăgĕ*, and so on. This sound could, without specifying its phonetic character, be classified and designated by a number in a table of Proto-Indo-European sounds. So the reconstructed form **ĕ*k_1*wŏs* means that the Proto-Indo-European form corresponding to Latin *equos*, Sanskrit *açva-s*, etc. comprised five specific sounds drawn from the inventory of sounds of the Proto-Indo-European language.

Within these limits, then, our reconstructions are fully valid.

CHAPTER IV [304]

Linguistic Evidence in Anthropology and Prehistory

§1. Languages and races

Linguists can, then, by the method of reconstruction go back in time and recover the languages spoken by certain communities long before there is any historical record of them. Can these reconstructions tell us anything about the peoples themselves, their race, their social structure, their customs, their institutions, etc.? In other words, can the language throw light on questions of anthropology, ethnography and prehistory? It is generally held that it can. But in our view that is largely illusory. Let us briefly consider a few aspects of this general problem.

First of all, race. It would be a mistake to believe that one can argue from a common language to consanguinity, or equate linguistic families with anthropological families. The facts are more complex. There is, for example, a Germanic race with very distinct anthropological features: fair hair, elongated skull, tall stature, etc. The Scandinavian type exemplifies it perfectly. But it is far from being the case that every population speaking one of the Germanic languages answers to this description. The Alemannic people at the foot of the Alps are very different anthropologically from Scandinavians. Could we say at least [305]
that a language in principle belongs to a given race, and that any others who speak it must have had it imposed on them by conquest? Certainly we can find many examples of nations adopting or having imposed upon them the language of their conquerors, as the Gauls did after being conquered by the Romans. But that does not explain everything. In the Germanic case, for instance, even granting that they subjugated so many different peoples, they can hardly have absorbed all of those. That would have required a long period of prehistoric

domination, and other conditions for which there is no established evidence.

Thus consanguinity and common language appear to have no necessary connexion. It is impossible to argue from one to the other. Consequently, in the many cases where anthropological and linguistic evidence do not agree, it is not necessary to suppose they conflict, or to choose between them. Each has its own validity.

§2. *Ethnicity*

What then do we learn from linguistic evidence? Racial unity in itself can only be a secondary factor and not a necessary condition where community of language is concerned. But there is another unity which is infinitely more important. It is the only essential unity, the unity constituted by social bonds: we shall call it *ethnicity*. By this we understand a unity based upon the many connexions of religion, civilisation, common defence, etc. which may become established between peoples of different races, without any political unification.

Between ethnicity and a language there becomes established a mutual connexion of the kind mentioned earlier (p. [40]). The social bond tends to bring about community of language, and perhaps gives the
[306] common language certain characteristics. Conversely, it is to some extent community of language which constitutes ethnic unity. Ethnic unity, in general, will always suffice to explain community of language. For example, in the early Middle Ages there was a Romance ethnicity linking peoples of very diverse origins and no political unity. Accordingly, for answers to questions of ethnic unity, we must look above all to what the language can tell us: here linguistic evidence takes priority over all other evidence. For example, in early Italy we find Etruscans side by side with Latins. Now if we wish to discover what they had in common, in the hope of proving them to be of the same origin, we can appeal to the evidence of everything they left behind them: monuments, religious rites, political institutions, and so on. But in these areas we can find no certainty comparable to the certainty given to us straight away by the linguistic evidence. Four lines of Etruscan are enough to show that the people who spoke Etruscan were quite distinct from the ethnic group that spoke Latin.

In this respect, within the limits indicated, a language can be considered a piece of historical documentation. For example, the fact that the Indo-European languages constitute a family forces us to infer an original ethnicity, of which all the nations speaking those languages today are, by social descent, the more or less direct heirs.

§3. Linguistic paleontology

Community of language may allow us to infer social community. But does it tell us anything about the nature of the common ethnicity?

For a long time it was supposed that languages provide an inexhaustible source of information about the peoples speaking them and about the prehistory of those peoples. Adolphe Pictet, one of the pioneers of Celtic studies, is chiefly known for his book *Les Origines indo-européennes* (1859–63). This work was the model for many others, and remains the most attractive of them. Pictet attempts to [307]
recover from the evidence provided by the Indo-European languages the basic features of 'Aryan' civilisation. He believes it to be possible to determine various features of this civilisation: its material equipment (tools, arms, domestic animals), social life (nomadic or agricultural?), family structure, and government. He attempts to locate the cradle of this civilisation in Bactria, and studies the flora and fauna of the land in question. This constitutes the most advanced investigation of its kind, and inaugurated a science called 'linguistic paleontology'.

Other efforts have been made in a similar direction. One of the most recent is that of Hermann Hirt (*Die Indogermanen*, 1905–7).[1] Hirt adopts Schmidt's theory (cf. p. [287]) as a basis for determining where the original Indo-Europeans lived, but he does not hesitate to appeal to linguistic paleontology. Their vocabulary shows that they practised agriculture, and he declines to locate them in southern Russia, which would be more appropriate for a nomadic people. He takes the frequency of names of trees, and particularly of certain species (fir, birch, beech, oak) to indicate a wooded country, somewhere between the Harz mountains and the Vistula, particularly in the region of Brandenburg and Berlin. It may be recalled that even before Pictet, Adalbert Kuhn and others had made use of linguistic evidence to reconstruct the mythology and religion of the primitive Indo-Europeans.

But it is doubtful whether information of this kind can be sought from the evidence provided by a language, for the following reasons.

The first is the uncertainty of etymologies. Only gradually has it [308]
become apparent how few are the words whose origins can be considered definitively known. We are now much more cautious than formerly. An example of the temerity of earlier days is the following. Latin *servus* ('slave') and *servāre* ('keep, guard') were – perhaps unjustifiably – assumed to be connected, and from this it was inferred

[1] Cf. also d'Arbois de Jubainville, *Les premiers habitants de l'Europe* (1877), O. Schrader, *Sprachvergleichung und Urgeschichte*, and *Reallexikon der indogermanischen Altertumskunde* (both publications slightly prior to Hirt's), and S. Feist, *Europa im Lichte der Vorgeschichte* (1910).

that the slave was originally someone who kept guard over the house. In fact it is not even clear that *servāre* originally meant that. But that is not all. Meanings of words change, and the meaning of a word often changes when its users migrate. The absence of a word has been interpreted as proof that originally a primitive civilisation lacked the thing in question. This is a mistake. Asiatic languages have no verb for 'to plough', but this does not prove that ploughing was originally unknown there. It may have been abandoned or replaced by other techniques, called by other terms.

The possibility of borrowing words is another factor which contributes to uncertainty. A word may come into a language at a later period, when the thing it designates is introduced in the life of the community. Hemp, for example, was introduced at only a relatively late date in the Mediterranean area, and even later in the countries of Northern Europe. But on each occasion the name went with the plant. In many cases the lack of extralinguistic evidence makes it impossible to say whether the presence of the same word in several languages is due to borrowing or to a primitive common tradition.

This is not to say that we cannot draw fairly firm conclusions about certain general features and even certain specific facts. The common Indo-European terms for family relationships, for instance, have come down to us very clearly, and allow us to say that originally the family, in Indo-European culture, was both a firmly established and a complex institution; for the language shows distinctions which have now been
[309] lost. In Homer *einắteres* means 'sisters-in-law' in the sense of 'wives of several brothers', whereas *galóōi* means 'sisters-in-law' in the sense of 'wife and husband's sister'. The Latin *janitrīcēs* corresponds to the former in form and meaning. Likewise the word for a sister's husband is not the same as the word for the husbands of several sisters. In such cases, very precise facts come to light, but usually only very general information can be gleaned. The same is the case with names for animals. With important species, such as cattle, one can count on the correspondence of Greek *boûs*, German *Kuh*, Sanskrit *gau-s*, etc. and reconstruct a Proto-Indo-European *$g_2\bar{o}u$-s; and even the flexional system of these forms is the same throughout the whole language family, which would not be possible if the word had been borrowed later from some other language.

A further example may be given here of a more detailed kind concerning a morphological fact which is both confined to one particular area and also related to social organisation.

Although much has been written about the connexion between Latin *dominus* ('master') and *domus* ('house'), linguists have not been fully satisfied because it is very extraordinary to find a suffix *-no-* forming secondary derivatives. There are no such examples as Greek *oiko-no-s or *oike-no-s from *oîkos*, or Sanskrit *açva-na- from *açva-*. But it is precisely this rarity which makes the suffix of *dominus* a valuable and interesting case. Several Germanic words, in our opinion, throw some light on the problem.

(i) **þeuđa-na-z* 'king, chief of the **þeuđō*', Gothic *þiudans*, Old Saxon *thiodan (*þeuđō*, Gothic *þiuda*, Oscan *touto* 'people').

(ii) **druχti-na-z* (partly changed to **druχtī-na-z*) 'chief of the **druχ-ti-z* ('army'), whence the Christian name for 'the Lord, i.e. God', Old Norse *Dróttinn*, Anglo-Saxon *Dryhten*, both ending in *-ĭna-z*.

(iii) **kindi-na-z* 'chief of the **kindi-z* (=Latin *gens* 'clan'). As the [310] head of a *gens* was, in relation to the head of a **þeuđō*, a viceroy, this Germanic term *kindins* (otherwise unknown) is used by Ulfila to designate the Roman governor of a province, because the emperor's appointee was, in the Germanic view, the equivalent of a clan chief in relation to a *þiudans*. Interesting as this assimilation is from the historical point of view, there is no doubt that the word *kindins*, which is quite alien to Roman culture, indicates that the Germanic peoples were divided into *kindi-z*.

So it appears that the secondary suffix *-no-* could be added to any stem in Germanic to express the idea 'chief of . . .'. It remains simply to point out that Latin *tribūnus* likewise means literally 'chief of the *tribus*' as *þiudans* means 'chief of the *þiuda*', and so too *domi-nus* 'chief of the *domus*', the *domus* ('house') being the smallest division of the *touta* (=*þiuda*). *Dominus*, with its remarkable suffix, looks like very convincing proof not only of community of language but also community of institutions between Italic and Germanic ethnicities.

But again it should be borne in mind that comparison between languages rarely yields specific information of this kind.

§4. Linguistic types and group mentality

Even if a language offers little precise, authentic information about the customs and institutions of its users, does it nevertheless indicate the mental type to which that community belongs? It is quite commonly held that a language reflects the psychology of a nation. But a serious objection can be raised. For a linguistic feature is not necess- [311] arily determined by psychological factors.

The Semitic languages express the relation of determination between two nouns (e.g. French *la parole de Dieu* 'the word of God') by simple juxtaposition of the nouns in question. The noun determined comes first, taking a special form called the 'construct state'. For example *dābār* in Hebrew means 'word' and *'elōhīm*[1] means 'God':

[1] The sign '(*aleph*) designates a glottal stop, corresponding to the so-called 'smooth breathing' in Greek.

'the word of God' is *dƀar 'elōhīm*. Can we say that this syntax reveals anything about the Semitic mentality? It would be rash to do so, since Old French regularly employs a similar construction: *le cor Roland* ('Roland's horn'), *les quatre fils Aymon* ('Aymon's four sons'), etc. Now this construction emerged in French purely by chance, both morphologically and phonetically. It was a novelty forced upon the language as a result of the drastic reduction of case flexions. Why, then, might not a similar stroke of chance have brought about a similar state of affairs in Proto-Semitic? A syntactic feature which appears to be one of the most inherent characteristics of the language thus offers no sure indication of Semitic mentality.

Again, Proto-Indo-European had no compounds with a first verbal element. But German has *Bethaus*, *Springbrunnen*, etc. (cf. p. [195]). Must we suppose that at a certain period the Germans modified the ways of thinking inherited from their ancestors? But this innovation, as we have seen earlier, is the result of an accident which was not only phonetic in character but negative: the fall of the *a* in *betahūs*. The development took place unconsciously, in the realm of sound change, and then immediately imposed strict constraints upon thought, obliging it to take the particular path made available by the material state of the signs involved. Many cases of the same kind confirm this interpretation. The psychological characteristics of the
[312] language community count for little as against facts like the fall of a vowel or a modification of stress, and many similar events capable at any time of disturbing the relation between sign and idea in any linguistic form.

It is always interesting to determine the grammatical typology of languages (whether they are historically attested or reconstructed) and to classify them according to the procedures they adopt for the expression of thought. But from these analyses and classifications no conclusions can be drawn with any certainty outside the linguistic domain proper.

CHAPTER V [313]

Language Families and Linguistic Types[1]

A language, as we have seen, is not directly subject to the control of the minds of its speakers. Let us conclude by emphasising one of the consequences of this principle: no family of languages rightly belongs once and for all to a particular linguistic type.

To ask which type a group of languages belongs to is to forget that languages evolve. It is to assume tacitly that there will be an element of stability in this evolution. But on what ground is a limitation imposed on developments which admit no limitation?

Many people, it is true, when speaking of the characteristics of a family of languages are thinking mainly of the characteristics of the prototype; and that is not an insoluble problem, since it is a question of one language and one period. But to postulate permanent features unaffected by time or space is to run counter to the basic principles of evolutionary linguistics. No feature is permanent as of right: it survives only by chance.

Consider the Indo-European family. The distinctive traits of the language from which this family evolved are known. Its sound system was very simple. It had no complicated consonant groups, and no double consonants. It had a restricted set of vowels, but sufficient to provide alternations of a very regular and essentially grammatical [314]
kind (cf. pp. [216], [302]). It had a pitch accent which could fall in principle on any syllable of the word and so contribute to the operation of grammatical oppositions. It had a quantitative rhythm, based solely upon the opposition of long and short syllables. It had a great facility for forming compounds and derivatives. Noun and verb flexions were very rich. The inflected word, carrying its own determinative markers, was autonomous in the sentence; and this allowed great freedom of

[1] Although this chapter does not deal with linguistics from the retrospective viewpoint, we place it here because it forms an apt conclusion to the entire work. (Editorial note)

construction, requiring very few grammatical words with determinative or relational values (preverbs, prepositions, etc.).

It is clear that none of these characteristics has entirely been preserved in the various Indo-European languages, and some of them (for example, the role played by quantitative rhythm and a pitch accent) nowhere survive. Some of the languages concerned have even changed the original character of Indo-European to such an extent that one is reminded of some totally different linguistic type (for example, English, Armenian, Irish).

It would be more justifiable to speak of certain changes more or less common to the various languages of a given family. The gradual weakening of the flexional system, mentioned above, is general throughout the Indo-European languages, even though there are some notable differences between them in this respect. Slavic has resisted this tendency most successfully, whereas English has virtually eliminated flexions. On the other hand, a more or less fixed order in sentence construction has become quite generally established, and analytic methods of expression have tended to replace synthetic procedures (case values rendered by prepositions (cf. p. [247]), verb forms constructed with the help of auxiliaries, etc.).

[315] A feature of the prototype, as we have noted, may fail to survive in one or other of the languages descended from it. The opposite may also happen. It is not unusual, indeed, to find that the features eventually common to all languages in a given family are not features present originally in the prototype. Vowel harmony (that is to say, the assimilation of all the vowels in the suffix of a word to the last vowel in the stem) is a case in point. This phenomenon is found in Ural-Altaic, a vast group of languages spoken in Europe and Asia from Finland to China; but in all probability it is the result of subsequent developments. It is thus a common feature but not a primitive feature, and as such cannot be invoked as evidence to prove the common origin of these languages (which is very controversial). Nor, likewise, can their agglutinative character. Similarly, it is recognised that Chinese has not always been a monosyllabic language.

When one compares the Semitic languages with their reconstructed prototype, one is at first sight struck by the persistence of certain characteristics. More than any other language family, Semitic gives the appearances of an unchangeable type, permanent, inherent in the family. It is recognisable by the following featurse, of which some contrast strikingly with those of Proto-Indo-European. There is an almost complete lack of compounds, and a restricted use of derivation. Flexion is relatively undeveloped (but more evolved in Proto-Semitic than in its daughter languages), and hence there is a word order governed by strict rules. The most noticeable feature concerns the constitution of roots (cf. p. [256]), which regularly include three con-

sonants: e.g. *q-ṭ-l* 'to kill'. These consonants remain in all forms, both in any given language (Hebrew *qāṭal, qāṭlā, qṭōl, qiṭlī*, etc.) and from one language to another (cf. Arabic *qatala, qutila*, etc.). In other words, the consonants express the 'concrete meaning' of a word, its lexical value, while the vowels, supplemented by certain prefixes and suffixes, mark solely grammatical values by means of alternations. [316]
For example, in Hebrew *qāṭal* means 'he killed', *qṭōl* 'to kill', *qṭāl-ū* with a suffix 'they killed', *ji-qṭōl* with a prefix 'he will kill', and *ji-qṭl-ū* with both prefix and suffix 'they will kill'.

In spite of these facts and the claims to which they have given rise, our principle remains unshaken. There are no unchangeable features: permanence is due to chance. If a feature is preserved over time, it can just as easily disappear over time. As regards Semitic, it should be noted that this three-consonant 'law' is not so characteristic of this family, for others present quite analogous phenomena. In Proto-Indo-European too, there are precise laws governing root consonants. For example, a root never has two sounds from the set comprising *i, u, r, l, m, n* following the *e*, so that a root like **serl* is impossible. As regards the vowels of Semitic, the same applies to an even greater degree: for Proto-Indo-European has an equally strict although less rich system. Oppositions like Hebrew *daƀar* ('word') vs. *dbār-īm* ('words') vs. *dibrē-hem* ('their words') are reminiscent of German *Gast* ('guest') vs. *Gäste* ('guests'), *fliessen* ('to flow') vs. *floss* ('flowed'). In both cases the origin of the grammatical device is the same. It is a question of purely phonetic modifications, due to blind evolution; but the alternations resulting were grasped by the mind, which attached grammatical values to them and extended by analogy the models fortuitously supplied by phonetic evolution. As for the immutability of the three consonants in Semitic, it is only approximate, and is in no way absolute. One might be convinced of this *a priori*, but the facts confirm it. In Hebrew, for example, whereas the root of *'anāš-īm* ('men') has the usual three consonants, the singular *'īš* has only two; and this is by phonetic reduction from an earlier form which had three. In any case, even granted this quasi-immutability, should one [317]
see it as a characteristic inherent in the roots? No. It is simply the case that the Semitic languages have undergone less phonetic change than many other languages, and the consonants are better preserved in this family than elsewhere. It is thus an evolutionary, phonetic phenomenon, and nothing grammatical or permanent. To proclaim the immutability of roots is to say they have undergone no phonetic changes, nothing more: and there is no guarantee that such changes will never occur. In general, anything time can do, time can also undo, or change.

While recognising that Schleicher distorted reality in treating languages as organic beings with their own intrinsic laws of evolution, we continue – without realising it – to believe that languages are organic in a different sense, inasmuch as the genius of a race or ethnic group tends constantly to direct its language along certain fixed paths.

From the excursions made above into regions bordering upon linguistics, there emerges a negative lesson, but one which is all the more interesting in that it supports the fundamental thesis of this course: *the only true object of study in linguistics is the language, considered in itself and for its own sake.*

Index

(Page references are to the pagination of the French editions from 1922 onwards, indicated in the margins of the present translation.)